57888A

S0-AXU-691

99BB
2400

The Neurosis of Our Time:

ACTING OUT

Adelphi University
Postdoctoral Program in Psychotherapy
Conference Series

The Neurosis of Our Time:
ACTING OUT

Compiled and Edited by

DONALD S. MILMAN, Ph.D.

Professor of Psychology, Institute of Advanced Psychological Studies
Co-Director, Postdoctoral Program in Psychotherapy
Adelphi University
Private Practice
East Norwich, New York

and

GEORGE D. GOLDMAN, Ph.D.

Clinical Professor of Psychology, Supervisor of Psychotherapy
Director, Postdoctoral Psychotherapy Center
Institute of Advanced Psychological Studies
Adelphi University
Private Practice
New York, New York

CHARLES C THOMAS · PUBLISHER
Springfield · Illinois · U.S.A.

Published and Distributed Throughout the World by
CHARLES C THOMAS • PUBLISHER
BANNERSTONE HOUSE
301-327 East Lawrence Avenue, Springfield, Illinois, U.S.A.

This book is protected by copyright. No
part of it may be reproduced in any manner
without written permission from the publisher.

© *1973, by* CHARLES C THOMAS • PUBLISHER
ISBN 0-398-02558-4
Library of Congress Catalog Card Number: 72-79194

With THOMAS BOOKS *careful attention is given to all details of
manufacturing and design. It is the Publisher's desire to present books
that are satisfactory as to their physical qualities and artistic possibilities
and appropriate for their particular use.* THOMAS BOOKS *will be true
to those laws of quality that assure a good name and good will.*

Printed in the United States of America
W-2

To our colleagues and students in the Postdoctoral and Doctoral programs at the Institute of Advanced Psychological Studies, who through the years have contributed so directly to our intellectual and emotional growth

Contributors

GERALD BERENSON, Ph.D.: *Graduate Postdoctoral Program in Psychotherapy, Adelphi University; Supervisor of Family Therapy, Doctoral Program in Clinical Psychology, Teachers College, Columbia University; Private Practice.*

MARIA V. BERGMANN: *Psychoanalyst, Private Practice.*

MATTHEW BESDINE: *Clinical Professor of Psychology, Adelphi University; President, National Psychological Association for Psychoanalysis; Faculty, Theodor Reik Psychoanalytic Institute.*

DANIEL H. CASRIEL, M.D.: *Co-founder and Psychiatric Director, Daytop Village, Inc.; Clinical Associate Professor, Temple University Medical School; Past President, American Society of Psychoanalytic Physicians.*

LAURA DEFREITAS, M.A.: *Staff Psychotherapist, Fifth Avenue Center for Counseling and Psychotherapy; Consultant in Nonverbal Communication, Manhattan State Hospital; Private Practice.*

MAGDA DENES-RADOMISLI, Ph.D.: *Associate Clinical Professor of Psychology, Institute of Advanced Psychological Studies and Supervisor of Psychotherapy, Postdoctoral Program in Psychotherapy, Adelphi University; Faculty, New York Institute of Gestalt Therapy; Private Practice.*

REUBEN FINE, Ph.D.: *Clinical Professor of Psychology, Adelphi University; Director, New York Center for Psychoanalytic Training; Member, Council of Representatives, American Psychological Association.*

RUTH FOX, M.D.: *President, American Medical Society on Alcoholism.*

HAROLD GREENWALD, Ph.D.: *Professor of Clinical Psychology and Chairman, Clinical Psychology Program, United States International University; Guest Professor, University of Bergen, Norway; Past President, National Psychological Association for Psychoanalysis; Member, Executive Committee, and Supervisor, Community Guidance Service.*

RALPH H. GUNDLACH, Ph.D.: *Associate Director of Research, Postgraduate Center for Mental Health; Senior Psychologist, Partial Hospitalization Program of the Mental Health Center, New York Medical College–Metropolitan Hospital; Private Practice.*

MILTON S. GURVITZ, Ph.D.: *Director, Great Neck Consultation Center; Senior Member, Training and Control Analyst, National Psychological Association for Psychoanalysis; Private Practice.*

HENRY GUZE, Ph.D.: *Adjunct Professor of Anthropology, Drew University; Council of Representatives, American Psychological Association; Past President, Society for the Scientific Study of Sex. (Deceased)*

EMANUEL F. HAMMER, Ph.D.: *Adjunct Associate Professor of Psychology, Graduate School of Arts and Sciences, New York University; Faculty, National Psychological Association for Psychoanalysis; Director of Training, New York Center for Psychoanalytic Training.*

LEON I. HAMMER, M.D.: *Adjunct Assistant Professor, Southampton College; William Alanson White Psychiatric Society; Associate Clinical Professor of Psychology and Supervisor of Psychotherapy, Adelphi University.*

LAWRENCE J. HATTERER, M.D.: *Associate Clinical Professor of Psychiatry, Cornell Medical School; Private Practice.*

BERNARD F. RIESS, Ph.D.: *Director of Research, Postgraduate Center for Mental Health; Vice President, Westchester Mental Health Association; Private Practice.*

MAX ROSENBAUM, Ph.D.: *Editor, GROUP PROCESS; Faculty, National Psychological Association for Psychoanalysis Institute; Private Practice.*

THEODORE SARETSKY, Ph.D.: *Director of Group Therapy, Brooklyn Psychiatric Centers, Pride of Judea and Catholic Charities; Adjunct Professor of Group Dynamics, Drew University; Private Practice.*

LEONARD J. SCHWARTZ, Ph.D.: *Director, Group Process Institute; Associate Clinical Professor, Postdoctoral Program in Psycho-*

therapy, Adelphi University; Group Process Consultant, New York City Board of Education.

Roslyn Schwartz, Ph.D.: *Staff Psychologist, Suffolk Rehabilitation Center; Faculty, Dowling College; Associate, Workshop Institute for Living Learning.*

Irving L. Solomon, Ph.D.: *Psychiatric Consultation Clinic, Mineola; Postdoctoral Psychotherapy Center, Adelphi University.*

George Stricker, Ph.D.: *Professor and Assistant Director, Institute of Advanced Psychological Studies, Adelphi University; Clinical Psychologist, Queens-Nassau Mental Health Center.*

Benjamin Wolstein, Ph.D.: *Clinical Professor of Psychology and Supervisor of Psychotherapy, Adelphi University; Faculty, William Alanson White Institute of Psychiatry, Psychoanalysis and Psychology.*

Introduction

I̲T̲ ̲H̲A̲S̲ ̲F̲R̲E̲Q̲U̲E̲N̲T̲L̲Y̲ been asserted by analytic therapists that there is a marked change in the types of neuroses seen by mental health practitioners today. In place of the classical symptom neurosis with a more focal presenting problem, we see patients with much more extensive characterological involvements. Today patients come to treatment with less ego-alien material clearly motivating them. Instead they have rigid ego elaborations that give them problems in living but usually maintain them at a state that is sufficiently anxiety-free so that their mode of adjustment is not seen as the needed locus of change. Frequently the patient's discovery of his need for treatment comes from an external source. For example, a man is confronted with the reality, after bankruptcy proceedings, that he has not succeeded in business as well as his potential indicated he could; or a beautiful girl who has been engaged five times, each ending abortively, has to have her aunt suggest that the problem may be within her before she recognizes it.

Ostensibly, then, we meet in our consulting rooms people with an entirely new species of disease. What factors account for this marked transformation in substance and structure? A generalization frequently provided is that the revolution in attitudes toward sexuality generated by Freud's discoveries made the usual repressive defenses impossible and, therefore, symptom neurosis untenable. Although this is a reasonable formulation and has within it the basic ingredients of truth, it neglects some very relevant alternative ideas. The most obvious one is that in Freud's day a relatively small number of analysts dealt with the vast majority of people in treatment. Those few who sought assistance had to be in real pain, for the stigma associated with neurosis precluded those with more general problems from seeking psychotherapy. Thus, changes in attitudes toward emotional problems, a larger body of professionals working in the area and a reorientation of the goals of psychoanalysis towards personality transformation could account for much of the shift in the character of the patient population.

The shifting of emphasis from repression of sexual functioning is in and of itself a much too simple explanation when applied to the rather elaborate libido theory of Freud's. This conception would neglect the intricacies of intrapersonal structure and interpersonal subtleties that generate the complex personalities with which we deal. This formulation also neglects the fact that in relatively simple cultures today, major hysterias are still frequently seen. Thus, complexity of culture seems to play some role in the drama of neurosis.

Continuing our search for an explanation of the change in the patient population, we find that it is an assumption of many mental health professionals that our culture has changed and that we have different forces at work within our society. They see many specific symptoms of this cultural disturbance, such as the several assassinations of leading citizens, the extent and intensity of riots, revolutions and wars, the increase of homicide and suicide, the insolvency and bankruptcy of our social institutions as exemplified in the high rate of divorce, and the addictive use of drugs by our youth which threatens to reach epidemic proportions. For them it is no longer a question of whether the character of our problems has changed, but what caused it and what can we do to stem the tide. For them, Toynbee's prognostication about the demise of Western civilization is in effect within the realm of our societal neurosis. It is also a basic thesis of the editors of this book that a major aspect of the change is exemplified in the symptoms previously cited, because they reflect the transformation from ego-alien to egosyntonic neuroses. Furthermore, we believe that the majority of present psychological ills includes the problem of acting out as a defense, symptom and/or characterological elaboration.

In order to place the question of acting out in proper perspective, it might be helpful at this point to outline some of the characteristics of this category of behavior. Generally, in acting-out behavior, a conflict from the past is expressed in behavior in a present situation as if it were the past situation repeated again. In contrast with most other defensive operations the repeated action is essentially nonverbal and acceptable to the person. Therefore, a critical aspect of this defensive process is its earlier psychogenetic foundation with concomitant regressive potential for other aspects of the personality structure. Individuals who use acting out as a major aspect of their behavior tend to have ego deficiencies characterized by an inability to tolerate frustration and a tendency to express their conflict through preverbal rather than verbal modalities. As with any defense, the motivations generating the countercathexis are usually anxiety and/or guilt. In contrast with most defenses, however, is the close relationship of acting out to symptoms in that there is within the expressed behavior both a defensive maneuver and a partial expression and gratification of the underlying unconscious impulse. Because it is repetitive and rigidly applied without an always accurate perception of the triggering site, it is still, in essence, neurotic. As with other defenses, the neurotic conflict and the related traits of behavior can be elaborated and generalized in broader character structure. Thus, in the overall perspective of defining acting-out behavior it is not always easy to distinguish the differences in the behavior, for defense, symptom and ego modification may blend almost imperceptibly into each other. As a form of resistance that may emerge during treatment, it is a particularly potent and difficult one to deal with since the behavior through which it is expressed is egosyntonic, its roots unconscious, and sufficiently gratifying so that the patient is not too willing to relinquish it. As a result, the therapist frequently has to infer the existence of the resistance and its resultant expression rather than have it reported by the patient.

In the context of the present-day emphasis on more active and interactive behavior on the part of the therapist, the concept of working through bears some discussion and comparison with acting out. Residual, repetitive infantile conflicts are not characteristic of working through. Insightful, conscious awareness of conflicts and insight with ability verbally to organize the dynamic interplay are most prominent in this stage in analysis or psychotherapy. However, since working through requires some modification of old patterns of reacting and usually entails some new action patterns, it could be confused with acting out. Additionally, as previously inferred, many modern therapists accuse more orthodox analysts of restricting patients' growth because of their anxiety about acting-out behavior. They cite therapists' responses to the patients as being conforming and constricting and developing from their countertransference needs. They suggest that less timidity about satisfaction of patients' needs would lead to faster development and growth for them. As a rebuttal, the arguments against these ideas are vehement and loud in pointing out the potential therapeutic destructiveness of acting out on both patient and therapist's part.

With those introductory comments on changes in the neurosis and a rough delineation of some basic concepts, we have a beginning outline of some of the issues that we feel are presently of significance. In the following pages we will summarize some further trends that we feel are germane to both the issues of acting out and changing neurotic structure. Our comments and observations are only meant to be a brief review of each issue since a more extended discussion and evaluation is not possible in the present context.

One explanation of the factors behind the genesis of many of our present difficulties is the extensive involvement and devotion to science within our society. Existential critics of our adjustment have indicated deification of knowledge as the guilty party in the genesis of many of modern man's difficulties. They point out quite concretely how this involvement with science and technology isolates us from those qualities of mankind that are most human. For them the alienation and anomie of this period is a logical development from this dehumanization and mechanization. Most markedly and meaningfully, it accounts for the schizoid and obsessive character of our society and would seem to bear a direct relationship to the isolation of affect and limited ability to experience often described as central to our national character structure.

A general trend also indicated as fundamental to the change in the economics of modern neurosis is the emphasis on aggression as central to man and his current conflicts. Some experts in evaluating aggression and its proper place within the psychic processes believe that aggression has not been given as much importance as is appropriate in evaluating different drive systems. These authorities would assign a more central role to the aggressive drive in their psychogenetic conception and structure, particularly in reference to energy systems. Whether or not we accept this shift in the importance of different drives, there are major forces at work in our civilization that could directly be related to an increase in aggressive energy level. Whether we conceive of the increase of aggression as being a possible result of frustration as suggested by Miller and Dollard, or as a defense against anxiety according to Sullivan or employing one of the many other theories, the possible direct increase in aggression is patently obvious in three major trends: hydrogen bomb development, ecological consensus about the end of civilization, and the population explosion. The population explosion and its effect on increased aggression could be derived almost directly from the work of Lorenz and his formulations indicating that decrease in life space is highly correlated with increased destructiveness. Thus, it means that there are major forces at work on all of us that can and do exacerbate our problems with aggression, and there is nothing on the immediate horizon that promises any relief.

Just as difficult to place in proper perspective as a factor in the structure of the neurosis of modern man is the influence of Freud and his theories upon child development. The interpretation of Freudian theory and its extrapolation to a conception of permissiveness as desirable in childrearing is cited as a source of much of our current dilemma. Many Freudians would say this was a totally misguided application of their principles and they would certainly be willing to shift the responsibility and credit to Dr. Spock, as some others in our society have also been willing to do. How would a generalized permissiveness affect the developmental pattern of our children? If we equate permissiveness with indulgence and gratification—and that equation certainly is an oversimplification if not a misrepresentation—then this could have had a drastic effect on ego development. Analytic theory posits fixation and developmental lag to overindulgence (among other alternatives as well). Additionally, frustration is essential to the development of adequate object relations, separation and individuation. The result then of permissive childbearing could be a poorly differentiated ego with inadequate strength for neutralization of drives. In modern ego psychology the inability to neutralize aggression leads very directly to the development of a more primitive and tyrannical superego. (We will not even attempt to bring in the possible interactive effects of an affluent society with permissive childrearing and their mutual effect on personality structure.) Therefore, in this oversimplified developmental schema that suggests parental permissiveness as characteristic of our "now" generation, we may have the seeds for developmental defects in two major structures of Freudian personality organization—the ego and the superego.

In our review of possible sources of personality difficulties and particularly those related to the increase in acting out, we have only superficially touched on the specifics of structural change. This is most true for the evaluation of the role of the superego in this area since, for many, a corruptible superego is the *sine qua non* for acting out. In psychoanalytic theory there tends to be an overemphasis on an early establishment of structure and its relative immutability. It is probable that groups and group norms can and do have, not only a temporary, but even a more permanent effect on this aspect of personality. Group values can be included as permanent introjects within the superego or temporarily produce shifts in the balance between standards of right and wrong. Lynch mob psychology and killing in the service of one's country are examples of transient but extraordinary shifts in values. Responses to the use of drugs despite legal prohibitions, women's liberation, and the new community marriages are some examples of what we believe are more fundamental changes in values. Some of these changes imply a major reorganization in superego standards and directly relate to questions of acting out.

In looking at some of the cultural phenomena we see at work, it often is difficult to distinguish acting out from working through or even sublimation. In the area of therapy, is the activity of the therapist a therapeutic progression necessary to deal with alienation and detachment or a rationalization for acting out the therapist's countertransferential needs? Are marathons and encounters mainly arenas for individuals to satisfy their needs for affection, contact and sex or genuine therapeutic techniques for dissolving defenses and emotional working through? In other areas in the social milieu it is also often difficult to determine whether there is a potential for growth in a particular piece of behavior or whether it is solely an expression of a conflict that will be repeated over and over again. For example, it is not clear whether student rebellions have as their basis a genuine need to change existent destructive institutions and, thereby, promote societal growth or whether they are displacements of hostility toward parental authority. Additional cloudy examples are: LSD use—regression in the service of the ego or narcissistic withdrawal? pot smoking—attempts to experience and deal with alienation or evidence of massive addictive problems in our society? long hair—a constructive solution to the identity crisis or an acting out of the same issue? lack of concern with dress—a constructive indictment of our hypocritical materialism or a regression to a more undifferentiated stage? All of these examples are unclear in their interpretation. The inability to label these samples of behavior easily and accurately serves to highlight the difficulty that each of us faces in trying to bring into focus the forces currently at work in our society. We hope that the contents of this book bring some clarification to these issues because we believe that the future of our society depends on channeling the forces of destructive acting out into constructive working through.

In structuring the sequence of papers for the book we decided to begin with papers of a more theoretical nature, then proceed with those contributions on the treatment approaches to specific nosological groups, ending with the treatment questions that seem to be broader in their application. The chapters concerning the broader issues of acting out begin with Dr. Reuben Fine's delineation of the issues of acting out and end with Professor Matthew Besdine's discussion of the genesis of acting out of hostility. Treatment and theoretical issues related to more circumscribed groups begins with Dr. Irving Solomon's paper and ends with Dr. George Stricker's presentation on his work with soft drug users. The transition to broader treatment issues begins with Mrs. Maria Bergmann's paper on psychoanalysis and ends with Drs. Leonard and Roslyn Schwartz's discussion of aspects of therapeutic acting out in groups.

DONALD S. MILMAN
GEORGE D. GOLDMAN

Acknowledgments

W E WOULD LIKE TO express our appreciation to Professor and Mrs. Matthew Besdine for their continued support of these conferences and the Postdoctoral Psychotherapy Center. Their generous contributions have made the conferences and the Center viable parts of the Postdoctoral Program. The conference from which this book was derived was in memory of Professor Besdine's daughter, Amy, who was a major in psychology at Adelphi University, Class of 1961.

We want to thank our secretaries, Miss Elyse Barry and Miss Rhonda Warshaw, who were extremely helpful in the tiresome task of administratively handling the details of compiling this book. We are most deeply appreciative of Mrs. Lorelle Saretsky's and Miss Deborah Janis' continuous professional assistance in so many areas, but most specifically now for their editorial work in the final preparation of this manuscript.

D.S.M.
G.D.G.

CONTENTS

The Neurosis of Our Time:

ACTING OUT

Publications from the Postdoctoral
Program Conference Series

Modern Woman: Her Psychology and Sexuality—George D. Goldman and Donald S. Milman, Editors.

Psychoanalytic Contributions to Community Psychology—Donald S. Milman and George D. Goldman, Editors.

Innovations in Psychotherapy—George D. Goldman and Donald S. Milman, Editors.

The Neurosis of Our Time: Acting Out—Donald S. Milman and George D. Goldman, Editors.

I N A WELL-FORMULATED presentation, Dr. Reuben Fine, a well-known authority on Freud and Freudian theory and a member of the Adelphi University Postdoctoral Program faculty historically examines the concept of acting out.

He begins by clarifying the difference between action and acting out. After reviewing Freud's conception of acting out, he discusses the problems that arise in distinguishing between acting out and action in patients with problems such as poor impulse control. The need for a more useful and less confusing classification is indicated by Dr. Fine's examination of aggressive and sexual acting out and the basic dichotomy between the two. Social values and attitudes serve further to cloud the distinction between action and acting out. The paper includes an interesting look at the translation of Freud's 1914 speech in which he first mentioned that the term *acting out* could have been translated as, and is, in fact, interchangeable with *action*. Believing that the differences between action and acting out are arbitrary, Dr. Fine offers his concept of destructive action to circumvent the inadequacies connected with the term acting out.

In his usual scholarly and original presentation, Dr. Fine critically explores and examines the origins and meaning of the term acting out. By returning to the original writings of Freud and by giving a "Fine" interpretation based on his own clinical experience, he broadens our theoretical and pragmatic knowledge about the concept of acting out.

D.S.M.
G.D.G.

Chapter 1

A Critical Examination of the Concept of Acting Out

Reuben Fine

T HE CONCEPT OF acting out is used so indiscriminately nowadays that both theoretical and clinical clarification are vital. As a guide to this clarification, the major question that must be resolved is this: What is the difference, both theoretically and clinically, between acting out and action?

At the symposium on acting out held by the International Psychoanalytic Association in 1967, Anna Freud[3] described the theoretical confusions surrounding the concept of acting out most succinctly in her remarks. She writes:

> Most psychoanalytic concepts owe their origin to a particular era of analytic theory or to a particular field of clinical application or a particular stage of technical procedure. They are carried forward, unaltered from there, only too frequently regardless of changes in these fields. Notwithstanding their having been firmly rooted in their home ground, they cease to fit the changed circumstances where they lead an uneasy existence and lend themselves to all kinds of theoretical misconceptions. It seems to me that the concept of "acting-out" belongs in this category and it is my hope that the present Symposium will make some contribution towards clarifying the confusion. . . .
>
> The term "acting-out" (agieren) made its first appearance in 1914 in Freud's essay on "Remembering, Repeating and Working Through" (1914). "Acting-out" is defined there in contradistinction to remembering as the compelling urge to repeat the forgotten past, and to do so within the analytic setting by actually reliving repressed emotional experience transferred on to the analyst and "also on to all the other aspects of the current situation" (1914, page 151). Such acting-out was understood to replace the ability or willingness

5

to remember whenever the patient was in resistance. "The greater
the resistance, the most extensively will acting-out (repetition)
replace remembering (ibid.)."

These quotes from Anna Freud and the corresponding quotes
from her father highlight the need for a more searching examination of the concept. In order to carry out this examination, five
questions will be asked and answers attempted:

    1. What is the relationship between acting out and memory?

    2. What is the difference between acting out and poor
impulse control?

    3. Are there any differences between acting out with regard
to the various instinctual drives? For example, is the acting out
of aggression to be put on a par with the acting out of sexuality
and the acting out of anal wishes?

    4. How is the notion of acting out affected by moral and/or
social judgments?

    5. How are we to distinguish the two types of patients, one,
those who act out a great deal, the so-called impulsive or acting-
out disorders, and those who act out very little, the so-called
passive or inhibited individuals?

ACTING OUT AND MEMORY

Freud originally defined acting out as the compelling urge
to repeat the forgotten past. This definition raises a number of
important questions.

First of all, what aspect of the past is being repeated in acting
out? Is it an actual event, or is it a fantasy which persists from
childhood? On this point Freud is silent. At other stages in his
work, Freud repeatedly was faced with the question about
whether the individual or the group was reacting to a memory
or to a fantasy. It will be recalled that the major thrust of his
work from the early days was to recall actual memories, but
as it became more and more impossible to recall these memories,
he replaced that demand by the need to reconstruct the event
from the known material. In the paper cited, on "Remembering,
Repeating and Working Through," for the first time he saw the
working through of resistances as the hallmark of analysis, in

contrast to the actual recovery of memories which had been his major goal up to that point. In other works, such as the *Case of the Wolfman* or *Totem and Taboo*, he finally came to the conclusion that it made no real difference whether the event that was being repeated was a memory or a fantasy. But if it makes no real difference, then the compulsion to repeat is less readily understandable; in fact it is the compulsion to repeat which becomes more prominent than the memory itself, which is inferred from repetitive actions on the patient's part.

Furthermore, it is a cardinal postulate of Freudian thinking that all human beings repeat the past in greater or lesser degree. On when this repetition can be considered acting out and when it can be considered ordinary action, the major distinction investigated in this paper, Freud is entirely silent, as are virtually all other analytic writers. Accordingly, Freud's definition of the compulsion to repeat the forgotten past is of little avail. A fresh look at the clinical material is needed.

Such a fresh look discloses two major groupings of patients: the acting-out or impulsive, and the inhibited. In the impulsive patients, formerly called perverts, or impulse disorders, and now most frequently referred to as the acting-out disorders, what is characteristic is not so much the action as the self-destructive character of the action, the weakness of the ego, and an underlying depression which is present in virtually all of them. In fact, it could be said that acting-out disorders are not infrequently direct or indirect suicide attempts. Thus, for example, it is well known that in alcoholic binges the number of suicides is quite high. In drug addicts the frequency of deaths, either directly or indirectly attributable to the drugs, is again striking and usually can be looked upon as a form of suicide, even though the intention of the person at the time of taking the overdose may not have been suicidal in itself. In other words more important than the acting out in these patients is the underlying depression. Parenthetically it may be noted that this depression becomes one of the major motives for seeking out analytic treatment, and the defenses against the depression by means of the acting out become one of the major forms of resistance in the course of analytic treatment.

Thus it is really not the memory that becomes important but the ego's capacity to tolerate a memory. Sullivan once said that it is not the trauma, but the scar. Memory arouses such a strong emotional reaction in the patient that he cannot sit back quietly and tolerate it; accordingly he tries to resort to some action which will obliterate this memory from consciousness. This is why acting-out patients produce so few memories, and the memories that they do produce are particularly significant.

By contrast, in the inhibited patient, action is held back by a variety of fears; many times these patients are outright phobic. Sometimes these patients produce many memories, sometimes they do not. Here the passivity is just as serious a problem as the activity in the acting-out patient. Thus again the differentiation does not lie in the action as such, but in the strength of the ego.

IMPULSE CONTROL

The concept of poor impulse control overlaps with that of acting out. In the patient with poor impulse control, there is usually a broader range of symtoms included, such as enuresis, hysterical attacks and the like. Nevertheless, the difference is more apparent than real. At different stages in the history of psychoanalysis, these have been called perversions, poor impulse control, or acting-out disorders, all with more or less the same dynamic structure.

The lack of impulse control is by definition a manifestation of ego weakness. It is differentiated from acting out primarily in that in poor impulse control the symptom is egodystonic, while in acting out, the symptom is egosyntonic.

How and why does a symptom become egosyntonic? This is a harder question to answer than how and why a symptom becomes egodystonic. It becomes dystonic by means of disapprobation from the parents, later the superego. But with egosyntonic symptoms it cannot be said that the superego really approves of what the individual is doing.

Two situations can be distinguished. First there are those

patients who have some anxiety about one kind of symptom, say homosexual practices, at the beginning, and then in the course of their acting out gradually lose the anxiety. Sometimes, in fact in many cases, the anxiety punishment is projected to the outside world so that the homesexual develops a whole paranoid system about the persecution of society, which is buttressed to some extent by the reality of stupid police actions. In these cases the egosyntonicity develops by a series of projections and denials.

In the second kind of patient, the symptom is egosyntonic from the very beginning. This may happen either because the parents consciously or unconsciously approve of the actions of the child (for example in overt aggression) or because the parents are totally indifferent to the activities of the child, so that he never really develops superego prohibitions in certain areas of living. Still a third possibility may occur when the child becomes anxious about the action but then pursues it anyhow as a form of rebellion against the parents. All these possibilities may occur at one time, as for example in many patients from deprived environments.

In all these cases of poor impulse control, it is very difficult to distinguish acting out from action. The patient for whom the acting is egosyntonic calls it action, but the outsider calls it acting out. The differentiation can only be made by a close metapsychological analysis of the total situation.

THE KIND OF IMPULSE

Generally speaking nowadays the term *acting-out disorders* refers to both aggressive and sexual actions. Quite often no distinction is made between the two. This is quite unfortunate, since these two impulses are markedly different in both origin, functioning, and outcome.

Sexuality should still be seen as the basic constructive instinct in human nature. It arises as a result of ascertainable physiological changes at certain ages in life, and although of course it is strongly influenced by psychological factors, it is nevertheless highly dependent on biological maturation. By contrast, hostility (a more precise term than aggression, which includes both hostility and assertiveness) arises primarily as the result of frustration. Although hostility has somatic consequences, it is essentially a psychological phenomenon and should be restricted to the wish to hurt another human being. Looked at in this sense, it is only human beings who have a hostile drive, since animals rarely consciously show a wish to hurt another animal merely for the pleasure involved in hurting them.

The main consequence of this theoretical distinction is that inherently sexuality is capable of gratification, while hostility is not. Hostility is generated by an inner discontent which can only be cured by an inner change; sexuality, however, is generated by an inner physiological change which responds to a normal process of discharge.

It is therefore highly confusing, both theoretically and clinically, to lump together all the various acting-out disorders involving both aggression and sexuality. It is true that a great deal of sexual acting out has a hostile meaning, yet it is equally true that a great deal of sexual action does not.

In the case of sexuality the difference between acting out and action lies in the capacity for gratification. The sexual impulse lends itself to a cyclical form of gratification; and this is its physiological base. After gratification there is normally a period of rest. As a result the person who has sex and then rests, can be looked upon as gratifying the wish, while the person who has to have sex incessantly without gratification is acting out.

In the case of hostility, however, the difference between acting out and action is of an entirely different order. If hostility is generated by some real damage to the individual or real danger in the environment, an action directed at removing that danger is perfectly normal and results in benefit to the organism. If, however, the hostility is generated by some internal threat, then no amount of external conquest can alter that internal threat. Thus whenever there is hostility resulting from internal imbalance, one cannot speak of constructive action; there is always acting out.

MORAL OR SOCIAL JUDGMENTS

All too often the label *acting out* is used to offer a moral or a social judgment, rather than a psychological evaluation. If the particular action pleases the observer, then it is called action, but if it displeases the observer it is called acting out. As we are going through a sexual revolution, in which the mores of the past give way to a new and different attitude toward sexuality, at each stage one group of theoreticians invariably refers to the newer behavior as acting out, while another group of theoreticians refers to it as part of the liberation or growth process. Different cultures have handled the sexual impulse in a variety of different ways. As Morton Hunt has shown in his book,[7] Western civilization has resorted to many variations of sexual activity in the attempt to reconcile tender and sexual impulses. Historically, Freud came at the height of a period of tremendous repression; had he come a century later or earlier, his theories would have been entirely different.

At the same time it is still impossible to tell from the action proper whether it serves a constructive or a destructive purpose in the psychic economy of the individual. Sexual intercourse itself may be and often is an act of aggression; in that sense for the person who is inherently aggressive all sexual activity becomes a form of acting out. This is particularly evident in our culture, where hostility is such a prominent feature of interpersonal relations. It would be improper, however, to extrapolate from our culture to other cultures, such as the Polynesians, who apparently regarded sex as a normal expression of the élan vital.

In the case of hostility, a reversal of cultural values by psychoanalytic thought is often apparent. Thus hunting in our culture would be considered a normal expression of a hobby for many people; in fact hunters themselves deny that there is any aggressive intent behind the hunting. A closer examination of the sport naturally reveals a great amount of latent aggression. From the inner-psychological point of view all hunting then becomes a form of acting out rather than a normal kind of action.

Again, the difference between acting out and action is not clarified by the moral or social judgments which are rendered.

The diagnosis of acting out in these cases really covers up an attempt to whitewash the particular values which are prominent or accepted in the culture at that moment.

THE INHIBITED AND IMPULSIVE PATIENTS

This grouping has already been alluded to above. Some further comments can be made here. In the impulsive patient what is striking is the activity, while in the inhibited patient what is striking is the passivity. It would be more correct to speak of the dichotomy between activity and passivity. But even this is not sufficient. What is striking in the impulsive patient is the overactivity, while in the inhibited patient there is underactivity. The question then is not so much one of diagnostic classification, but of seeing the difference between extremes of one kind or another. In both cases there is acting out rather than action. The inhibited patient frequently shows a pattern of a good deal of passivity alternating with outbursts of violence or sexual activity. The acting-out or impulsive patient frequently shows alternations of self-destructive actions followed by a tremendous amount of depression or sleep, the acme of passivity. Once more the difference between acting out and action disappears.

REEVALUATION

Both theoretical and clinical reevaluation point up the difficulties involved in distinguishing between acting out and action. Only a close meticulous examination of the total ego structure can lead to the conclusion that any given action is a form of acting out rather than a constructive activity in any given situation. Consequently it must be doubted whether the concept of acing out has any real conceptual clarity, or a sufficiently defined clinical meaning.

It is known that acting out is (1) compulsive, (2) based on underlying depression, (3) relies on a weak ego, (4) shows a lack of capacity to delay gratification, (5) shows a lack of capacity to accept gratification, (6) is found in masochistic individuals, (7) attempts to resolve an unpleasant feeling by action, and (8) usually confuses sexuality and aggression. These clinical observations can be reversed into a definition of normal action. An action could be considered normal if it is (1) noncompulsive, (2) based on an underlying desire, (3) tied up with a strong ego, (4) shows a capacity to delay gratification, (5) shows a capacity to accept gratification, (6) is nonmasochistic or self-damaging, (7) shows a natural transition from feeling to action, and (8) differentiates adequately between sexuality and aggression.

However, no differentiation is possible without a careful examination of the total personality, the total situation, and the meaning of the action within the psychic economy of the individual. These considerations are relevant to both theoretical research and therapy. What is of most significance is not whether something should be considered acting out, but the degree of ego weakness and depression which is present in the individual.

REVIEW OF THE ORIGINAL LITERATURE

Inasmuch as no clear-cut distinction has been found between acting out and action, except in a deep metapsychological sense which makes it more or less equivalent with the weak ego, the problem deserves further investigation.

To begin with, the term *acting out* has a jarring effect on an American's (or Englishman's) ears. It is obviously not correct idiomatic English and must have been invented for the purpose on some occasion. But when? Tracking down the sources reveals the following interesting material.

The term *acting out* was first mentioned by Freud in his paper on "Remembering, Repeating and Working Through" (1914). The original German in Gesammelte Werke reads:[4]

Von diesem erfreulich glatten Ablauf ist nun bei Anwendung der neuen Technik sehr wenig, oft nichts, uebrig geblieben. Es kommen auch hier Faelle vor, die sich ein Stueck weit verhalten wie bei der hypnotischen Technik und erst spaeter versagen; andere Faelle benehmen sich aber von vornherein anders. Halten wir uns zur Kennzeichnung des Unterschiedes an den letzteren Typus, so duerfen wir sagen, der Analysierte erinnere ueberhaupt nichts von dem Vergessenen und Verdraengten, sondern er agiere es. Er

reproduziert es nicht als Erinnerung, sondern als Tat, er wiederholt
es, ohne naturerlich zu wissen, dass er es widerholt.

In the Standard Edition[5] the passage is translated as follows:

Under the new technique very little, and often nothing, is left
of this delightfully smooth course of events. There are some cases
which behave like those under the hypnotic technique up to a
point and only later cease to do so; but others behave differently
from the beginning. If we confine ourselves to this second type
in order to bring out the difference, we may say that the patient
does not *remember* anything of what he has forgotten and repressed,
but acts it out. He reproduces it not as a memory but as an action;
he repeats, without, of course, knowing that he is repeating it.

But in the *Collected Papers*,[6] which was published earlier
under the supervision of Joan Riviere, this same passage is translated as follows:

To return to the comparison between the old and the new
techniques; in the latter there remains very little, often nothing,
of this smooth and pleasing course of events belonging to the
former. There are cases which, under the new technique, conduct
themselves up to a point like those under the hypnotic technique
and only later abandon this behavior; but others behave differently
from the beginning. If we examine the latter class in order to define
this difference, we may say that here the patient *remembers* nothing
of what is forgotten and repressed, but that he expresses it in
action. He reproduces it not in his memory but in his behavior; he
repeats it, without of course knowing that he is repeating it.

Thus what Strachey translated as "acting out" is translated
as "action" in the *Collected Papers*. Further, in Fenichel[1] the
term "acting out" is not listed in the index. Fenichel does have a
paper entitled "Neurotic Acting-Out," Chapter 22, in his *Second
Series of Collected Papers*.[2] Here he says the following:

Obviously, all "neurotic acting-out" has the following in common:
it is an acting which unconsciously relieves inner tension and brings a
partial discharge to warded-off impulses (no matter whether these
impulses express directly instinctual demands, or are reactions to
original instinctual demands, for example guilt feelings); the present
situation, somehow associatively connected with the repressed
content, is used as an occasion for the discharge of repressed
energies; the cathexis is displaced from the repressed memories to
the present "derivative" and this displacement makes the discharge

possible. This definition is certainly correct but it is insufficient. . . .

"Acting-out," as distinguished from the other phenomona is an acting, not a mere feeling, not a mere thinking, not a mere mimic expression, not a mere single movement. This fact distinguishes it from symptom formation. It is true that there are also symptoms which involve a certain acting; but these symptoms actually could also be called "acting-out." . . .

Upon what does it depend whether the displacement substitute for what has been warded off is expressed in mere thoughts or single movements or whether it results in acting? It is not easy to give an answer to this question immediately.

It is clear from this discussion that the term "acting out" is an arbitrary introduction by Strachey, who in spite of his enormous contribution through the *Standard Edition*, nevertheless obviously suffered from the need to retranslate everything in highly original form. His language could just as well have been translated as action, and in fact it was so translated by an earlier expert. The term "action" more readily expresses the sense of the German and fits into the English language more smoothly. It is thus no surprise that a careful examination reveals no significant difference between acting out and action; the two terms express essentially the same idea.

The problem is, What leads to action? Obviously this question is so broad as to permit no simple answer. The literature is full of uncertainties and contradictions.

SEXUALITY AND AGGRESSION

Action involves some gratification or acting out of instinctual drives. In the current context it is used almost entirely in relation to the sexual and aggressive drives, although as the passage from Fenichel quoted above points out, symptoms could just as well be considered a form of acting out. It is therefore necessary to distinguish more carefully between sexuality and aggression.

Sexuality is inherently a constructive form of action, motivated by the physiological and psychological needs of the human being. The work of many brilliant researchers since Freud has served to amplify, but not alter his basic discoveries. The understanding of sexuality still relies most heavily on Freud's Three Essays. As is well known, sexuality becomes neurotic when (1) it is pregenital, (2) it is carried out inadequately (frigidity, impotence and so on), (3) it fails to lead to any satisfaction.

On the other hand, aggression should be looked upon as a reactive instinct. Here Freud's later theories have created a great deal of confusion. The death instinct has been almost universally rejected by psychoanalysts as a totally inadequate concept. But real clarification of the problem of hostility has still not appeared on the scene. Freud[8] himself in a letter to Marie Bonaparte dated May 27, 1937 wrote:

> "I will try to answer your question (about aggression). The whole topic has not yet been treated carefully and what I had to say about it in earlier writings is so premature and casual as hardly to deserve consideration."

Essentially aggression should be divided into assertiveness and hostility. Hostility is a reaction to frustration; in this respect the earlier Freud is more convincing than the later. If it is applied to an external danger, the individual meets the danger and the hostility disappears. As mentioned above this means that all hostile action is neurotic unless directed towards a real enemy.

As is well known, hostility can be expressed as sexuality and sexuality can be expressed as hostility. These displacements can be disentangled easily enough in the clinical situation, but not in superficial behavioral research.

CONSTRUCTIVE AND DESTRUCTIVE ACTION

Since acting out and action are essentially the same, a clarification must be reached by distinguishing between *constructive* and *destructive action*. Since this is both the clinical and theoretical point at issue it should be approached directly rather than by the roundabout locution of acting out.

In general it can be said that constructive action is (1) purposeful in a rational sense, (2) conscious, and (3) leads to satisfaction. By contrast destructive action is (1) purposeless, (2) unconscious, and (3) leads to frustration.

The specification of the nature of destructive action should replace the concept of acting out entirely. This is a question which is readily approachable in terms of both clinical and theoretical knowledge. Action is destructive when it is inappropriate to the reality situation.

Two aspects of destructive action can be singled out: (1) There is the resort to action in an attempt to resolve some underlying feeling such as depression. This is the case with most of what we ordinarily classify as acting out nowadays such as homosexuality, drug addiction and the like. Such action may bring temporary relief, or it may not; in either case the underlying disturbance remains and returns to disturb the individual. (2) The second case where action may be destructive is where it is specifically based on some hostile fantasy which is then carried out towards another human being or situation. The alternative to such destructive action is an internalization of the rage, the neurotic consequences of which are well known. The individual is thus faced with the choice of neurotic activity or neurotic passivity, each of which is destructive in its own way. The only real solution is to overcome the inner-psychological conflict.

THEORY AND THERAPY

Theory has immediate relevance to the problems of therapy. An important misunderstanding of theory has led to the development of the lunatic fringe of psychotherapists who incessantly urge their patients to carry out all kinds of actions without regard to their destructive or constructive consequences. This lunatic fringe of psychotherapists represents a dangerous trend in psychotherapy, especially since it offers more immediate relief than the more systematic and more effective forms of psychotherapy. Furthermore it offers, surprisingly, a therapeutic rationale for the release of hostility.

If a clear distinction is drawn between sex and aggression it can be seen that the lunatic fringe group bases its position on a combination of ignorance and foreplay. The ignorance appears in the indiscriminate relief of hostility in both the therapist and the patient. There are already some therapists who deliberately beat their patients, and with our knowledge of human nature it can only be predicted that the number will grow, unfortunate as that may be. Generally this school justifies this position with a number of statements about therapy which are completely at variance with the historical and clinical facts. For example, the oft-repeated absurdity that Freud had a touching phobia must be set off against the fact that for many years Freud used to massage his patients from head to foot and only gave up this procedure when he found it therapeutically ineffective.

The question of foreplay instead of real gratification through intercourse can be seen in many of the writings of the lunatic fringe group. A typical example is that of a girl who was told by her analyst that she could not have any feelings unless he held her hand. So he held her hand. This naturally led to feelings of sexual excitement (which she had anyhow) but when she experienced these the therapist told her she was angry at him. In desperation she finally left. After she left the therapist called her to establish a social relationship with her. Again he held her hand. She expected him to go on to have intercourse with her but he refrained, this time on the grounds that it would "hurt her." Actually one of her problems was that she had sex with too many men so that it would not have hurt her in the slightest. It was rather his fear of being hurt which he was projecting on her.

Proper theory leads to a proper therapy. The first problem is to differentiate between constructive and destructive actions. Constructive action moves towards the development of a happy life based on love with full sexual freedom. What is destructive is the overemphasis on hostility and actions which either bring temporary relief or internalize them in a destructive manner.

The replacement of the concept of acting out by destructive action leads to immediate theoretical and clinical gains. In practice on the current scene acting out is used more as a term of opprobrium than a scientific description. It is everyday clinical experience that what one analyst considers normal behavior another looks upon as acting out. To take but one example, the whole field of group therapy is looked upon as acting out by certain rigid Freudians, whereas others regard it as a serious contribution to the problem of therapy.

If the emphasis is placed on the destructive character of action the onus is upon the analyst to help the patient see in what way any particular action is destructive. This is in fact the way analysis works. For example in the analysis of homosexual patients the emphasis is generally on the destructive consequences of the homosexual activity for the patient. In other clinical situations a relatively simple differentiation is frequently possible. For example, an occasional smoking of a marijuana cigarette does no obvious harm, but continuous resort to marijuana is as destructive as continuous resort to alcohol.

SUMMARY

This paper began with an attempt to differentiate between acting out and action. A consideration of questions of impulse control, memory, different kinds of impulses, social and moral judgments, and the passive versus the impulsive patient reveals no clear-cut distinction between acting out and action. Further, a review of the original literature indicates that Freud's original language can be translated as action more appropriately than acting out. Acting out is an artificial word especially created by Strachey for the *Standard Edition*. Thus to some extent the whole argument rests on a spurious semantic basis.

In order to clarify the question it is necessary to draw a sharper distinction between sexuality and aggression. Sexuality is a constructive instinct which leads to gratification while hostility is a destructive instinct which leads to frustration.

In the light of this distinction it is proposed that the concept of acting out be dropped and replaced by the dichotomy of constructive as contrasted with destructive action. Clinical and theoretical criteria for this differentiation are much easier to establish than those for acting out.

REFERENCES

1. Fenichel, O.: *The Psychoanalytic Theory of Neurosis.* New York, Norton, 1945.
2. Fenichel, O.: *Collected Papers,* Second Series. New York, Norton, 1954, pp. 296-297.

3. Freud, A.: Acting out. *Int. J. Psychoanal.*, 49:165-170, 1968.
4. Freud, S.: *Gesammelte Werke*. London, Image Publishing Co., 1946, Vol. X, p. 129.
5. Freud, S.: Remembering, repeating and working-through. In *Standard Edition*. London, Hogarth Press, 1958, Vol. XII, pp. 149-150.
6. Freud, S.: Recollection, repetition and working-through. In *Collected Papers*. London, Hogarth Press, 1948, Vo. II, p. 369.
7. Hunt, M.: *The Natural History of Love*. New York, Knopf, 1959.
8. Jones, E.: *The Life and Work of Sigmund Freud*. New York, Basic Books, 1957, Vol. III, p. 464.

D r. Benjamin Wolstein is a long-time member of our Adelphi University Postdoctoral Program faculty and a past contributor to earlier volumes in this series. He is one of the more prolific writers of the new breed of psychoanalysts who have been critically examining and evaluating various aspects of analytic theory. In this paper he puts acting out in clearer perspective by contrasting it with "acting" and "action" in behavior.

Dr. Wolstein begins the paper by recounting a brief history of behaviorism from which he concludes that this development does not replace psychoanalytic studies of unconscious processes. Next, he presents the biological and sociological models of psychoanalysis, which, again, are demonstrated as inadequate. This discussion prefaces Dr. Wolstein's presentation of the psychological "action" model unifying experience and behavior which, he feels, are artificially separated by the preceding models. As a result, it is concluded that the interminable controversy between experientialists and behaviorists is based upon one-sided concepts used by each school. The paper concludes with a proposal for a modified approach which would ideally encompass and integrate conceptualization.

In this erudite and stimulating theoretical paper on acting out, Dr. Benjamin Wolstein has given us much material to ponder in our understanding of the neurosis of our time.

D.S.M.
G.D.G.

Chapter 2

"Acting Out," "Acting," "Action": Three Views of Behavior in Psychoanalysis

Benjamin Wolstein

IF THE "ACTING-OUT" disorders are, as the organizers of this Conference suggest, the neurosis of our time, then the behaviorist program of theory and therapy may be its most important symptom in psychological knowledge today.

The notion of behaviorism, itself, is a vague and ambiguous scientific usage. While it claims to label the science of activity of organisms without break from animal to human species, it emphasizes the need, in fact, for moral controls of activity. Strange though it may appear, science of behavior is less science of psychology than morality of behavior. It views human activity from the standpoint of rightness of outcomes rather than description of inputs, products rather than processes, consequences rather than motives. In short, it studies human behavior from the standpoint of adjustment and adaptation rather than affective and cognitive human psyche.

Behavior is not mere activity, then, but activity in accordance with established moral, ethical and legal standards. Take behavior in such rather common usages as "Behave yourself!" or "I'm not misbehaving!" and this moral, ethical and legal dimension of behaviorism is practically self-evident. It is, therefore, more likely that laws of behavior will be found in the legislative actions of Congress in Washington than in the operant conditioning experiments at Harvard and Columbia. So the fact, if no other, that behavior is a term of the individual's biological and moral adjustment to his environment, or social and ego-interpersonal adaptation to his culture, limits its usefulness for the empirical

23

and systematic requirements of scientific psychology in general and psychoanalytic inquiry in particular.

But the notion of behavior is vague and ambiguous for still another reason. Consider, again, what happens to the meaning of behavior when taken actively as behaving. It is, clearly, a secondary elaboration of a primary having, and I shall hyphenate it as be-having for the following discussion. For if, in a significant sense, the be-having of experience relates to having the original experience, it suggests a real and distinct duality inherent in the theory and research programs of all behaviorisms, which, in turn, suggests that no matter how thorough and extensive any analyses of behavior are or may become, they do not extend through the surface adaptive functions down into the deeper structure of a field of experience. The self divided between having and be-having experience cannot, under any conditions, be put back together again. If, in other words, you start with a divided self, you end with a divided self.

In most histories of psychology, John B. Watson is the commonly accepted founder of laboratory behaviorism, his *Psychology from the Standpoint of a Behaviorist*[7] its seminal work. His behaviorism most probably traces back to the physiological side of William James's *Principles of Psychology*,[5] John Dewey's "The Reflex Arc Concept in Psychology,"[3] and to the functional behaviorism of the Chicago School of George H. Mead, Addison W. Moore, James R. Angell and others in addition to Dewey around 1900. But it is Watson who first hit the vision of behaviorism dead-center and then took it all the way to its most consistent, extreme statement.

Now, it seems certain that some workers in psychoanalysis were aware of these developments in American psychology. At one time or another, Sigmund Freud, Alfred Adler, Carl G. Jung, Sandor Ferenczi, Otto Rank and others visited this country at various times, for varying periods, to lecture, supervise or practice. Why, then, did they never—not one, even—take behaviorism seriously? They did not, I think, because it does not extend their respective visions and metapsychologies of psychoanalysis. But in light of the distinction between having and be-having a thought or feeling, it is easier to see why they did not rush to become behaviorists. Behavior, being a secondary elaboration, does not replace the psychoanalytic study of the relation of unconscious to conscious experience.

Introduced into the field of therapy, as ego-interpersonal psychoanalysts discovered, behavior tends to carry with it a series of masks, shields, disguises—ego defenses and interpersonal security operations—that cover up the motives, thoughts and feelings, the dreams, fantasies and aims, the distortions, disturbances and difficulties of human psyche. It encourages the use of "acting"—to be discussed as part of the sociological model. The id psychoanalysts understood this so well, in fact, that they never modified their suspicious attitude toward behavior. They clearly indicate this in their notion of "acting out"—to be discussed as part of the biological model. A third approach, to be discussed as part of the psychological model, treats behavior directly as experience be-haved or enacted, which, simply, is "action."

In the movement from havior—if I may coin the term—to be-havior of experience, then, systems of beliefs, values and ideals are established for both. This distinguishes psychology from metapsychology, a distinction underlying the whole problem of choice, judgment and decision in all other psychotherapies as well. See Table 2-I for its representation in psychoanalytic structure. If be-having, therefore, covers and extends the having of experience into moral, ethical and legal considerations, it is again clear that be-having a motive, as secondary elaboration, may cover up the primary having of it. Study of be-haved consequences, by the same token, is an important source of information about the motives originally had. As long as the James stream of experience retains its temporal, continuous and cumulative flow, the be-having of experience will remain a second having of it.

THE BIOLOGICAL MODEL—"ACTING OUT"

Using this distinction between having and be-having thoughts and feelings, the id psychoanalysts are, as a general rule, mainly interested in inner experience of dreams and motives, fantasies and impulses as primarily had. They are far less interested in the

TABLE 2-I

SYMBOLS OF REPRESENTATION

Orders of Psychoanalytic Inquiry

Empirical Observation	*Definition*	*Systematic Postulation*	*Theory*	*Interpretive Metapsychology*
(1)	(2)	(3)	(4)	(5)
transference t_n	transference t	genesis G	unconscious experience U	Freudian [M₁]
resistance r_n	resistance r	function F		Adlerian [M₂]
anxiety a_n	anxiety a	structure S		Jungian [M₃]
counter-anxiety ca_n	counter-anxiety ca	dynamism D		Rankian [M₄] .
counter-resistance cr_n	counter-resistance cr	immediacy I		. .
counter-transference ct_n	counter-transference ct	reflection R		. . [Mₙ]

From Wolstein.[8]

outer experience of beliefs and values, ends and ideals as secondarily be-haved. Reports of ongoing experience in the first person are the significant data; second-person reports about their outcomes are significant only as a source of cues, clues, hypotheses and inferences. The direct study of experience with the person having it, above all, constitutes the unique and revolutionary procedure of the late nineteenth century hypnotists and psychotherapists—H. Bernheim, Josef Breuer, J. Charcot and their gifted student, Freud. Nothing quite like it had ever been done before: to study the ongoing stream of experience without the established philosophy of a power structure of religion or law, politics or education, but with the single aim of increasing self-knowledge. And though Freud and his followers later speculated about a ponderous instinctual metapsychology—which, unfortunately, was to become an establishment in its own right—the psychoanalytic experience was probably the most frank and open human experience then extant involving two people.

In the biological model, id psychoanalysts take behavior

seriously enough to admonish the patient against doing anything about the outward conditions of life while his psychoanalysis is in process. He is not to change occupation, marital status and so on. They prefer to study his inner experience in, as they say, statu nascendi of thinking and feeling, dreams and fantasies, transference and resistance. "Acted out," this inner experience would be placed beyond the scope of therapeutic inquiry for the reason that pleasure of enacting them ordinarily outweighs the pain of exploring them. Id psychoanalysts, here, are guided by the difference between the unfolding edge of experience and its hardened realization as behavior. We are, I believe, all familiar with this difference in our daily lives. Experience of fantasy and actuality of behavior are polar opposites. One way to change or lose a fantasy is, simply, to do something about it. The futuristic, expansive aspect of fantasy may be defined by contrast to the past-oriented, reductive aspect of behavior.

In this perspective, id psychoanalysts are inspired by a grand humanistic ideal of expanding awareness by transforming unconscious into conscious experience. It is the lasting merit of late nineteenth-century hypnotists and psychotherapists, already mentioned, that they turn this ideal into working theory for all later psychoanalytic inquiry. And they join both the perspective and the theory into a special procedure designed to anticipate and control a patient's "acting out" of experience as behavior. For this purpose, however, the biological model set special conditions for the collaboration of psychoanalyst and patient.

The id psychoanalyst interposes his own ego and superego between his patient's id, on the one side, and ego and superego on the other. In so doing, he also carefully excludes his own id from the experiential field of therapy. Though Freud has not yet fully stated the relations of ego and superego to id when he first formulated the biological model (see, for example, his 1915-1917 *Introductory Lectures*,[4] especially Chapters 27 and 28), he clearly recommended that the psychoanalyst exclude the patient's and use his own ego and superego to interpret the patient's id. From the other side, the patient is, moreover, prevented from using his ego and superego to consider his psychoanalyst's id. Recall, here, that while transference and resistance of id process and pattern constitute the core of this new theory, counter-transference and counter-resistance of these same materials are beyond the context of inquiry of the biological model. How does this clarify the definition of "acting out?" When the id psycho-analyst interposes his ego and superego between the patient's ego and superego and his id, leaving his own id out of therapeutic field, the id patient can only have—but not be-have—experience of his id life. The patient cannot control and direct his be-haved experience because, in short, he surrenders his ego and superego to his psychoanalyst who does.

In sum, the target of id therapy is symptom removal; the means is reorganization of inward experience. This focus on experience at the expense of behavior leads to the genetic fallacy.

THE SOCIOLOGICAL MODEL "ACTING"

During the 1930's, the biological model was completely trans-formed. The problem of therapeutic inquiry no longer simply reflects disorders of the id. After Wilhelm Reich's character analysis, Anna Freud's and Heinz Hartmann's new ego psychology and Harry S. Sullivan's interpersonal relations, among others, it is now possible to include character armor, defense mechanism or security operation as part of the working context of therapeutic inquiry. And once character, ego or interpersonal self is admitted, it becomes necessary, as well, to admit all the beliefs, values and ideals that concern a particular patient. In this way, psycho-analytic therapy becomes, to put it briefly, egoic and inter-personalized.

The sociological model is split into two wings: the ego wing seeking to extend the original biological metapsychology to these new social concerns, and the cultural and interpersonal wing seeking to introduce categories of social and cultural anthropology as new interpretive metapsychology of psycho-analysis. These differences in metapsychology aside, however, both ego and interpersonal psychoanalysts try to work the be-having of experience into therapeutic inquiry. And for the first time, behavior, as character armor, defense mechanism or security operation, begins to dominate the working context such that ego-interpersonal experience be-haved is now as important as id experience had.

Given the average expectable environment, the patient learns to "act" in order to meet the environing expectations on average. So his self is divided between the self-system and its security operations, the ego and its mechanisms of defense, the character structure and its armoring—in short, the persona and its bearer. The armored, egoic, interpersonalized self is one step removed from the thinking, feeling, personal self. The ego-interpersonal self, however, is so divided as to correlate it with the new principle of adaptation in metapsychology. Hartmann, for example, answers the question of development of defenses, arising from a context of ideas set mainly by Reich and A. Freud, as well as the elder Freud, with the adaptative point of view postulated as directly applicable to the ego and its defense mechanisms. Influenced by the pragmatic movement in American thought— above all, I believe, by Mead's philosophy of the act—Sullivan puts special emphasis on the relation of pursuing satisfactions and securities to the social order. They both join the procedures and goals of ego-interpersonal therapy, inextricably, to the prevailing beliefs, values and ideals of the social order that supports its practice. If you cannot become sane, in other words, at least learn to "act" as though you were.

The sociological model focuses on ego-interpersonal operations of defense and security, or, in terms of our discussion, not on having but be-having experience. With this new respect for behavior, the point is to learn to "act" properly and meet the requirements of a selected environment. The psychoanalytic problem is not whether character armor, defense mechanism or security operation is wrong or false as such; it is, essentially, whether these patterns succeed or fail to meet the environing expectations for purposes of adapting the patient to his field of social and ego-interpersonal relations. But ego-interpersonal psychoanalysts, not unlike their colleagues in behavior therapy, overlook the duality inherent in all "acting" or be-having. I have already suggested this duality, above, as the difference between primary having and secondary be-having of experience, and discuss some further implications below.

To this point about the sociological model, it suffices to note the common dictionary definition of "acting" as both doing and performing, as both enacting unself-consciously and playing a social and ego-interpersonal role for others. The possibilities for feigned behavior, deceit and distortion, hypocrisy and duplicity and the whole range of politics of experience are practically self-evident, since, from an ego-interpersonal point of view, it is most difficult to tell the ego and its defense mechanisms apart, to distinguish the interpersonal self from its operational security. For in any selected piece of social and ego-interpersonal behavior, there is no need to determine whether it represents the social persona or its maker, a fictional facade or its author.

In strictly behaviorist and ego-interpersonal psychology, this whole question is itself questionable. The behavioral outcome finally counts; it outweighs the experiential input by far. If the outcome can be made to stick, it is pointless to explore the true and false constituents of the "act." Grossly pragmatic, the "act" that works out is, in fact, the right behavior. This view fosters the unwarranted assumption that a person is what, "acting," he can make others believe he is—as though they did not have thoughts and feelings, spontaneous intuitions and unconscious resources of their own, as though they were capable of knowing him only as he represents himself to be, nothing more. And this view turns the psychoanalytic field of inquiry into a psycho-dramatic stage for ego-interpersonal "acting," as though real "actions" spontaneously innovated were no different from distorted "acting" calculated for deceptive purposes—as though, in short, nothing within a person extended beyond his behavior. The ego-interpersonal point is, in principle, that what is not be-haved cannot be known—which leaves the sociological model unable to account for change, creativity, novelty and the psychic processes and powers, even, required to produce the ego defense and interpersonal security so central to this perspective.

In sum, the target of ego-interpersonal therapy is personality change; the means is reorganization of outward attitude and behavior. This focus on behavior at the expense of experience leads to the functional fallacy.

THE PSYCHOLOGICAL MODEL—"ACTION"

A psychological perspective on psychoanalytic therapy requires a direct, straightforward view of "action." In this view, "action" represents the unity of experience and behavior. Interest in the id problem of "acting out" is declining for the reason that the environment is no longer consistently either average or expectable. The happening, the be-in and love-in, the mass social and political psychodramas about Vietnam, pollution, overpopulation, black power and women's liberation and so on make the organization of wide-ranging behavior much easier to imagine, rehearse and carry out; therefore, paradoxically enough, less significant for psychoanalytic therapy. Standard inhibitions of behavior are becoming much vaguer and harder to define. Conventional standards are so changed since World War II that almost anything reasonable and rationalizable is now average, expectable and appropriate behavior for a selected environment. Even the sexual inhibitions, with the rise of unisexual values, are being less frequently observed in current psychoanalytic inquiry. I hear more from patients and, from students in supervision, about patients involved in bisexual and group relations that deprive the "act" of any special sanctity or uniform patterning.

And interest in the ego-interpersonal problem of "acting" is also declining for the reason that success of behavior no longer identifies the personal quality of life. The duality of having and be-having experience may, during psychoanalytic inquiry, lead as directly into a simplicity of "action." Here again, of course, is the gap between having and be-having experience; that is, one can "act" as though a given state of affairs existed—when it is not, in fact, the actor's experience—in order to influence another's experience, change his mind, manipulate his behavior, manage his life. In this gap flourish all the politics of experience; for "acting" both expresses as behavior yet disguises as experience the unconscious psychic processes and patterns. Having experience is direct, presentational, immediate; be-having experience is reflective, representational, mediate.

The behaviorists, incidentally, would be right if the ability

to produce the right behavior were all there is to the understanding of human psychology. If that were all there is, then
why bother with anything more than the manipulation of
behavior? But if a real distinction does exist, however, between
inner experience and its enactment in outer behavior, behaviorists
are short-sighted and, therefore, wrong; they lack the leverage
by which to transform new experience into enlarged behavior, or
new behavior into deeper experience. Now: if new experience
actually did not at all affect behavior, then the id psychoanalysts
would, of course, also be wrong; if new behavior actually did
not at all affect experience, then so would the ego-interpersonal
psychoanalysts; and if — per impossible — human psyche were
nothing but behavior, there would, strictly speaking, be no
science of psychology, no structure of psychoanalytic inquiry,
no psychopathologies.

The point of this third view of behavior in psychoanalysis—
"action"—may now be clear. It is not simply that "acting out"
and "acting" are no longer very instructive beyond the modes of
relatedness and models of therapeutic inquiry for which these
id and ego-interpersonal notions were first sketched out. For
these types of be-having derive from basic postulates of psychoanalytic psychology—those of immediacy and reflection; see Table
2-I for their placement in the overall structure of psychoanalysis.
The point is, rather, to foster the unity of immediacy and reflection, the unity of having and be-having thoughts and feelings, the
unity of experience and behavior. While "acting out" derives
directly from instinctual experience, and "acting" expresses as
behavior what it represses as experience, "action" unifies experience and behavior through mediation of the psyche.

The third view marks the declining significance of behavior
altogether in the working inquiry of psychoanalysis. This major
shift in emphasis is supported, mainly I believe, by new efforts
to answer questions the biological and sociological models do
not even ask. Who, in the biological model readjusts infantile
sexual conflict? Not the biological or id self, obviously, because
it is that self that is in conflict. Who, in the sociological model,
readapts distorted behavior to the average, expectable environment? Not the social or ego-interpersonal self, obviously, because

it is that self that is in distortion. The answer, here, can only be a psychic self—an individual and personal psyche that has thoughts and feelings as experience and, again, as behavior. It is this psychic self, then, that mediates experience and new behavior as well as behavior and new experience.

EXPERIENCE AND BEHAVIOR

I now turn to some aspects of the recent controversy between experientialists and behaviorists. It endures, I believe, because both sides deal with two distinct perspectives on psychology—experience and behavior—that they develop and state on a derivative level. They do not usually term them derivative since there is no recognized principle of metapsychology, or factual basis in psychology, according to which they derive them. In this way, the distinction of experience from behavior turns into a spearhead of controversy between therapists of experience and therapists of behavior who end up unable to address one another.

The established canons of behaviorism treat experience as an inadmissible construct on the critical ground that its processes and patterns are mentalistic, subjective and not directly observable or checkable. According to Robert Bolles who takes a hard behaviorist line in his *Theory of Motivation*,[1] human experience "cannot be invoked to lend ancillary validity to a construct that is otherwise anchored in behavioral phenomena . . . its reference is outside the theory . . . it does nothing to bind together the structure of the theory." As might be expected, the bulk of this work on behaviorism is devoted to theories, methods and results of laboratory experiments with infrahuman species—cats and dogs, mice and rats. For in such animal studies, any human experience is not only considered irrelevant as construct but, because of possible anthropomorphism, also in fact.

In this way, the hard-line behaviorist also excludes from the structure of his perspective, of course, all relatedness and communication of all primarily psychological therapies. Taking this view to its logical but, I hope, unintended conclusion, studies of human psyche and its distortions, disturbances and difficulties somehow disappear from his domain of science because human

experience—inevitably, a necessary construct for these studies—
is outside behaviorist theory. Though the relations of experience
and behavior are complex, they are still critical for contemporary
psychology and psychoanalysis; and they will not soon be resolved
without a notion of individual, human psyche. Because of such
behaviorist views, however, studies of human psyche and its
distortions, disturbances and difficulties do not seem to be fading
away either—not, at any rate, by simply manipulating this major
distinction of behavior from experience.

Why this methodological impasse and what will resolve it,
however, are not simple questions. Even a brief consideration of
nineteenth-century biological metapsychologies would indicate
that the relations of experience and behavior became increasingly
strained from 1859 onward. After Charles Darwin's *The Origin
of Species*[2] appeared, instinct and drive theorists adapted the
implications of evolutionary biology to studies of the human
organism, extending a long overdue emphasis on animal behavior.
In this light, any enduring change in the relations of experience
and behavior depends on creating large enough perspective to
encompass the three categories peculiar to human species—id or
need satisfaction, social and ego-interpersonal security, individual
psyche and its direction—without the currently undue Darwinist
emphasis on animal behavior and therapy of natural selection.

There is real need in contemporary psychology and psychoanalysis for this change but, I think it is clear, the change is not
about to happen. Hard-line behaviorism is usually articulated,
curiously enough, as the complementary but unreachable opposite
of hard-line experientialism; and differences between them are
not being resolved in the language and thought of current controversy. The line between the two continues to harden—and,
as a result, keeps them so far apart—because their differences cut
far deeper into presuppositions about their relations than previously suggested in public discussion. To appreciate how far
apart they actually are, see Wann's *Behaviorism and Phenomenology*[6] for various approaches to this hard duality of experience and behavior, especially those of Carl Rogers and B. F.
Skinner. It is from various biological and social Darwinist
presuppositions, then, that this basic split between distinctly

human experience and generally animal behavior derives. Without getting beyond such Darwinist presuppositions, it is not reasonable to expect behaviorists and experientialists, however, to resume constructive relations in the near future. And if this were not so, the hope of getting through and beyond this impasse would be very slim indeed.

THE PSYCHE

The controversy between the two perspectives, in their own terms, tends to create more sparks and argumentative heat than light and real penetration. While it may be stimulating, it has, unfortunately, so far proved unproductive of new vision and metapsychology beyond itself. It is, as controversy, literally interminable because both sides use one-sided concepts to develop their respective positions. They fail to move through the two notions of experience and behavior—which refer to the self-same human processes and patterns seen from different sides—to a central notion of individual, personal psyche out of whose affective and cognitive resources such processes and patterns are generated. To state it in current transactional terminology, the behaviorist studies games people play; the experientialist studies their motives for playing games; the psychoanalyst would, I propose, study their resources for making them up. If, in others words, experience is latent behavior, and behavior is manifest experience, then psyche is the affective and cognitive resources for experience be-haved or behavior experienced.

The distinction between experience and behavior is, fundamentally, a distinction between duration and outcome—between undergoing thought and feeling and thought and feeling undergone and done. In actual psychological inquiry, the significant factor, here, is time. The other's behavior is always directly observable to us before we infer his experience; our own personal experience is always directly observable to us before the other infers it from our behavior. When "action" translates experience into behavior, then, and no social and ego-interpersonal barriers filter out the experience of certain misbehaviors or reinforce the behavior of certain proper experiences, that is, when experience translates directly into behavior and behavior translates directly into experience, then the distinction between them is temporal rather than substantive.

At some future date, perhaps a mutually modified experiential-behavioral reconstruction may be worked out, in other language and thought, no doubt, and with other presuppositions, and then be applied to such fields of human-scientific inquiry as psychoanalysis. If any such reconstruction is to be useful, it will have to modify and extend the limits of biological, social and ego-interpersonal Darwinism and, of course, supplement its perspective on human species. A reconstruction of experience and behavior moving deeper into the individual, personal psyche is the most probable way of changing it, however, because neither the having nor the be-having of experience can persevere without, at some point, also referring to the other; neither can sustain itself without the other's support. Both experience and behavior, in this view, extend the individual affective and cognitive resources of human psyche into all fields of human relatedness and communication.

Consider this proposal against the backdrop of the following ideas: As the influence of Darwin's evolutionary hypothesis declines, together with such root metaphors as struggle for existence and survival of the fittest, or the indelible instincts for competition and self-preservation, the hard line now dividing the self as experience and behavior will probably dissolve into a deeper psychic perspective on human living of individuals who think and feel, decide and choose, innovate and reconstruct or, at the risk of disapproval from both sides, who have experience and be-have it. For if, in truth, behaviorist theory sets off its program of research and therapy so sharply from all aspects of human experience, it may then be asked, who is it that knows? for whom? or what? Or how can behavior ever reunite itself with experience as derivatives or extensions of individual affective and cognitive resources of human psyche? How get them back together again so that they be seen to exhibit the unity they may actually possess as attributes of a single psychic continuum, as be-haved experience or experienced behavior?

However anyone, experientialist or behaviorist, appraises and applies knowledge in clinical and laboratory inquiry—even in the personal experience, indeed, of his own social and ego-interpersonal behavior—he cannot deal seriously with such questions without first accepting, as a matter of simply being human, that behavior is as much a function of experience as experience is a function of behavior. To paraphrase that great philosopher of science, Immanuel Kant: without experience, behavior becomes empty and, therefore, both futile and pointless; without behavior, experience becomes blind and, therefore, both fruitless and frustrated. If it is true, then, that experience and behavior articulate the self-same processes and patterns from different sides, the question about their psychological origins and functions remains the only serious question for psychological science. And the relation of their conscious to their unconscious dimensions remains, by the same token, the only serious question for psychoanalytic inquiry.

REFERENCES

1. Bolles, R.: *Theory of Motivation.* New York, Harper & Row, 1967.
2. Darwin, C.: *The Origin of Species.* New York, Modern Library Giant, n.d.
3. Dewey, J.: The reflex arc concept in psychology. *Psychological Rev.,* 3:357-370, 1896.
4. Freud, S.: *A General Introduction to Psychoanalysis.* Garden City, Garden City Publ., 1943.
5. James, W.: *Principles of Psychology.* New York, Holt, 1890.
6. Wann, T. (Ed.): *Behaviorism and Phenomenology.* Chicago, University of Chicago, 1964.
7. Watson, J. B.: *Psychology from the Standpoint of a Behaviorist.* Philadelphia, Lippincott, 1919.
8. Wolstein, B.: *Theory of Psychoanalytic Therapy.* New York, Grune & Stratton, 1967, p. 157.

Dʀ. Mᴀx Rᴏsᴇɴʙᴀᴜᴍ, a practicing psychoanalyst and a prolific contributor to the literature on group psychotherapy, has been quite concerned recently with the encounter movement and the potential destructiveness of the acting-out behavior of both patients and therapists. Therapists, Dr. Rosenbaum posits, have a value system based upon internalized values and beliefs that could and should govern their treatment.

He approaches his topic by first defining and discussing sexual acting out in a group therapeutic situation. Causal factors including transference, countertransference, and their interrelationship are described in the presence of acting-out behavior on the part of the patient. In a section on countertransference, Dr. Rosenbaum distinguishes between classical and active analysts in terms of cognizance and use of countertransference. His paper concludes with an especially timely warning to psychotherapists: in order to insure maximum benefits to patients one must be wary of fads in psychotherapy and remain faithful to personal ethical and moral values.

Dr. Rosenbaum, in his usual combination of scholarliness and hard-hitting directness, provides us with an intellectual manifesto detailing those reasons for maintaining the integrity of our ethical and scientific standards. Currently, such issues are particularly relevant to the concerns that many of us have regarding the increase in acting out on part of both therapists and patients.

D.S.M.
G.D.G.

Chapter 3

Acting Out and the Ethic of the Psychoanalyst

MAX ROSENBAUM

Today psychoanalysts are increasingly confronted with behavior that interferes with the movement of the analytic process. They encounter patterns of acting that becloud the recognition of the patient's basic problems. Obstructive behavior may be said to take place when the patient instead of verbalizing his feelings, substitutes motor activity. In place of verbalizing his feelings of love and hostility he may engage in acts of seduction or aggression. The patient who substitutes motor activity for verbal activity in a transference relationship is acting out. Acting out has been described as a disturbance of superego control as a result of unusually strong transference reactions. Such reactions are based on an unconscious misunderstanding of present external objects in the sense of the past.[8]

A basic rule of analysis is to provide for free association and free verbalization of affect. This rule is broken whenever the patient begins to act out instead of containing his feelings on a verbal level. At that point his actions prevent his gaining insight by means of interpretation and working through, and the analysis is said to be at a standstill.

In the literature such acting out is considered to be a common and deplorable occurrence. Emch[7] regards acting out as a repetition of the past. Loeser and Bry[18] and Roth[22] see it in terms of the related phenomenon, transference. Bry[5] regards acting out as resistance. Weiss,[27] Fenichel,[9] and Kasanin[17] say that acting out is the reappearance of an inner drive, the expression of or relief from it, that it is unpredictable and irrational. Johnson and Szurek[16] state that the person who acts out is one with a superego defect. Reich[21] has used the term "impulsive

41

character" to describe people who act out, and Alexander[2] feels that individuals who need punishment tend to act out. Schmideberg[23] states that patients who act out their conflicts are constitutionally unable to tolerate frustration, as compared with more repressed and inhibited individuals. Aichhorn,[1] in his studies of antisocial behavior, and this was confirmed by Healy and Bronner,[15] pointed out that at times children who act out have identified themselves with the ethical distortions of their parents. Healy and Bronner formulated the concept that the rejected child cannot develop a normal superego that would enable him to control acting out.

The literature suggests that acting out is seen as a persistent problem and a therapeutic difficulty. In only a few isolated instances is there admission of the possibility that acting out may contain a positive element. Rarely does an author indicate that acting out can be used constructively in the therapeutic process. In the literature, then, acting out is generally considered obstructive and negative. Sexual acting out is rarely a subject of discussion as such.

It has been generally agreed, starting with Freud,[11] that successful psychoanalysis is based on the concepts of working through of resistance and transference. Acting out may become the expression of an evidence for the transference relationship. In analysis the patient displays behavior originally repressed when his conflict was in the making. At this earlier period his characteristic behavior patterns were becoming ingrained into his character structure. Some of the behavior patterns have been compulsively employed over the years at the slightest frustration. Others develop in the course of analysis as an attempt to act out the repressed incestuous or aggressive fantasies of childhood. In both cases acting out manifests itself in repetitive, irrational behavior, as an outgrowth of the person's history.

Why does acting out occur? It does so always in the frame of strong transference relationship, when the impulse is strengthened and the defense is weakened. Before therapy, transference behavior may have been directed at a definite person or persons who have become representatives of some significant figure of the past. Likewise, in therapy, and especially in the group, acting out may be directed at any member who also becomes a significant figure of the past.

With the practice of psychoanalytic group therapy the mixed therapeutic group provides a familial setting, often including for the first time the experience of truly permissive parental figures. The "alternate sessions" meetings unattended by the analyst reinforce this permissive milieu. Often in this atmosphere free verbal and nonverbal communication of sexual feelings occurs, sometimes stimulated by certain group members. For some individuals, such communication is erotically stimulating, particularly under conditions of physical proximity, and the resultant tension may lead to sexual acting out with members of the same group or with individuals outside the group. Significant group reactions may serve to inhibit sexual acting out. In one group two patients, both married, were on the verge of acting out sexually, but countertransferences of the other group members, who saw them as parental prototypes, forced them to work through their feelings and prevented them from acting out.

Group members who act out sexually with one another evoke, in other members of the group, conscious and unconscious feelings that the family pattern is being disrupted by a violation of the incest taboo. The sexual acting out elicits anxiety in them with respect to their own incestuous feelings. This may in turn lead to constructive working through, enabling these other group members to resolve their own incestuous conflicts which they have hitherto been unable to face.

Bromberg[4] has pointed out that it is difficult to make a distinction between acting and acting out in practice, although the theoretical distinction seems clear. Acting itself has many roots of psychological and realistic origin: one of the latter may be an attempt to master anxiety by repetition or by dramatization. He sees *acting out* as an unconscious repetition of the past in the present which occurs instead of remembering repressed events. Acting out is discouraged in psychoanalytic treatment because it represents resistance to the recovery of unconscious memories in the transference relationship. On the other hand, acting and acting out are essential parts of psychodrama. Bromberg notes the confusion when he points to words as substitutes for motor activities and wonders whether they are effective enough. It seems to this writer that acting out, transference and countertransference must always be seen as part of the scheme when we try to explore acting out in the culture of 1970.

Countertransference

Transference, to begin with, is a regressive process. Waelder[26] has discussed this in detail. He described transference as follows: ". . . (It) may be said to be an attempt of the patient to revive and re-enact, in the analytic situation and in relation to the analyst, situations and phantasies of his childhood." ". . . Changes of this (analytic) situation through technique can considerably alter the transference phenomena. Among the means of influencing it are the confrontation of the patient's phantasies with reality, and analytic interpretations."

This has every relevance to discussion of acting out. The therapist must be clear as to which behavior is a response to the immediate and which behavior is a response which is transference-based. The important point is that countertransference is the analyst's transference reaction to the transference of the patient in the analytic situation. It is an error to include all the responses of the analyst to the patient, since there are conscious reactions to the patient as a reality object.

Because of countertransference there is the danger of the analyst using the analysis for "acting out." Here the activity of analysis begins to have some hidden meaning for the analyst. This is particularly seen in group therapy where the analyst may include patients in a group since because of countertransference he cannot tolerate a one-to-one relationship. He therefore places the patient in a group and often encourages the group to "act out" his own anger toward the patient. Or the analyst may keep patients in a one-to-one relationship to indulge his own needs to be seen as the benign and protective parent. Often, patients serve as substitutes for the analyst's own family and he lives his life through them. There are therapists who encourage patients in patterns of social activism which really mask the therapist's own reluctance to take part in life outside of his office. Increasingly, this writer has received referrals of patients who have become locked into patterns with therapists where the patient defies authority relationships which are basically related to unresolved transferences. Tragically, some therapists encourage patients in rebellious behaviour with nonverbal messages that communicate approval. There are therapists who, because of their own problems, feel that every young adult who defies his parents has achieved emancipation. They take the easy way out when they use therapy to attack parenthood.

It was in April, 1910 that Freud first introduced the term countertransference in a lecture on "The Future Prospects of Psychoanalytic Therapy," given at the Second Psychoanalytic Congress. He was quite definite and stated: "We have become aware of the countertransference which arises in the physician as a result of the patient's influence on his unconscious feelings and we are almost inclined to insist that he shall recognize this countertransference in himself and overcome it. . . ." For almost fifty years the area of countertransference lay dormant. It was acknowledged as the problem of the analyst to be worked through by him. But then the tide changed. A renewed interest in countertransference was accompanied by questions as to whether the countertransference might be accepted and worked through as a useful part of the analytic process. The more traditionally oriented psychoanalytic psychotherapists continue to see countertransference as an unconscious neurotic problem of the analyst and an impediment to therapy. These analysts are generally nonactive. The second group who may be fairly called the active analysts value all of the responses of the analyst and believe the countertransference to be very useful. In the group of active analysts are included the advocates of Melanie Klein's theories who generally interpret very early in treatment. These Kleinians also emphasize the revival of early primitive object relations.

This writer has noted Waelder's succinct statement of transference. To repeat, transference is perceived as a regressive progress. According to Waelder, the definition of the transference is critical to an understanding of the primary goals of psychoanalytic therapy which is the resolution of the infantile Oedipal problem in the structure of a transference neurosis.

All this has been repeated in another way because there must be some baseline when we discuss what is appropriate and inappropriate behavior. Currently analysts who study transference and countertransference are much more cautious about labeling all responses of the analyst to the patient as countertransference. It would appear that responses which are inappropriately sexual or aggressive and seem to be based on unconscious infantile feelings and therefore very intense in nature can be called countertransference. All of this relates to the analyst or therapist being "neutral." The therapist may like or dislike something which the patient is doing. But the analyst is conscious of these feelings. But again when the feelings become intense enough to preclude objectivity there is the genesis of *acting out* on the part of the analyst. At this point the needs of the analyst are being worked out through the person of the patient. Specifically the method of analysis has become distorted, for the activity of psychoanalysis has an unconscious meaning for the analyst. The problem will always be there as far as this writer is concerned. But it is a matter of degree. Fliess has quoted Hanns Sachs, the pioneer analyst, in this regard: ". . . the analyst's own shortcomings, the deficiencies of his individual development, the gross defects of the society in which he lives, the imperfections of psychoanalytic insight and method—these will always impose serious limitations on his efficiency, however incessantly he strives to overcome them."[10]

Racker[20] did not appear too worried when he stated that we are still children and neurotics even when we are adults and analysts. Orr[19] was more specific. He confirms this writer's observation when he wrote of two large groups of analysts when he discussed transference and countertransference. *The first group* of analysts has a *more classical* view of countertransference where it is seen primarily as an unconscious transference response of the *analyst* to the patient's transference which interferes with treatment. *The second group* of analysts adopts a different concept which encompasses all responses of the therapist and uses the countertransference as a therapeutic tool. Here the analyst becomes quite active. Today this is to be seen in the active approach of many analysts. For some years the Kleinian analysts have been interpreting very early.

There is a difference in the theoretical and clinical approaches of the Freudian and Kleinian schools. In the Freudian viewpoint, there is emphasis on the superego developing through resolution of the Oedipal conflict; there is stress on ego formation, defenses, the therapeutic alliance, resistance. Interpretation in this scheme is cautious and determined by the working alliance between therapist and patient.

The Kleinian view stresses a great emphasis on early superego formation. There is a primary emphasis on regression and the revival of early primitive object relations. More important in the Kleinian schema, there is a need for appropriate interpretation regardless of the ego structure and this is at any depth. The interpretation is done with or without a therapeutic alliance. This difference of approach accounts for why some more traditional analysts feel there is a quality of wildness when they hear of a particular technical innovation in work with patients. They simply do not think about the fact that there is a theoretic base which is quite different from anything that they have ever been exposed to or are knowledgeable about.

Spotnitz[24] says that the therapist should ". . . not function in any way contrary to his own feelings." He has done much work with acting-out patients (and their resistance patterns and narcissistic transference).*

Current chaos in many social settings leads to a great deal of discussion about the patient's tendency to "act out" destructively.[6] Most patients today do not fit the classic picture of the hysteric or compulsive neurotic, the cases described by Freud and many of the early psychoanalysts. The political and social climate is vastly different. Psychotherapy today is not conducted within the father-led structure of the Austro-Hungarian empire or the upheaval of post-World War I or even the depression

---

* In the opinion of this writer the development of a theory of treatment for the narcissistic disorders is perhaps the most vital issue in modern practice. Our hedonistic culture is very much part of this problem, with escapist reaction-formations (nomads searching for utopia). It is therefore critical that psychoanalysts be quite clear as to "where they are at."

culture of the early 1930's. Quite the contrary. The culture today moves under the threat of total destruction and atomic warfare. The more common patient today is an individual with anal and oral character problems and severe ego disturbances. These patients show a tremendous need for attention and a minimal threshold for frustration. Freud felt that the analyst should keep his reality reactions to a minimum and should restrict even his ordinary human sympathy for the patient's current reality problems.[12, 13] This is more easily said than done in 1970 when patients come to sessions fresh from meetings of the Women's Liberation Movement, or a mass meeting against the war in Vietnam. Or young adults come to a session directly from students rioting on a university campus. Or instructors come from a college campus direct from a Black Power confrontation. Or physicians come from a hospital where the community social activists have occupied the admitting room. Or lawyers come from a court where political trials are held. What is there to say when an analyst writes: "The problem of acting out is resistance and the therapy is difficult. . . ." In dealing with acting out (1) the patient must realize he is acting out and why and (2) interpretation must come quickly. . . ." "The therapist must be on guard concerning his own countertransference feelings. . . ." "In sum, acting out is a character disturbance and not a diagnostic entity. The patient has no insight into it at all."[25] There are no simple answers such as this analyst gives.

When dealing with young adults or older adolescents the intensity of the patient's reactions often produces a therapist's countertransference. While countertransference has been defined in many ways, we may at this point describe countertransference as all the feelings aroused in the therapist during the treatment of his patients. We noted that according to classical theory a therapist had no countertransference if he was properly psychoanalyzed. Currently, contemporary psychotherapists recognize their countertransference and use it as a tool in therapy. Winnicott[28] has pointed out that feelings of dislike or hate of the patient can be appropriate if what the patient does is hateful. Bion[3] has not hesitated to use his countertransference. On occasion the therapist can become so confused about what is attributed to him that he is no longer certain of his own identity and is unable to apply his therapy skills. Indeed, the therapist may *act out* what is attributed to him.

If there is a theoretic state of being "thoroughly analyzed" it is still true that there are extra-analytic satisfactions which may lend themselves to acting out. Violent emotions on the part of the analyst impel the patient toward acting out which often reflects the analyst's own needs. The analyst can and should be sensitive and empathic but his function is to move toward contemplation and objective observation. This writer would *not* ignore the feelings of the therapist and the important nonverbal messages that occur between patient and therapist. The analyst should explore his own negative and positive feelings and constantly make use of them, but *not* burden the patient with them. Borderline psychotic patients as well as acute character disorders have intense and wildly swinging transferential responses and this often evokes intense countertransference reactions on the part of the analyst so that acting out ensues.

The less neurotic patient is able to reflect and observe. The more disturbed patient, with less ego structure, calls forth more activity on the part of the therapist. The activity, if not carefully assessed, simply leads to acting out on the part of the patient, who interprets the motoric behavior of the analyst as a go-ahead for his own acting out. In short, the analyst is bombarded by the patient's own distortions and his own regressive forces come to the fore with intensification of transference and countertransference. The patient acts out and in turn promotes the therapist's acting out.

Glover[14] has noted that analysts are generally able to remain objective as long as the patient is talking about external events or fantasies that do not directly involve the analyst. The situation becomes quite different and the analyst is far more vulnerable when he is being attacked or he is the object of the fantasy. Further, when his value systems, political orientations and social goals are under direct attack there is every danger that he will counterattack. One of my colleagues, a dedicated analyst and professed political conservative, was denied entry to a psychoanalytic organization because his political philosophy was alien to his colleagues who are, for the most part, social activists. So, in a sense, they "acted out."

To repeat, current depth psychotherapists recognize that the total response of the therapist merits attention. They do not respond to countertransference as a dirty word and do not have phobic reactions to the word. The nonverbal messages that exist between patient and therapist merit close attention. But all of this makes great demands upon the analyst who must be a sufficiently analyzed and mature individual whose reactions shall for the most part be nonhostile to the patient. His own infantile needs and personal difficulties should not be a burden on the patient. In our culture, where there seems to be an increasing need for more structure rather than less structure on the part of the patient, many analysts are moving toward a more active position with their patients. Unlike Freud, we are not dealing with Victorian patients who need emancipation from their sexual inhibitions. More often, we are working with people who bombard therapists with massive demands and express a quality of orality which is very wearying.

More than ever before, it is the increasing responsibility of the therapist to know the facts and not become caught up in social crazes. Today radical youth searches for alternative institutions and cultures. This could be a significant move in our culture of the U.S.A. But easy solutions are often quite neurotic. For example, it is my impression that the search for the commune is doomed to failure. In the United States almost a hundred thousand people tried this approach to living during the past century (19th). In Europe as well there were commune experiments. These experiments were isolated and lacked formal structure. Between 1780 and 1860 ninety-one utopian communities were founded in the United States, and only eleven lasted more than sixteen years.* The American commune has attempted historically to exist outside of the mainstream of society. But the only successful commune concept, the kibbutz system of Israel, was never seen as a social goal in and of itself, but always as a means of achieving the specific socialist and

---

* Personal communication from Menachem Rosner.

national goals of the Zionist-Socialist labor movement. The kibbutz was never a place where someone could take refuge from society and isolate himself. The kibbutz was, and is, a part of the larger social struggle. Consider, if you will, that in spite of Bruno Bettelheim's concern about lack of individualism as a result of the kibbutz experience (*Children of the Dream*, 1969), the kibbutz population, 4 percent of the State of Israel, contributed 25 percent to the command level of the Israel armed forces and over 50 percent of the fighter pilots of the Israel Air Force. It is not my intent to recruit supporters for the State of Israel, but psychotherapists should know facts and be clear when they treat young adults or older adults who, in their frustration, look for unreal ways to cope with the American culture.

We require in the field of psychotherapy, and particularly in group psychotherapy, where social norms of the group can be used to promote and justify acting out on the part of the patient, therapist, or both, psychotherapists who are clear as to their value systems. Patients should be encouraged to combine maximum self-actualization and social responsibility. For this writer the internationalization of collective goals and the commitment to them results in an experience where the individual does not feel that societal needs are alien forces that are oppressing him.

Ernest Jones daydreamed in his later years that in the future the analyst or medical psychologist, like the priest of ancient times, might serve as a source of practical wisdom and a stabilizing influence in this chaotic world. According to Jones, the community would consult this figure before embarking on any important social or political enterprise. This writer questions Jones' wish. Therapists will be swept up in new crazes that erupt in the field of psychotherapy as long as they are confused about their own value systems and, more importantly, the ethic that guides them as human begins. The great figures of psychoanalysis, the early pioneers, did not look for an ethic in psychotherapy. They brought an ethic to the field. The same cannot be said for most of the psychotherapists this writer has observed. All kinds of bizarre therapeutic approaches are tolerated under the guise of an emancipated therapy. Therapists who are busy playing the role of the all-accepting parent have never learned to distinguish between the parent who has self-respect and is in turn respected, and the parent who is trying to be "one of the crowd." It is difficult in a world where parents are encouraged to dress and look like adolescents and where sex roles are supposed to blend to a unisex. More than ever before, psychotherapists who work in depth have to be at one with themselves about their own philosophy of life, what they are doing and why they are here. If the all too eager effort of many psychotherapists to enter into every social movement under the guise of their professional expertise has any merit, and this writer has many doubts as to whether expertise in one area automatically qualifies a person for another field, there will have to be a lot of clarity about what the function of psychotherapists is. We are not the high priests of the culture. We can only bring our patients to the point where they will have to confront the unfairness, duplicity, ambiguity, beauty and challenge of life. Current fads in psychotherapy merely encourage many patients in the belief that motoric activity is growth. Vandalism is condoned by therapists who are fearful of being perceived as "square." Immediate intimacy as spawned by the encounter group movement is no substitute for the arduous struggle toward personal maturity. Psychotherapists should speak out on this. Psychotherapists should not be deceived by gimmicks. Clinical training appears to have missed the boat in the year 1970 if both therapists and patients have not learned Max Weber's comment in his famous lecture on "Politics as a Vocation": ". . . Experience has not hardened them to imperfection."

REFERENCES

1. Aichhorn, A.: *Wayward Youth*. New York, Viking Press, 1935.
2. Alexander, F.: The neurotic character. *Int. J. Psychoanal, 11,* 1930.
3. Bion, W.: *Experience in Groups*. New York, Basic Books, 1959.
4. Bromberg, W.: Acting and acting out. *Amer. J. Psychotherapy,* 12(2):264-268, 1958.
5. Bry, T.: Acting out in group psychotherapy. *This Jl.,* 3:42-48, 1953.
6. Durkin, H.; Glatzer, H.; Kadis, A.; Wolf, A., and Hulse, W.: Acting out in group psychotherapy—panel discussion. *Amer. J. Psychotherapy,* 12:87-105, 1958.

7. Emch, M.: On the need to know as related to identification and acting out. *Int. J. Psychoanal.*, 25:13-19, 1944.
8. Fenichel, O.: *The Psychoanalytic Theory of Neurosis.* New York, Norton, 1945.
9. Fenichel, O.: Neurotic acting out. *Psychoanal. Rev.*, 32, 1945.
10. Fliess, R.: Counter-transference and counteridentification. *J. Amer. Psychoanal. Assoc.*, 1, 1953.
11. Freud, S.: *An Outline of Psychoanalysis.* New York, Norton, 1949.
12. Freud, S.: Observations on transference love. *Collected Papers.* London, Hogarth, 1946, Vol. II.
13. Freud, S.: Analysis terminable and interminable. *Collected Papers.* London, Hogarth, 1950, Vol. V.
14. Glover, E.: *The Technique of Psychoanalysis.* New York, International Universities Press, 1955.
15. Healy, W., and Bronner, A.: *New Lights on Delinquency and Its Treatment.* New Haven, Yale, 1936.
16. Johnson, A., and Szurek, S. A.: The genesis of antisocial acting out in children and adults. *Psychoanal. Quart.*, 21, 1952.
17. Kasanin, J. S.: Neurotic acting out as a basis for sexual promiscuity in women. *Psychoanal. Rev.*, 31, 1944.
18. Loeser, L., and Bry, T.: The position of the group therapist in transference and countertransference: An experimental study. *This Jl.*, 3:389-406, 1953.
19. Orr, D. W.: Transference and countertransference—a historical survey. *J. Amer. Psychoanal. Assoc.*, 2, 1954.
20. Racker, H.: The meaning and uses of countertransference. *Psychoanal. Quart.*, 26, 1957.
21. Reich, W.: *Der Triebhafte Charakter.* Wien, Internationaler Psychoanalytischer Verlag, 1925.
22. Roth, N.: The acting out of transferences. *Psychoanal. Rev.*, 39:67-78, 1952.
23. Schmideberg, M.: The mode of operation of psychoanalytic therapy. *Int. J. Psychoanal.*, 19:310-320, 1938.
24. Spotnitz, H.: *Modern Psychoanalysis of the Schizophrenic Patient.* New York, Grune & Stratton, 1969, p. 167.
25. Vass, I.: The acting out patient in group therapy. *Amer. J. Psychotherapy*, 19:302-308, April, 1965.
26. Waelder, R.: Introduction to the discussion of problems of transference. *Int. J. Psychoanal.*, 37, 1956.
27. Weiss, E.: Emotional memories and acting out. *Psychoanal. Quart.*, 11, 1942.
28. Winnicott, D. W.: Hate in the counter-transference. *Int. J. Psychoanal.*, 30:69-74, 1949.

$\sim\sim\sim\sim\sim\sim\sim\sim\sim\sim\sim\sim\sim\sim\sim$

Dr. MAGDA DENES, a practicing psychoanalyst and a professor in the doctoral and postdoctoral programs at Adelphi, is quite conversant with both Gestalt and existential thinking about man and his problems. In her erudite paper, she clearly and thoroughly traces the history of theories of acting out from its inception and ends with her own theory as applied to our time.

Dr. Denes begins with a historical survey of the concept of acting out from the time it was first introduced by Freud in 1914. Following this with a theoretical discussion of her conception of anxiety within the framework of existentialism, Dr. Denes asserts that acting out is an expression of non-being and tells why, in today's cultural milieu, acting out has become the prevalent malady. She vividly examines technology's role in our world and the hopelessness and despair which are the natural result. Dr. Denes asserts that the consciousness which shaped the new generation is a result of an all-encompassing feeling of non-being in the existential sense.

Dr. Denes discusses the cultural and psychological milieu in our present environment and concludes that all of our society, with the exception of the blacks, is in fact acting out. Although violent behavior on the part of minority groups is self-asserting and denotes intentionality, it also contributes to the destruction of our civilization.

Dr. Denes offers an exciting, provocative and stimulating paper on acting out and its implications in current society.

D.S.M.

G.D.G.

Chapter 4

Acting Out: Private Symptom or Political Expression

MAGDA DENES-RADOMISLI

H ISTORICALLY THE CONCEPT of acting out was introduced by Freud in 1914 in an essay entitled "Remembering, Repeating, and Working Through." He distinguished, in the analytic situation, between remembering the past and the compelling urge to repeat the past through action without benefit of memory. The latter contingency is termed acting out and it is said to occur whenever the patient is in resistance and replaces remembering with repetitive action in the transference.

The analytic aim is to minimize acting out through the techniques of free association and dream interpretation which enable the patient to recover the "forgotten past." However, certain kinds of repressed psychic contents cannot be recovered in this manner, but have to be re-lived and re-enacted, and so acting out in the transference becomes an addition to remembering, provided that the acting out is circumscribed by certain analyst-imposed restrictions, such as its stopping short of motor action and it not affecting the basic treatment alliance between patient and analyst.

With time, the concept underwent some major changes. For one thing, as Anna Freud[2] points out, the concept was evolved with the fairly intact neurotic in mind whose acting out was induced by the analytic situation through the lowering of his defenses. In other words, the need to repeat the past in action was not an integral aspect of these patients' behavioral repertoire but represented an analytically induced temporary artifact.

Now, when psychoanalytic therapy was expanded as applicable treatment procedure for diagnostic categories other than the original intact neurotic, that is, when addicts, character disorders, psychotics, and so on, began to be thought of as treatable through psychoanalysis, the concept of acting out became radically altered although the term was retained as if it still referred to the phenomenon described in 1914. The reason for the radical alteration, says Anna Freud, is that in contrast to neurotics, the patients in the new diagnostic categories act out as an expression of their life style and in the real world rather than just in the transference.

> Unlike the neurotic, the delinquent, the addict and the psychotic act-out habitually without the releasing benefits of the analytic techniques. With them, the upsurges from the Id which cause their impulsive behavior have to be understood as belonging to their pathology not to a curative process. If one wishes to apply the term to them at all, it has to be defined anew; this time not as repeating in contradistinction to remembering as with the neurotic, *but as Id controlled action in contradistinction to the ego controlled actions* of the normal individual.[2]

She further points out that the direction of the two types of acting out differs in that neurotic acting out originates in the transference and is induced by it whereas in the other diagnostic categories the impulsive behavior "begins in the external world from where it has to be dislodged and drawn into the transference,"[2] for treatment to take place.

Although there is no general agreement among the Freudians regarding this distinction, to my mind it seems the most plausible one within the framework.

My own theoretical framework, however, is not Freudian and so I should like now to reexamine the concept of acting out from an Existential point of view. To begin, permit me to describe some pertinent existential concepts.

Existence analysis is concerned with ontology, the science of being, and with *Dasein*, that is, the particular existence. Dasein is a German word composed of "da" meaning "there" and "sein" meaning "being." It refers to the conception that man is the being who is there and who by virtue of his consciousness can know that he is there. Being as used here is not a static noun

but a participle connoting a dynamic process which implies both
the potential for, and the process of becoming; that is, the
being who is there is there as a being who every minute is
becoming what he is. Moreover, the "there" is the particular time
and space at the given moment of existence of the particular
being.[5]

What I want to get across here, somewhat awkwardly, is that
Dasein is an inclusive concept (as opposed to ego or self for
example) and it implies the dialectical relation that existentialists
presuppose between man and his world. Since the particular
world of a human being cannot exist without that human being—
and since there can be no being for a particular human being
without his world—the Dasein concept encompasses both members of the dialectic.

Rollo May posits three points as corollaries to the concept of
Dasein. First, and I am quoting him here,

> One corollary is that we can understand another human being
> only as we see what he is moving toward, what he is becoming
> and we can understand ourselves only as we project our potentialities
> in action.
>
> Another distinctive aspect of "being" in the human sense is that
> it is not given once and for all; it does not unfold automatically, as
> the oak tree does from the acorn, but can be forfeited or sloughed
> off. An inseparable element in human being is self-consciousness;
> man (or Dasein) is the particular being who must become aware
> of himself if he is to become himself.
>
> A third distinctive aspect is that man is the being who knows
> that at some future moment he will not be; he is, in other words, the
> being who is in a dialectical relation with non-being, death.[5]

This brings us to a second crucial concept in existential
thought, namely the concept of nothingness. Most simply put,
this concept refers to the fact that since man is both mortal
and conscious, he is a being who knows that at some, as yet
undetermined but definite time in the future, he will cease to
be, that is, he will die. This knowledge, this consciousness, of his
potential for non-being (which as potential is a dynamic aspect
of his being) subjects him to ontological, or more properly put,

ontic anxiety.* In other words, the potential dissolution of one's being is experienced as confrontation with nothingness, with no-thingness, and it results in ontic anxiety.

To quote Paul Tillich:

> Anxiety is the state in which a being is aware of its possible non-being. The same statement in a shorter form, would read: Anxiety is the Existential awareness of non-being. "Existential" in this sense means that it is not the abstract knowledge of non-being which produces anxiety but the awareness that non-being is part of one's own being. It is not the realization of universal transitoriness, not even the experience of the death of others, but the impression of these events on the always latent awareness of our own having to die that produces anxiety. Anxiety is finitude experienced as one's own finitude. This is the natural anxiety of man as man.[7]

Anxiety strikes at the very center of a person's being. It is a threat to his continuing person-ness, or in existential terms, anxiety is a threat to the Dasein. The anxious person cannot stand outside his anxiety and observe it. He is overwhelmed by it and he cannot even imagine to himself what it would be like not to be anxious. As Kurt Goldstein points out, anxiety is not something we have but something we are. Now the answer to the threat of non-being is courage. When confronted with the anxiety of loss of being, a person can affirm his being despite the anxiety. This affirmation "in-spite-of" is what we refer to as courage. It is the affirmation of an inner aim or entelechy; the affirmation of one's essential nature. The alternative to courage, that is the inability to affirm being in the face of anxiety, results in despair.

Ontological anxiety is common to all of us. In that sense it is "normal" and we all experience it whenever we come face to face with a measure of our human vulnerability.

Both Tillich and May contrast ontological anxiety with pathological anxiety, the latter of which is characterized by a sense of utter helplessness and the need to shrink the self rather than to affirm it. Rollo May enumerates four distinguishing characteristics of pathological anxiety:

---

* Onto-logical designates the philosophical analysis of the nature of being, whereas Ontic, from the Greek word "On"—being refers to being in simple existence.[7]

First, neurotic anxiety is anxiety which is inappropriate to the threat of a situation. Secondly, it involves repression into unconsciousness. Thirdly, it is expressed in symptom formation. Fourthly, it has destructive rather than constructive effects upon the organism.[5]

May sees the aim of therapy in relation to pathological anxiety as that of converting it into normal anxiety so that the patient can live with it more constructively.

Paul Tillich views pathological anxiety as the result of an escape from despair after appropriate courageous self-affirmation in the face of ontological anxiety has failed. In his words:

He who does not succeed in taking his anxiety courageously upon himself can succeed in avoiding the extreme situation of despair by escaping into neurosis. . . . Neurosis is the way of avoiding non-being by avoiding being. . . . Self-affirmation is not lacking . . . but the self which is affirmed is a reduced one.[7]

My own view is somewhat different from both of these. I do not think it necessary or accurate to posit pathological anxiety as separate and distinguishable from ontological anxiety. I do believe that anxiety strikes at the core of being, that it is a centrally overwhelming experience and that it is the result of a person being faced with the potential dissolution of his Being. I do not believe that there are two types of this crucial experience. To my mind, *all* anxiety is ontological, and it is only the response, the relatedness of the person to his anxiety, that becomes pathological. Contrary to Tillich then, I do not think that one escapes despair through neurosis, but rather that neurosis contains large elements of despair. That to the extent that a reduced self is being affirmed that self despairs over the shrinkage. Again I see as pathological, not the anxiety at all, but the response of partial self-affirmation.

Similarly, in relation to May's points, first, since anxiety by definition is the response of a being to his possible non-being, no anxiety can be inappropriate to the threat of a situation since the threat is always the same. This is especially so when one considers that Tillich for example believes that even fear is fear only because ultimately the anxiety of non-being stands behind it. Secondly (and this subsumes May's three additional distinctions of neurotic anxiety), I think that what is destructive to the organism is its own inadequate response to the anxiety and not the anxiety as such. One could conceive of it almost like a chain reaction in fact, in that the more inadequately ontological anxiety is met, the more destroyed, fragmented and reduced the person becomes; therefore, the more inadequately he responds to the anxiety next time, and so on. Repression and other symptom formation then does not reside in the quality of the anxiety, but rather it resides in the quality of the person's response to it.

In my view then, all of us are confronted with ontological anxiety, we all relate to it in some fashion, and all of us to some degree despair because a completely courageous affirmation of one's total being is virtually impossible. And I would regard as pathological *any* response that only partially affirms being. The more partial the response the more pathology derives from a person's relatedness to ontological anxiety.

Both Tillich and May regard ontological anxiety as a constructive though tragic force in life that positively challenges man to courage. Here, too, my view is a little different. I see ontological anxiety as an existential given in human life—tragic, yes—but neither constructive nor destructive in itself, but rather simply there for man to responsibly choose his own committed relation to it, be that creative courage or truncating despair.

Now I propose that acting out is the aftermath of the inability to affirm being in the face of ontological anxiety and that it represents the actions without intentionality* of a person in a state of despair. It is the response of a diminished self to a reduced world. Or to put it in other words, acting out is the expression of Dasein curtailed and despairing. It represents the objective pole of the subjective sense of powerlessness to design and mold the world in accordance with one's wish and will—that

---

* Intentionality is defined as man's relation to meanings. In Paul Tillich's words: Intentionality is "being directed toward meaningful contents."[7] It is in direct correlation to vitality and the expression of both is the courage to be. Rollo May also regards intentionality as the meaning-matrix of human experience both cognitive and conative, the expression of man's orientation to himself and to his world. He defines it as "the structure which gives meaning to experience . . . it is man's capacity to have intentions."[4] Intentionality then can be seen as man's integrated, vital, courageous commitment toward his future and his becoming.

is, in accordance with one's intentionality. Acting out is the paralysis of intentionality, the inability to bring the self's power to bear on the world in such a way that the self is affirmed and Dasein expanded.

I see acting out then as not confined to a specific diagnostic category but as potentially universally present in the human behavioral repertoire but which manifests itself in actuality when constructive action, that is, action expressive of intentionality and leading to an increment of growth, has failed.

Just as affirmation of being in the face of threat to being does not always consist of action, acting out is not the only manifestation of a being in despair. But I do contend that action which occurs in the face of anxiety that does not affirm being and does not result in an increment of growth and mastery, always represents acting out. Thus, it is possible for a human being to refrain from purposeful behavior for periods of time, but once he does not refrain he can do only one of two things: act or act out. That is, he can either implement his intentionality which is accompanied by choice, consciousness of meaning and consciousness of responsibility and results in the enlargement of Dasein; or he can with intentionality paralyzed or temporarily destroyed, act out, which is accompanied by lack of consciousness of meaning, the inability to express one's power positively in being-in-the-world, and results in further shrinkage of the Dasein.

Let me give you a somewhat oversimplified but concrete example of what I mean. Suppose that as I am writing this lecture (a self-affirming action expressive of my intentionality) I begin to imagine the lecture hall, the audience, and their reaction to what I say, which is unknown to me, and I become anxious. I become anxious because my listeners' reaction to me constitutes a threat to my being as I live my being today. Whether the reaction is positive or negative it will alter me in some way and therefore my prior-to-the-lecture-being (for complete accuracy I should really say "my-prior-to-the-lecture-being-in-the-world") will cease to be and I will have to forge my post-lecture-being out of the matrix of what I am today and what I will have become through my encounter with this audience. This is true of all serious committed engagement: one risks one's being in encountering it. Now this perceived risk to my being arouses my anxiety because it involves the possibility of non-being since I cannot yet know what I will become but I already know that I will not remain the same as I am, since I have committed myself to writing and giving this lecture, that is, to risking myself in encountering this task and this audience.

Now, as I become anxious I can do one of two things: I can continue writing with and through my anxiety, perhaps even write a little more carefully or better, in order to insure that I bring to the encounter my best powers, in which case I will have affirmed myself in the face of the threat of non-being and will have become re-engaged with my intentionality and my committed and conscious choice to give this lecture and to give it at the best level I know how. In other words, I will have reaffirmed myself through courage and I will have potentiated my possibilities. Or as an alternate to this, I can, in the face of my anxiety, get up and drink a glass of water, eat an apple or read the newspaper. If I do these latter actions, as avoidance of my anxiety, I am acting out. My intentionality toward being a good lecturer is paralyzed. I truncate my potentials for a creative encounter with my writing at the moment and with my lecturing in the future. I diminish myself through the truncating of these potentials and I reduce my world which I now can no longer mold, i.e. I cannot lecture without having written a lecture and I cannot encounter with impact my audience without lecturing.

Now I further propose that acting out invariably leads to existential guilt, particularly guilt in the *Eigenwelt* or more properly put, the vehicle of existential guilt in the Eigenwelt is acting out. Let me explain what I mean.

Existentialists distinguish three simultaneous aspects of world which are characteristic of the existence of each of us as "being-in-the-world." These words are hyphenated to reflect the dialectical relation that obtains between being and world.

First there is *Umwelt*, literally meaning "world around." All organisms share in this world, not just human beings. This is the biological world of drives, instincts and deterministic forces.

Second, there is *Mitwelt*, literally "with world," the world that one shares with other human beings, the world of interpersonal relatedness. Relatedness in the Mitwelt however, is that relatedness which is characterized by encounter, by the meeting of two persons wholly and awarely as persons not as objects.

The third mode of world is *Eigenwelt*, meaning "own world." This is the world of the self in relation to the self. Since Eigenwelt is dependent on self-consciousness, it is unique to human beings. It does not, however, refer to merely subjective experience but rather it is in the Eigenwelt that I grasp the meaning of things in the world outside me—in the real world as it were—and therefore Eigenwelt is the basis for my orientation to reality.

It is crucial to remember that these delineations do not represent three separate worlds but that each person lives simultaneously in all three. Also, that pathological disturbance in one, whether culturally induced or privately developed, will produce alterations and disturbances in the other two.[5]

Guilt in existential thought is also an ontological characteristic of man; that is, guilt inheres in man's existence much the same way as does anxiety. Man's mortality, his finiteness, implies his anxiety; man's potential and actual estrangement from nature, from his fellow men and from himself implies his guilt. Thus again guilt is not something one has but what one existentially is.

Martin Buber writes:

> Existential guilt occurs when someone injures an order of the human world whose foundations he knows and recognizes as those of his own existence and of all common human existence.[1]

And Paul Tillich puts it this way:

> Man's being, ontic as well as spiritual, is not only given to him but also demanded of him. He is also responsible for it; literally, he is required to answer if he is asked, what he has made of himself. He who asks him is his judge, namely, he himself, who, at the same time stands against him. This situation produces the anxiety which, in relative terms, is the anxiety of guilt. . . .[7]

Ontological guilt then is to be seen as an inescapable aspect of man's basic nature. In actuality, it manifests itself in all three modes of world. In the Umwelt (the world around) it arises as man's guilt for his separation from nature. In the Mitwelt (the with world) guilt exists in relation to one's fellow man. Guilt in this realm inheres in the very nature of individuality and it places man in a state of paradox. Guilt in the Eigenwelt (own world) can be most simply defined as the guilt of self-betrayal. It is the guilt that arises when a person forfeits his potentials and settles for being less than what he could become. As Meddard Boss puts it, it occurs when we "forget being." When we fail to become authentically ourselves, then we become guilty against our "core." Another way of saying this is that whereas anxiety arises at the point where a being confronts non-being, guilt in the Eigenwelt arises when non-being has triumphed; when some part, some aspect of our being, has been betrayed by us and allowed to atrophy or die.

Acting out, then, as I have defined it in this paper, is the expression of non-being, it is a malady of the will, a sickness of action; and as such action and acting out are polar opposites in their form, directionality and consequence.

One last theoretical consideration before I turn to the examination of acting out as it displays itself in the culture in the form of political expression. "World," says Rollo May, "is the structure of meaningful relationships in which the person exists and in the design of which he participates."[5] Differently put, world is always a dynamic pattern which the person within the limits of his freedom continually molds and remakes.

World and self, as I have said earlier, always stand in dialectical relation to each other; that is to say, the person and his world represent a unitary structural whole wherein neither can have existence without the other and where alteration in one must perforce produce change in the other.

Man, then, makes himself, chooses his being, through his participation in the design of his world and what makes a man uniquely himself are the concrete choices he makes within the given limits of his existence.

To go back to my earlier example, this lecture room is my world this Saturday morning because a week ago I had chosen to affirm myself and finished writing my lecture in spite of my anxiety. But suppose that there were to be a sudden law against existentialist speakers. I could then not choose this lecture room as my world. I could still choose to affirm myself as an existentialist in spite of the law, even choose to write, if I hid the writings or if I were willing to be jailed, say, for having written, but I could *not* choose my participation in this lecture-room-world.

Under these circumstances, my self would be effectively curtailed by the shrinkage of the world. A shrinkage in which I did not participate. The number of my choices in affirming myself would be diminished, and certainly the realms of my self-affirmation would be lessened—at least by one possibility. It is not that I would no longer be free to choose my self and be free to participate in the design of my world; but that the law would force my hand in terms of the direction and scope of my design. This is a crucial issue inasmuch as it implies that it is possible for conditions to exist in which the self is presented with a "pre-shrunk" world. The crucial question that arises then is, is it also possible that in a "pre-shrunk" world self-affirmation is so arduous and so fraught with perilous obstacles that increasingly larger numbers of people succumb to the sickness of will and action, that is to acting out.

On the sociocultural level, acting out has in fact become the epidemic of our time. In addressing myself to this issue, allow me to begin by examining a widespread general change in the Zeitgeist, especially among the young, the expression of which is the shift from a cultural orientation of "why" to one of "why not."

The question "why" is the tool of reason. It is a query of the questing objective intellect of rational man that achieved its pinnacle of significance and meaning with nineteenth-century determinism. The laws of conservation of energy, of thermodynamics, of natural selection, all represent achievements prompted by a dispassionate "why." The key to nature and its control, the key to knowledge and its mastery, the key to the universe in fact, lay in the question "why" for Victorian man. And it served for a while. "Why" produced the Industrial Revolution, the Age of Reason, the visions of Mankind in eventual scientifically attained bliss. It also produced the split between subject and object, the division between body and mind, the rift between production and pride, the separation of language from reality, of environment from heredity, the divorce between man's nature and his systems. The newly joined reason and mechanics of the nineteenth century served to fragment the culture, to fragment man's personality and to dehumanize his relation to others and to himself. It served to banish individual significance and to sicken the will. At the same time these developments dislodged man's anthropocentric world view and through "why" man lost his place as center of the universe. He lost the theologically provided meaning of his existence, and the assumption that there surely was a sustaining friendly presence rooting for him somewhere in the great beyond became absurd. By the end of the nineteenth century, then, Western man, through his "why" stands alone in an alien world whose meaning to him is dubious. He is anxious, estranged, dehumanized and lonely.

There were various reactions to this state of affairs. One was psychoanalysis—itself too much allied with the question of "why" to effectively alter the tide. Another was existentialism with its emphasis on "how" and "what," with its focus on existence as opposed to essence, and with its Western tradition and Oriental empathies.

Nietzsche, Kierkegaard, and all the early existentialists fought to repair the rifts that "why" had caused and to reestablish man's wholeness and integration, his human meaning, in spite of the knowledge of his own cosmic insignificance. They fought to de-mechanize man, to counteract the industrial objectification and levelling of the individual, to rejoin intellect with passion and commitment. They did not succeed very well. The influence of existentialism turned out to be too sparse and too obscure to make a real difference in the culture at large. And so, at least this is what I think, we witness now a third reaction, the emergence of "why not." "Why not" is a query of the id, of the Umwelt, it is not mediated by the intellect and its concern is not order. It is alien to responsibility, estranged from commitment. The quest of "why not" is sampling at random on the side of the world, and indiscriminate availability on the side of the self.

What I mean by that is that in the self-world dialectic the attitude of "why not" implies the taking in of the world passively,

at random in so far as possible, rather than actively participating
in its design. Under such conditions whatever happens in the
world, one need not be responsible for it. Similarly, through
the attitude of "why not" the self is made, again passively,
available to experience without commitment to it. It is note-
worthy here, that many young people today confuse the passivity
of their "why not" orientation, with oriental acquiescence, with
the Taoist "stand out of the way" or with William James' "let
it be," to which it bears no psychological relation.

"Stand out of the way," and "let it be," as expressions of
philosophy, are rooted in the conviction of man's intentionality.
They are rooted in his commitment to openness, yes, but also
in the conviction that he has an essential nature which he can
actively fulfill by suspending his voluntaristic will but not his
decisiveness and not his responsibility.

"Why not," on the other hand, is anarchy in the realm of the
possible. It implies that no choices are organically rooted in
one's being; it implies a paralysis of intentionality, an arrest in
self-determination, a sickness of willing. It implies an attitude
of detached indifference and dispassionate experimentation. As
such, it is mechanical and fragmenting, much the same way as
"why" had turned out to be. This is not surprising if one views
"why" and "why not" as a structural whole of two polarities,
where the presence of one implies the other. Nineteenth-century
Western man's "why," then, contained in itself all along its "why
not" as smoldering, passive potential in the unconscious waiting
to be activated by some force that had irreversibly, unalterably,
discredited the query "why." I believe this force to have been
"The Bomb." With the dropping of the atom bomb evil
acquired a new meaning. Along with Hiroshima the foundations
of Western morality went up in smoke.

I do not mean to say here that the bombing of Hiroshima
as such destroyed Western morality. It is true that war in
general is immoral—it is an atrocity—but within that context I
am not evaluating here the significance of Hiroshima as a single
specific act of war. Rather I regard Hiroshima as the tragic
beginning of both the fact and people's consciousness of the

fact that technological power ended up by supplying the means for a dominant minority to eliminate mankind.

It was in the shadow of this consciousness that the parents of the current generation reared their children in America, in France, in Japan, in the entire world. And it was this consciousness that shaped the development of the current generation.

I do not agree with Margaret Mead[6] that what ails the current generation is that they do not have the reassurance of competent models, or with Paul Goodman,[3] who puts his hopes in the belief that the young are undergoing a new Reformation (meaning the religious revival).

I see the young as reacting to a state of siege where the enemy is invisible, and so one segment is all for giving the enemy shape in Vietnam and the other larger segment is for giving the enemy shape at home as parents, authority, establishment. Life is threatened, the young and everyone else knows it. But the structure of our lives has reached such complexity that no one knows anymore the real source of the threat. What is good for General Electric is not good for the country, that is clear. But what is not clear, in fact what is more and more obscured, is that General Electric is not a monolithic computer. At least not yet. General Electric is composed of real live individual people, who bleed when stabbed, and what is good for the Yippies is not good for them. My point is that the declaration of segments of the population as non-people is not confined to the establishment. We are all running scared, every single one of us, and we are all, at the same time, looking to name the threat, to give it human shape, to have it out with some recognizable others, who at least have palpable existence because to be scared of and do battle against systems and power structures and fictional "Thems" and bombs whose composition and consequence defy comprehension, images without referents, messages without meaning, politics without platforms, is to have the mind blown.

And so homosexuals battle heterosexuals, liberated women battle bondaged man, students battle deans. (In case you are wondering, I am leaving out deliberately blacks battle whites because I think that this battle constitutes a special case and I shall turn to it in a minute in detail.)

At any rate, I believe that the social structure has succumbed primarily to the threat of imminent non-being—to which a self-affirming response was made impossible by the automated complexities of twentieth-century life.

As I pointed out earlier, a curtailed world implies a reduced self. And when curtailment consists of the absence of an arena for meaningful action in the realm of a primary concern, the reduction of self occurs in the faculty of willing.

Incidentally, I am as aware as anyone that preoccupation with the bomb is at the moment not fashionable and is regarded a cultural cliché. But that is just exactly a major aspect of our tragedy—that consciousness not aided by decisiveness, lacking the understructure of will, ceases to be consciousness.[4] We know, but we don't know, because we cannot act. In this passivity, in this absence of personal significance, is where symptom formation begins. This is the hothouse where acting out flowers. And flower children act out—as does everybody else.

My point is very simple: I am proposing that under certain conditions of social disaster, there is no action in relation to that disaster that does not qualify as acting out. As you remember, I have defined acting out as action which is the aftermath of the despair of having not been able to affirm the self with courage in the face of the ontological anxiety of non-being. Now it seems to me that our entire Western society is prey to this despair traceable to the consequences of a technology that has gotten out of hand and produced a world incomprehensible to people and inadequate to their nature.

Technology produced on the one hand, the bomb (by now thermonuclear) which proved to be a social challenge of such magnitude that no existing institutions were capable of dealing with it. It became evident that the leaders had no creative solutions to safeguard mankind; and more, that for any mistaken or foolhardy action on their part everyone would die. Not even the possibility of voting every four years—as is the privilege of all sane adults in a democracy—made this risk seem either less or reasonable.

On the other hand, technology with all its systems and media produced social conditions in the context of which the development of an authentic sense of personal identity became more and more problematic, not to say (and there is considerable evidence that one has to say it) impossible.

There is ample evidence both in fact and in theoretical papers that the culture is fragmented, passive, dehumanized, dehumanizing, and detrimental to the growth of its members. The psychological environment is schizophrenogenic in that all of its values are in the context of a double-bind. This applies to the values of all factions. Double-bind means that two mutually exclusive ideas are simultaneously held and/or communicated. Thus students fight prejudice but are prejudiced against their parents; or hippies abhor technology but advocate chemical enlightenment, and so on. Further, the culture is schizophrenogenic in that a great deal of its public language utilizes reasoning by predicates. This is true of virtually all advertising, most propaganda, and a good deal of political communications. It is invariably true whenever an "image" is being sold.

Finally, and as a function of the product (in the sense of multiplication) of the first two factors, the psychological environment is schizophrenogenic in that through the use of conditioned stimulus signals, referentless language, and behavioral models unrelated to actual persons, the culture renders a transcendental relatedness to reality impossible. In the absence of such a possibility, the development of identity is blocked and large-scale identification with segmental groups occurs. Now identification to my mind is in direct opposition to the development of identity. And to the extent that an environment is conducive and favorable to one, it is detrimental and unfavorable to the other.

Identity, genuine self-hood, represents a developmental achievement. It is the result of personal evolution through active, vigilant self-discoveries and successive differentiations, in realistic interaction with one's world. It is characterized by courage. Identity is the core of autonomous functioning and it involves the conviction that one is both peculiarly one's self, and in that way different and separate from everyone else, and also peculiarly human, and in that way related to everyone else, albeit not the same.

Identification, on the other hand, is a process based on a passive attitude, where the individual, in order to obtain gratifications, sacrifices his autonomy and the fulfillment of his primary capacities.[3a]

It is my conviction that our contemporary culture with its attendant systems and media fosters in people passive, cowardly, parasitic attitudes and spurious identifications, while it effectively obstructs the development and affirmation of an authentic sense of self. Now what this amounts to is that our overextended technical development has stripped man of his powers on the one hand and stripped him of a manageable world on the other. Activity in this context involves a sacrifice of identity, a loss of intentionality, a curtailment of Dasein. I maintain that all relevant activity then must, in this circumstance, take on the character of acting out.

I have said earlier that I shall consider the black-white battle as a separate issue and I would like to do that now. It seems to me that the tragedy of our social disintegration and psychic fragmentation does not, cannot, apply to militant blacks. It is true that ostensibly they are subject to the same social forces as the whites but in reality their consciousness of these forces is radically different.

The phenomenal world of the blacks in America has always contained the threat of imminent annihilation not only through metaphysical reality, but through the reality of an angry white mob's rope or shotgun. The bomb then is not perceived (correctly) by the black man as his most immediate danger; *his* most immediate threat to being is and has been the white man. Now when blacks take action against whites—the activity is self-affirming, courageous action in the face of the anxiety of non-being—it is directed toward the appropriate source of danger and it results in an increment of growth and dignity. The black man in America had no world worth preserving prior to the bomb, which the bomb threatened. The American black man is designing his own world now for the first time in American history. And in the process he is forging, also for the first time, his identity as different and separate from white identifications. Perhaps I can make clearer what I mean by saying that when I say "affirm being," I am not referring to mere physical survival. When man consciously chooses to commit himself to life and to affirm his being, he is committing himself to the conviction that the quality and meaning of his life matter.

It was the meaning of life that the bomb exploded as it undermined morality and the structure of the white man's social order. The black man was not a part of this world before or after the explosion.

Let me give you a personal example. During the Second World War, I was imprisoned with my family in a Jewish ghetto. My family had been Hungarian Jews for countless generations and the immediate family with whom I was imprisoned, including grandparents, had lived for many years in Budapest where I was born. Budapest was a good and beautiful city before the war and each of us was tied to it with memories *and* love. I remember one very distinct night watching from the rooftop of our ghetto house the saturation bombing of the city and being overjoyed. It is true that we could have been hit by a bomb, as in fact we were some months later, but that is not what mattered. What mattered was that a world of which we were no longer a part and which threatened our existence was being destroyed. There was no Jew in Budapest at that time who was afraid of air raids. Air raids represented a general disaster—in which a Jew accidentally might be caught—but the focus of attention was on the Jewish disaster, that was the locus of Jewish concern because that was the personal matter, the world of the self.

My point is that no black action directed against the white order can be regarded as acting out however violent or even fruitless it is, because in the black phenomenal world the immediate source of ontological anxiety is the white man. And accurately so. The same activity then as performed by Jerry Rubin is random acting out, but as performed by Rap Brown it is committed action. I am not implying here that I advocate a black revolution—I very much don't. But that is only so because I am white.

And incidentally, among others, being white is the single most embarrassing paradox for the white new left, who claim, as do Women's Lib and Gay Liberation, to be faced with the same psychic environment as the blacks and to battle the same foes. Nothing in my opinion could be farther from the facts as I have attempted to demonstrate earlier. The invoked similarity to the blacks emanates from a misunderstanding of both the white and the black situations. Understandably, the blacks do not make the same mistake, for *them* the lines of battle are clearly drawn. For the black man in America today violence is self-assertion; it is a political platform; it is the embodiment of intentionality. The opposite is true of white violence (both police and SDS) although it masquerades as political stance it is not even strategy. It is the ultimate expression of the despair of human beings sickened in will and routed by their world.

Finally, I wish I could conclude by suggesting a brilliant solution to these predicaments. I cannot. Or at the very least conclude with a statement of faith that we are at a time of transitory turbulence but also at a new beginning where in time men will transcend their limits and through constructive action bring about a new order of harnessed power devoted to fraternity and peace. I cannot say this. I do not believe it.

All I can say to you in conclusion is that I am, as I ponder these matters, profoundly anxious for I fear the destruction, if not of the species, certainly the destruction of what, to a middle-age square like me, appears as civilization.

REFERENCES

1. Buber, M.: *I and Thou*. New York, Charles Scribner's Sons, 1958.
2. Freud, A.: Acting out. *The Int. J. Psychoanal.*, 49:165-170, 1968.
3. Goodman, P.: Fringe political movements. *New York Times Magazine*, November 29, 1970.
3a. Lomas, P.: Passivity and failure of identity development. *The Int. J. Psychoanal.*, 46:438-454, 1965.
4. May, R.: *Love and Will*. New York, Norton, 1969.
5. May, R.; and Angel, E., and Ellenberger, H. F.: *Existence: A New Dimension in Psychiatry and Psychology*. New York, Basic Books, 1958.
6. Mead, M.: *Culture and Commitment: A Study of the Generation Gap*. Garden City, New York, Natural History Press, 1970.
7. Tillich, P.: *The Courage to Be*. New Haven, Yale, 1952.

Professor Matthew Besdine, a member of our Adelphi University Postdoctoral Program faculty, has been widely heralded for his fascinating and innovative studies of mothering. In a very timely and original synthesis he elucidates the acting out of violence in the context of his theories of mothering.

Professor Besdine begins by exploring the premise that the violent acting out so prevalent in our society is, in fact, rooted in the mothering processes of our times. Discussing man's dehumanization as portrayed in the mass media, Besdine postulates that in struggle for identity, the seeds of future violence are planted. He proceeds with his continuum of mothering styles, ending with an elaboration of the aptly labelled Jocasta complex. Through the development of his theory he accounts for the fact that through adolescence and young adulthood violence is more likely to erupt in individuals for whom identity is unclear.

In his conclusion, Besdine explores the problems that arise when an individual breaks away from the home and the mothering role is taken over by the university or business world where the person is further discouraged in his efforts to achieve identity development.

Professor Besdine, in this stimulating and original paper, not only demonstrates a clear picture of a socially pertinent phenomena—the acting out of violence—but elaborates by an interesting and stimulating explanation of its etiology: defects in the mothering process.

D.S.M.

G.D.G.

Chapter 5

Cradles of Violence

MATTHEW BESDINE

THIS ESSAY WILL attempt to describe the mothering styles that generate the neurosis of our time. Violence is merely one example of the compulsive acting-out process. The predominant neurotic pattern is a schizoid withdrawal, with many defenses that all too frequently explode in violence. Mothering is central to child development, and if we would understand the personality, character structure, or neurosis of our time, we must seek its roots primarily in the styles of mothering that prevail and discriminate benign and malignant aspects wherever possible.

So many of our patients live in what is a schizoid prison, using the world not in any psychotic sense, but more as Fairbairn and Guntrip use it, as a description of the defenses against being touched by human contact. The imprisonment was expressed by a patient in a dream. He was living in a concentration camp and I, his analyst, was on guard to help keep him there. His associations to the dream were connected to his unsuccessful efforts to break out of the isolation and his feeble attempts at dating. The anxieties developed by human contact powered the dream. It represented a wish that I and he accept the schizoid prison in which he was more comfortable than in the real world of people and that the analysis be perverted to featherbed him and keep him comfortable without undue anxiety and tension.

One of the obsessive fears of this patient was that he would burst into open violence, assault people, first with angry words, and then get into physical brawls. Though he was a professional in his thirties, with no record of violence, his fear persisted. The close relationship between distrust, isolation, alienation, and paranoid furies that can culminate in violence were clearly observable.

The patient comes in like a moth from the loneliness and cold, seeking the light and warmth of human relations, but gets burned consistently by the flickering evanescent candle of human contact. All the distancing operations leading back to the isolation of his schizoid prison are utilized. To escape from tender, friendly, intimate, human feelings, fury, anger, disappointment, and a sense of betrayal are mobilized. Periods of withdrawal, detachment, apathy and depression follow as the defenses and resistances are again manned against the enemy. And who is the enemy? It is love, friendship and intimacy that are experienced as snakes that strike and Trojan horses that destroy. This paranoid fear of friendship and love as a two-faced experience that cannot be trusted is central to understanding the neurosis of our time, the alienation it breeds and the violence of our age.

The schizoid development of our patients and our culture has been portrayed by the novelists, playwrights and artists. Even the pioneers in the psychoanalytic world were behind Kafka, Camus, Beckett, Cezanne, Van Gogh, or Picasso in understanding it.[13]

The dehumanization of man and the reduction of even sexual intercourse to another experience devoid of tenderness is portrayed regularly in the mass media as a casual encounter designed to stimulate lust. A recent film, *Loving*, portrays it as a ludicrous spectacle and reduces it to the ridiculous, just as the throwing of pies served an earlier generation for laughs and kicks. The theme of ridiculing sexual intercourse and making it a human foible naked to laughter is repeated in *M*A*S*H*. It is interesting to note that these two pictures were acclaimed by the critics. The dehumanization of people is at peak when sexual intercourse is portrayed as another aspect of the absurdity of man and another target for the theater and art of the absurd.

It is a curious fact that as the prudery about sex disappeared and more sex manuals began to appear, less satisfaction in sexual intercourse became apparent. The many technical and procedural questions examined logically could not replace the absence of a substantive serious intent, spontaneity, and the mutuality of tenderness and affection that are alien to our age. The capacity to love is missing and with it what is most human and meaningful in sexual intercourse and human relations. Two mechanically perfect, cold-hearted fornicating machines, tabulating orgasms, are no substitute for a love relationship. The intimate ways in which lovers communicate and touch one another intellectually, spiritually, emotionally and physically, are missing. It is all too logical, stereotypical and "cool," according to the latest manual.[13]

It is this viewing of life *In Cold Blood* that is described in the murderers portrayed by Truman Capote. It is one with the massacres of Mai Lai, the apathy of the world to the exterminations in the concentration camps, Hiroshima, the bombing of open cities, the use of napalm, or defoliation, to mention a few of the characteristic unconcerns for human life and feelings. It is all played quite "cool" by more or less dehumanized computers.

This basic estrangement from the self shows clinically in extreme cases, where all emotions are repressed and never experienced. In other cases, where some faint echoes of feeling are present, it is possible to observe the repression and suppression. Some patients, aware of their woodenness and inability to feel, try to cover up by acting as if they had these missing human attributes. It is this estrangement from the self and others that is dramatically portrayed by Camus in *The Stranger*, who eventually explodes compulsively in violence.

As indicated previously, the clues to the roots of this character structure are located in the fundamental area of trust and distrust.[5] It must be sought in family life and patterns of mothering. As psychologists and psychoanalysts, we must make our contribution in this area, aware also that the human condition cannot be explained by one specialty alone.

In line with the findings of Erikson, Mahler, Anna Freud, Kris, Spitz and others working in the field of ego psychology and child-rearing styles, and with my own clinical observations, studies of Jewish mothering, of reluctant mothering in ghettos, and the family life of geniuses,[2, 3] my impressions are confirmed that for good or ill, the mothering patterns prevalent in a culture are a crucial ingredient that decisively affects the character

structure, intelligence, achievement, creativity and even survival
—in fact, all aspects of child development.

Too little is known about the mothering process and its
decisive influences. Freud in a sense neglected the period of
infancy and childhood.[21] What was known came from the analysis
of adults. Only recently has psychoanalysis taken an interest
in the direct observation of mother and child. The process which
began quite early with the birth of Darwin's first son, was finally
picked up by Piaget, Anna Freud, Bowlby, Kris, Mahler, Spitz
and others. There is a woeful lack of precise knowledge of just
how and to what extent mothering influences child development.
The emotional factors in nurturing have hardly been explored
sufficiently; yet clinically, and even experimentally, there are
sufficient data and clues present to warrant some statements,
even tentative generalizations about the mothering process in
our time and why it tends to breed the schizoid cerebrals that
resort to violence.

In examining the roots of violence in modern youth from the
vantage point of our own speciality, psychoanalysis, I have
discriminated a facet of the problem which I would like to bring
to you for consideration and which has its roots in the pre-
Oedipal period. There exists a need of all people for an identity
as an aspect of human striving, natural growth and development
on the road from fusion and helplessness in infancy and childhood,
toward adulthood and independence.

The much used and abused term "identity" came into vogue
in the literature when used by Erikson some twenty years ago.
In his latest thinking, he reviews its historical development,
confusions in the popular usage, and the changes in meaning
that have evolved even when used by professionals. He lists
three necessary preconditions for understanding this term, namely,
"a psychoanalysis sophisticated enough to include the environment . . . a social psychology which is psychoanalytically sophisticated . . ." and, "a new field which would have to create its
own historical sophistication."[6]

Aware of the inadequacies of definition for the purposes of
this paper, identity is defined tentatively as the result of a
normative growth process, from the dependence of infancy,

toward a growing, meaningful sense of self and independent adulthood. It embraces an ever-expanding self-discrimination of a satisfying life, lived with a sense of autonomy and fulfillment. In its early stages it is a search. As it matures, tempered by experimentation, crisis and *weltschmerz*, it becomes a positive affirmation. In adulthood, it is an ever-refining and developing entity.

It is my impression that the roots of violence in our youth are located in the earliest struggles for identity during the pre-Oedipal period. The threatening frustrations and furies that develop as a consequence of faulty family constellations and defective mothering that ignore identity needs set the pattern of a paranoid dynamism that culminates in violence.

The basic function of mothering is described by Mahler to be at optimum when it meets the changing needs of the growing infant and child.[12] There are two broad areas involved. They can be described as dependency needs and needs for independence, both of which are essential for identity growth.

The need for closeness, bodily contact, coddling and playing during the early period of symbiosis and fusion are the more obvious dependency needs of the infant. The loving action-interaction cycle of communication and mutual responsiveness that meet the child's needs are necessary for its normative growth.[19] After locomotion sets in, these needs continue in changing proportion. Autonomous needs to explore the environment, to relate to father, siblings and others, develop. These needs of the infant and child are also essential to growth, independence and identity. Different styles of mothering thwart different aspects of identity development.

Roughly and descriptively, mothering can be seen as a continuum:

Negligible Mothering	Reluctant Mothering	Average Mothering	Dedicated Mothering	Jocasta Mothering
/	/	/	/	/

Three of these styles tend to defeat the establishment of identity: negligible, reluctant and Jocasta.

In attempting to describe the types of mothering on the continuum, there is an awareness of the paucity of research into mothering patterns and a lack of precise scientific knowledge in this area. Perhaps the extremes are a little better known based on the research into negligible and Jocasta mothering. However, these types can be delineated descriptively and clinically because of the broad recognition of these general trends.

Negligible mothering is a clinical entity observed in hospitals and institutions caring for foundlings. It is an outgrowth of socioeconomic and psychological circumstances that deprive children of a home. It is also affected by all the intangibles that lead institutions to depersonalize human relations. It is characterized by extremes of deprivation of a one-to-one relationship where the infant does not experience sufficient stimulation, coddling, playing or communication from a mother or surrogate. Such mothering is lacking in intensity, quantity and quality, and at no time is the infant an important person in the life of the mothering one. Little dedication, commitment or involvement in a loving, joyful, mothering experience is present. Spitz has described the traumatic effects of extreme deprivation during this early period, when negligible mothering prevails. It includes death, anaclitic depression and permanent incapacities for intellectual and social growth.[17, 18]

Reluctant mothering is a depriving type of nurturing but does not go to the extremes of negligible mothering. It exists in all populations but flourishes mostly in modern urban ghettos and in impoverished large families. It develops out of socioeconomic and psychologic conditions that make the child a burden the mother is reluctant to assume. Such children are frequently reared by part-time makeshift, reluctant surrogates, such as grandparents, friends, aunts, or baby-sitters, with the mother much more involved in other pursuits, seeking her satisfactions and fulfillment outside the home.

Reluctant mothering is characterized by a lack of sufficient coddling, listening and playing. There is insufficient intensity, quantity and quality. The homes are unstable and children are frequently born out of wedlock. The infant and child does not experience a child-centered home. The mothering is sporadic, unreliable and basically reluctantly administered. It lacks the wholehearted commitment, involvement and enjoyment that are essential aspects of mothering. Much of our violence, crime and educational retardation have roots in the sociopsychological conditions found in ghettos. The unstable, fatherless homes, the insecurity and reluctant mothering make a large contribution to our increasing crime rates and the violence of our age.[15] These two depriving types of mothering breed the very characterological disorders previously described.

The effects upon the personality of people having experienced such mothering deprivation take the following forms: "Depression, a sense of abandonment, feeling of emptiness or hollowness, deep dependency needs, inability to maintain consistently intimate human relationships, psychoticlike rage attacks and frequent use of a projection mechanism giving paranoid coloring to the personality."[8]

I have found similar symptoms in patients reared exclusively by "Jocasta" mothers who made them their chief love objects. One sees this frequently in family constellations characterized by a strong dominating mother and a weak, inept or absent father. When a woman is deprived of basic human and biologic needs and suffers affect-hunger due to long yearning for children, the death of a child, a loveless life or the disappearance of her husband, she will make her child the chief love object. I have called the type of mothering developed from this severe affect hunger, Jocasta mothering.[4] Drawing on the Oedipus myth, I have shown there is a dynamic, the Jocasta complex, that is quite as definitive, fatalistic and symbolic as is the Oedipus complex. One sees this rather frequently in illegitimate children, in adopted children, when fathers are drafted into the army, or any circumstance where a father is absent as a loving, masculine force in the family either psychically or physically or where the mother suffers serious emotional deprivation.

Jocasta mothering has had a number of not entirely satisfactory tags placed upon it, such as overprotective, seductive, close, binding, intimate, doting, narcissistic, and momistic. While they describe aspects of the configuration, they do not see it as having an inner dynamic of its own, powered as it were by the biologic yearning for children and the complicated sexual and emotional needs of women. There is general agreement that this type of mothering, far from depriving the child of dependency needs, if anything, gives too much—but not based on the child's needs. It is rather the mother's emotional starvation that is central and causes her to resort compulsively to Jocasta mothering.

In the normal growth process the child and mother are fused in a symbiosis for the first eight months to a year. When locomotion sets in and the child moves to explore the world on his own, the normal mother will permit him his freedom, watching carefully and standing by. She will permit him to move toward a second love object, to play with his father. When he comes back frightened and crying, she will be there to meet his dependency needs. Not so the Jocasta mother who compulsively fulfills her own jealous needs for an exclusive relationship with her child. Even if the father is around, she will find ways to exclude him. She prevents the necessary growth toward separation-individuation, autonomy and a separate identity. The father does not play his historic role in the family of helping to break the loving symbiosis of infancy and childhood and introduce the child to broader experiences. The separation-individuation never occurs or is defective.

The Jocasta mother maintains the symbiosis long after the natural cut-off point and fails to meet the child's increased needs for an independent life of his own. As a result, the child begins to feel the intimacy, love and affection of the mother as a bondage against which he rages in frustration inwardly or overtly, but from which he cannot free himself psychically. He comes to the Oedipal period with exaggerated lust for his mother and exaggerated patricidal feelings. He is unable to cope with the problems that ensue and remains with an unresolved Oedipus complex.

As the Jocasta mother continues the symbiosis on into the Oedipal period and beyond, the child, young adult and adult, experiences love and intimacy as a contaminated, incestuous, guilty bondage. It forever undermines his human relationships. His defenses are miles high, varying from paranoid furies to dissociation of emotional states. They come crashing down again as he repetitiously and compulsively repeats the cycle of love and hate that he first experienced in the loving symbiosis and the separation-individuation frustrations.

Such Jocasta-reared children have a definite character structure marked by an unresolved Oedipus problem, the fear of love, strong ambivalence in human relations, strong paranoid trends, a tenuous ability to conform or accept authority, an underlying sense of guilt and masochism, a strong homosexual component, latent or overt, and high ambitions. They are unusually oral and demanding, easily disappointed and regress readily to panic, furies, anger and rage, with states of emptiness, withdrawal and depression. The Jocasta-reared child differs from the emotionally deprived child in several important respects, among them his intelligence, his creativity and his leadership qualities. He is usually above average intellectually, may have unusual gifts and talents and frequently provides the leadership in rebellious movements. It is the personality found most frequently in geniuses and extraordinary achievers.

Thus I tend to see the violence of modern youth as having its roots in the pre-Oedipal period and as a direct outgrowth of frustration in identity growth due to defective nurturing, either negligible or reluctant, depriving mothering which disregards necessary dependency needs or Jocasta mothering which disregards independency needs. This frustration in infancy, childhood and beyond leads to paranoid dynamisms that are later transferred to other establishments than the home. It is at the root of class, racial, student, criminal and the national violence of our age. The increased matriarchal character of our society and the fact that men tend to be more absorbed in the business world or the armies creates a problem. Children are reared almost exclusively by their mothers or mother surrogates which tends to generate Jocasta mothering and the pre-Oedipal problems at the root of violence.

In singling out the family, the father and especially the mothering process of the first five years as critical, there is no intent to place the burden of error on the parents. The fact that 40 percent of ghetto homes are fatherless and that a matriarchal setting prevails most decisively in ghetto homes is a cultural fact

that has its roots in many causes outside the family.[8] Nevertheless, the home establishment cheats, frustrates, deprives the
growing infant and child of his identity. It is this primal experience that repeats later in youth, adolescence and young manhood.
All the regressed emotional states are transferred to new objects
and institutions.

It is important to note that criminal violence is mostly a
male problem and occurs most frequently during the ages of
eighteen to twenty-five. It is the age when youth must meet the
problems of the larger culture. It is the crucial transition period
from young manhood to adult citizenship. It is the time when
Jocasta-reared sons most keenly feel their need to be people
in their own right, with their own ideas, ideals, opportunities,
concepts of life—their own identity.

Adolescence presents a critical point in the development of
identity. Furious battles and even physical violence frequently
occur. The Jocasta mother continues the fused relationship and
desperately attempts to control through manipulation. It is this
violation of identity that underlies the furies and violence we see
today. Whenever authority invades and violates the fundamental
sense of self, or when the paranoid dynamism, ever trigger-happy,
feels that it does, or when the human being is stripped of
dignity and opportunity to be himself and "do his thing" in the
continuing search and growth into that fulfilling, unique, individual with his own sense of identity occurs, he regresses to
his old behavior, the extremes of which are his defenses, paranoid
fury or the computer-like, alienated stranger of Camus who
eventually explodes in violence.

Because the separation-individuation development was
thwarted, the Jocasta-reared person distrusts commitments of
any kind to a person, alma mater or any institution. Because
the deprived child experienced a mothering that was defective
and could not be trusted to meet his needs, he also has a tenuous
capacity for trust and commitment. This expresses itself in his
estranged relations to all people and establishments. It is the
essence of the schizoid personality. The struggle against this
thwarting of identity becomes a way of life. He becomes a rebel,

frequently without a cause, locked in hostile integrations with family, lovers, school and society.

The universities have become vast factory complexes, depersonalized, lacking in human considerations. The students feel themselves reduced to numbers on an IBM card.[9] They feel like computers evaluated by other computers. They experience a sense of violation that alienates them, sets them in fierce competition for grades and leaves them without recognition and identity as people. Their lives are controlled and manipulated by heartless institutions, universities, businesses and war machines that do not take their ideals, needs, hopes and ambitions—their lives—their identity into consideration. They are furiously anti-establishment.

Berkeley's best student, after sixteen years of success in the rat race of the grade-point system, could say, "It wasn't worth it. . . . I copped out on myself . . . my ideals . . ." and yielded to a "dehumanizing system."[16] Youth has found many ways of protesting during adolescence and young adulthood; dropping out, becoming hippies, using drugs, and resorting to violence and crime are the most common. This has seized not only the culturally and psychically deprived, but affects students from every social class level at the universities—and 46 percent of all our youth are located in the universities.[16] They feel their identity denied, violated, unrecognized and insulted. Their very existence as human beings is threatened by a slow dehumanizing process, by rejection if they fail in the rat race, and by seizure for military service.

The "establishment" tends to provoke all the frustrating experiences generated by the mothering procedures that originally discouraged identity growth. The schizoid cerebrals, confused and frustrated in their identity, tend to resort to violence. It is important to note that the absent father plays a significant role in the defective mothering. This is true in all three cases that thwart identity needs.

One of the effects of the absence of a father, psychically or physically, appears to be a tendency toward homosexuality and identity confusion. Clinically, it has been well established that homosexuality and paranoid trends are closely connected. In spite of this, it is one of the illusions of our age that homosexuals are "pansies," "sissies," and peaceful. Historically, this is not so. In Roman society, especially the period of the greatest violence during the civil wars, the outstanding leaders were strongly homosexual and bisexual. This was especially true of Sulla, Julius Caesar, and Marc Anthony.[20] Ancient Greece, the Doric States, with Sparta outstandingly so, were the most warlike.[11] It was there that homosexuality was most firmly entrenched and institutionalized. The outstanding warrior of the Homeric epic was Achilles whose lover was Petrocolus. The noble band of 300 Thebans, who gave so good an account of themselves as warriors and died to the last man defending Greek liberty, were matched homosexual lovers.[11] They were the chosen warriors of their day.

The unresolved Oedipus complex develops paranoid furies not only against the father as highlighted by Freud, but also against the mother. The matricidal murderous feelings developed against the mother who betrays is clearly present in *Hamlet*.[7] It is even more so in Shakespeare's *Coriolanus*.[7] The unresolved Oedipus complex develops murderous hatred toward the father.[10] Shakespeare deals with this theme in the great tragedies. The furious rebellions versus the father who is the establishment is a consistent theme in song and story, myth and legend.[14]

This unresolved Oedipus problem is a direct result of ghetto life with its absentee father, but also of the rest of our society. It is especially true where Jocasta mothering prevails.

In conclusion, I tend to see the violence of our age from the point of view of our own specialty, based on the three mothering processes that thwart identity needs and make difficult the resolution of the Oedipal conflicts and a firm sexual identity.

REFERENCES

1. Besdine, M.: Jewish mothering. *The Jewish Spectator*, 35(2):7-10, 1970.
2. Besdine, M.: Jocasta complex, mothering and genius. *Psychoanal. Rev.*, 55(2), 1968.

3. Besdine, M.: Jocasta complex, mothering and genius. *Psychoanal. Rev.*, 55(4), 1969.
4. Besdine, M.: Jocasta and Oedipus: another look. *Pathways in Child Guidance*. Bureau of Child Guidance, New York City Board of Education, March, 1968.
5. Erikson, E. H.: *Childhood and Society*. New York, Norton, 1963.
6. Erikson, E. H.: *Identity, Youth and Crisis*. New York, Norton, 1968, p. 21.
7. Faber, M. D.: *The Design Within: Psychoanalytic Approaches to Shakespeare*. New York, Science House, 1970, pp. 79-153, 287-339.
8. Freudenberger, H. J., and Overby, A.: The patient from emotionally deprived environments. *Psychoanal. Rev.*, 56(2), 1969.
9. Jencks, C., and Riesman, D.: *The Academic Revolution*. Garden City, Doubleday, 1968, p. 12.
10. Lederer, S.: Historical consequences of father-son hostility. *Psychoanal. Rev.*, 54(2), 1967.
11. Licht, H.: *Sexual Life in Ancient Greece*. New York, Barnes and Noble, 1963, pp. 418, 443.
12. Mahler, M. S.: *On Human Symbiosis and the Vicissitudes of Individuation*. New York, International Universities Press, 1968, Vol. I, p. 22.
13. May, R.: *Love and Will*. New York, Norton, 1970.
14. Moloney, J. C.: Oedipus Rex, CuChulain, Khepri and the Ass. *Psychoanal. Rev.*, 54(2), 1967.
15. Report of the President's Commission on Law Enforcement and Administration of Justice. *The Challenge of Crime in a Free Society*. Avon Books, 1968, Ch. III and p. 130.
16. Schlesinger, A., Jr.: Joe College is dead. *The Saturday Evening Post*, 241st Year, No. 19, September 21, 1968, p. 27.
17. Spitz, R. A.: Hospitalism. *Psychoanalytic Study of the Child*. New York, International Universities Press, 1945, Vol. I.
18. Spitz, R. A.: Hospitalism. *Psychoanalytic Study of the Child*. New York, International Universities Press, 1946, Vol. II.
19. Spitz, R. A.: *The First Year of Life*. New York, International Universities Press, 1965.
20. Weigall, A.: *The Life and Times of Marc Anthony*. Garden City, Garden City Publishing Co., 1931, pp. 51, 56, 91.
21. Winnicott, D. W.: *The Maturational Processes and the Facilitating Environment: Studies in the Theory of Emotional Development*. New York, International Universities Press, 1965, p. 39.

IN THIS ILLUSTRATIVE and informative paper, Dr. Irving Solomon, a candidate in the Adelphi University Postdoctoral Program in Psychotherapy, explores the acting-out and acting-in resistances as manifested by the hysterical personality.

Dr. Solomon begins by describing the female hysteric, tracing many of her overt symptoms back to their origins in the patient's early relationship with her parents. He clearly accounts for the patient's "nongenuine" reactions to the therapeutic situation and openly discusses his own behavior towards these patients in the past. Disturbed by the hysteric's resistance to therapeutic progress and noting his difficulty in coping with this "nongenuineness," Dr. Solomon suggests alternative methods for dealing effectively with patients acting out in this manner.

In his treatment-oriented paper, Dr. Solomon has delineated his personal feelings and reactions to the acting-out and acting-in resistances of certain of his patients. He enables us not only to understand and treat acting out somewhat better, but also provides methods of handling therapists' reactions to that behavior we label as "nongenuine."

D.S.M.
G.D.G.

Chapter 6

The Non-genuine Resistance of the Hysterical Personality

Irving L. Solomon

There is a kind of patient—mainly the female hysterical personality—who gives forth a great deal of feeling. She may talk about happenings with a sense of involvement, but in the session what emerges is a phony, unreal affect. It is as if she were acting on a stage. Out there, away from the analyst she seems to be feeling; for she talks about crying, about being passionately angry, about raging with yearning desire. Once in therapy, on the other hand, we see only phoniness.

What does the analyst do to obtain some genuine feelings? I have faced this resistance problem many times and always experienced difficulty in resolving it. Does it depend on an intractable transference resistance? Might I have experienced some subtle countertransference which prevented my patients from experiencing genuine feelings both in and out of therapy? The intention of this paper is to try to answer these questions. Above all, I want to clarify the experience of being stymied by what proved to be for me often an insurmountable egosyntonic acting-out and acting-in resistance closely associated with the hysterical personality but occasionally linked to other nosologic groups. Hopefully, the possible reasons for the difficulty in resolving what I term the "nongenuine" resistance will benefit other therapists should they face this same type of blockage to constructive therapeutic progress.

The hysterical personality has been described in the literature as a dependent little girl in the body of a woman, strikingly youthful, manipulative and imbued with magical thinking and an abundance of pregenital fantasies[5] as a neurotic who has set up a barrier to and also the symbolic satisfaction of incestuous sexual wishes[6] and as a transference neurosis characterized by repression, isolated reaction formations, phallic qualities, emotionality, somatizations, conversions, genitalizations and identification with lost love objects and guilt-producing objects.[4]

As one might suspect the mother of the hysterical personality plays a key role in the dynamics of the egosyntonic behavior of pseudoemotionality. Mother, in essence, hypocritically acted out love and protection. Her daughter may have recognized this duplicity at one level, and this perception was too painful to try to deny or wish away. Mother was also seen as a phallic woman, glamorous and sexually exciting. Along with this perception there was considerable anxiety, for to be like mother meant to be destroyed or castrated. Yet, mother attracted and excited the hysterical patient. Mother's very emptiness acted like a powerful magnet which beckoned the hysteric to fill the void. When she drew closer to mother she met rejection and the overwhelming ominousness of emptiness. One way to defeat terror was to make emotional noise or "static." Thus nongenuine feelings served in a sense as a means of quieting the emptiness of mother and the emptiness within the hysteric.

Of course, unmet orality needs, too, played a great role in making the hysteric greedy for new experiences. Analysis, therefore, is seen as a delightfully delicious tidbit; something which sends erotic chills down the spine of the hysteric. But all the time the hysteric is not really there. She is really in bed as a child listening to her version of the primal scene; that is, listening to a mother and father who bickered, listening to a mother who taunted father, provoking him into a crescendo of impotent rage. She knows and is very much aware that feelings are important and thus feelings are not given. She fantasizes herself wrecking therapy, urinating on the analyst. Perhaps, the analyst in frustration will begin to shriek like father.

When the analyst confronts the hysteric with her chronic pseudo-emotionality she simulates concern. When every pseudo-reaction is touched upon she finally retreats into passivity. Her main claim now becomes "I don't know," "I can't help it," or "help me." The analyst feels as if the patient is dead weight, like a child who crumples to the floor when she does not have her own way. Obviously, this is a passive-aggressive resistance. Yet, there seems to be more to it.

What I did not take sufficient notice of is that every interpretation is seen as a phallic thrust. The patient may frequently keep her legs tightly shut and is frigid. Nothing gets in or comes out. She is neither man or woman now; she is a blank screen or better still seemingly dead. Now she is her emotionally dead mother and nothing can touch her, or like the deer by being perfectly still she avoids death.

Death, then, I propose is one main issue in the treatment of the hysterical personality, an issue I did not sufficiently apprehend or deal with in the past. The hysteric fears death and outfoxes it by being emotionally dead. Every outside romance brings her back to life. The aging process is seemingly arrested and she has found eternal youth. Like the fairy-tale princess, she sleeps the sleep of simulated death, waiting as Sleeping Beauty waited for her Prince Charming to bring her back to life with a kiss of love. She compulsively seeks her Prince Charming and just as inevitably finds him a "frog" dressed in royal garments, or worded another way, already castrated or ready-to-be castrated. No wonder she fights the analyst "tooth and nail!" He wants to make her feel, and to feel is to experience life and, therefore to age and die. Perhaps the hysteric is afraid that her genuine feelings will pour out of her unchecked by thought, leaving her a dry dead husk. She may recall how her mother remained ageless and powerful. Mother did not deteriorate, only the men about her.

I suppose one could also consider the hysteric as alienated from her true feelings, predominantly phallic-aggressive ones. As Bychowski[1] has pointed out, "alienation seems that last resort of the ego which found repression an insufficient and uncertain protection against the danger of destructive hostility." It is hypothesized that the hysterical personality was early subjected to repeated visual sensitization traumas (namely the primal scene) and the ego learned to use alienation, dramatization and non-genuine behavior (derivatives of exhibitionism and scoptophilia) as a protective barrier against excessive external and internal (fantasied) stimuli. Fenichel,[2] especially, emphasizes the ego's need compulsively to repeat and act out stimuli once passively received, to bring down the dosage to an acceptable level. Greenacre[3] also focuses on early intense visual sensitization, correlating it with a proclivity for dramatization, and she perceives these people utilizing speech more for catharsis than for communication.

It is therefore theorized that the hysteric had an intense influx of primal scene stimulation creating a traumatic experience. She may have seen father expressing what appeared to be genuine sexual feelings and mother not relating in kind. Here it is assumed that the hysteric is exquisitely tuned in on her mother as a frustrating, depriving object. She saw the head of father's penis or fantasized it as lost during coitus; thus she equated "losing one's head" with losing one's penis. Since a part of the hysteric identifies with father's penis she strives mightily not to "lose her head." The result is nongenuine behavior, for to feel is to "lose one's head."

The hysterical personality may have the screen memory of father being provoked to such a fury by mother that in frustration, he "banged" his head against the wall. This memory may then elicit the recollection of father masturbating in mother's absence and of the patient's Oedipal anxiety about father possibly molesting her. The obvious frustration, occurring during the primal scene and elsewhere between her father and mother, leads the hysteric to cause other people to "lose their heads," mainly men, while she keeps hers. She transfers this need to the analyst, whom she fears will "lose his head" in the face of her frustration of him through nongenuiness, and therefore he cannot be relied upon. The extent to which the hysterical personality can get men to "lose their heads" and thus seek penis substitutes is graphically revealed by the number of their husbands that I have seen who became interested in collecting or playing with guns, a hobby they may not have considered prior to their marriage.

When the hysteric keeps her legs tightly closed together in the treatment session she creates a wall to drive the analyst, like father, into masturbation; that is, to "beat his head against the wall" in an attempt to work through the "nongenuine" resistance. As the analyst repeatedly confronts the hysteric with her nongenuine behavior he appears to her as if he is masturbating against her, a sexualized occurrence all too welcomed by the hysteric. Once this kind of father transference is established the patient settles down to a waiting game; her passivity, her spiteful, noncompliant identification with mother versus the analyst's need to experience the patient as genuine.

It is here that we make a significant error. We should *not* actively confront the hysteric with her pseudoemotionality. My hunch is that I became terribly anxious over what appeared to be the psychic death of these patients. I can recall many sessions in which they would lie, legs rigidly together and arms tightly at their sides, and not utter a word. Looking back I can now see I was made terribly uncomfortable by being present before a profoundly regressed state resembling death. It evoked a need to rescue like Prince Charming, a need doomed to failure; for it coincided, as previously mentioned, with the hysteric's acting out of the primal scene, masturbatory fantasies, and a need to be magically transported without any effort into the land of life. One patient actually dreamed she was being lifted on a flying carpet away from her problems.

We may then say that the analyst, when confronted with the "nongenuine" resistance, must remain silent excessively longer than in other types of treatment situations. He must remain silent until the patient speaks despite the simulated corpse lying before him. When the patient breaks the silence the analyst might say "you see you are not really your dead mother."

The patient will then begin to voice a repeated chant; namely, "I don't know," "I don't know how to feel." This can be handled as a query or a seeking of reassurance of the analyst to not "lose his head" when the patient "loses" hers. Thus the analyst might say "you're afraid that I will not be able to help you control your feelings should you bring them out." This interpretation will be more constructive at this point for the hysteric had had the prior experience of the analyst's nonanxiety and nonmasturbation in the face of the semblance of death. In other words, by the analyst's waiting for the hysteric to emerge from her psychic death, he demonstrates that she and only she is responsible for coming back to life.

REFERENCES

1. Bychowski, G.: The archaic object and alienation. *Int. J. Psychoanal.*, *48*:384, 1967.
2. Fenichel, O.: Neurotic acting out. *Psychoanal. Rev.*, *32*:197, 1945.
3. Greenacre, P.: *Trauma, Growth and Personality.* New York, Norton, 1952.
4. Greenson, R. R.: *The Technique and Practice of Psychoanalysis.* New York, International Universities Press, 1967, p. 93.
5. Murphy, W. F.: *The Tactics of Psychotherapy.* New York, International Universities Press, 1965, pp. 599-612.
6. Tarachow, S.: *Introduction to Psychotherapy.* New York, International Universities Press, 1963, p. 40.

D r. Emanuel F. Hammer, a psychoanalyst who has worked extensively with sexual deviates, offers his expertise to clarify and elaborate the dynamics and treatment of those patients with acting-out sexual disorders.

Dr. Hammer's paper focuses upon the particular group of sexual deviates who have characterological rather than neurotic problems; theoretically, because they have little capacity for symbolic defenses and, therefore, a greater propensity to act out in an egosyntonic manner. The task of therapy, according to Hammer, is to help the deviate develop the capacity for delay and reflection and to encourage feelings of discontent as a motivating factor to change; that is, to convert the acting-out character disorder into a "simply straightforward neurotic condition" more readily accessible to traditional psychotherapy. With this latter thesis in mind, Dr. Hammer uses case material to illustrate the pitfalls and principles of various therapeutic interventions. Group therapy, pictorial and sensory communication and other innovative techniques are elaborated as beneficial and appropriate methodology.

The reader will appreciate, as we did, Dr. Emanuel Hammer's concise, well organized, and meaningful presentation.

D.S.M.
G.D.G.

101

Chapter 7

Sexual Disorders, Character Neurosis and the Therapy Technique of Confrontation *

EMANUEL F. HAMMER

In an earlier paper[6] on "Symptoms of Sexual Deviation" the writer pointed out that individuals suffering such symptoms manifested a concrete orientation with lowered capacity to employ fantasy and sublimatory outlets. The "sex offender" releases his antisocial sexuality directly, because he operates on a concrete level. He does not have the abstract capacity for sublimation available to handle these impulses in another way. The neurotic, in contrast, having more symbolic capacities available, builds a defense of symptoms to guard against the emergency of forbidden impulses.

Kubie[8] points out that it is because of the capacity for symbolization that neurosis can come into being. But in the perversion, in contrast to the neurosis, it is just such a capacity for symbolic transformation which has not developed.

Diagnostically, most individuals suffering symptoms of sexual deviation fall into predominantly two categories: secondly, neurosis and, primarily, character disorder. The neuroses involving sexual deviation are treated essentially like any neurotic condition. But character disorders are a treatment challenge of another order. It is to that challenge that this paper addresses itself.

We are all well aware of the egosyntonic vs. ego-alien differentiation between a character disorder and neurosis, one

* Warm appreciation is extended Naomi Goldstein, M.D., Director, N.Y.C. Criminal Court Psychiatric Clinic, for her reading of the ms. and helpful suggestions.

where in the egosyntonic condition the ego gets drawn into the symptom itself. I would like to suggest another difference.

Neurosis represents a maladaptive compromise between impulses and defenses. So does a character disorder. But the difference is that in this compromise, the sexual character disorder (in contrast to the neurosis) expresses relatively more of the impulses than the defenses against them. It is nearer to raw impulse and less impulse-derivative, and because of its unvarnished gratifications it is more difficult to treat. Impulsivity and acting-out tendencies spur the patient in the direction of immediacy, and against delay of satisfaction or insight.

Others, or society, suffer the pinch of the individual's character disorder. And then society retaliates—with arrests, imprisonment, rejection, punishment, etc. Only *then* does the individual (and only indirectly) suffer from his "symptoms."

In these patients, here-and-now action has not relinquished that part of its domain which, with maturation, is ordinarily given over to the primacy of thought. Their psychic condition is one dominated by sensorimotor levels of development. They can neither mobilize much tolerance for frustration, nor hold back instinct and impulse discharge.

In sexual character disorders the clamorous impulses and the seeking of direct gratification drown out the voice of reflection. The task in their therapy is to activate: first, motivation, and second, capacity for such delay and for reflection. The goal is to help the patient to grow in his use of secondary thought processes for preliminary "trial" action.

The aim here is to stimulate the patient's interest in the motivating power of his inner trains of thought and feeling and to have him learn to attend more to the anticipatory affects and "small actions" in his head before they bubble over into overt behavior.

TREATMENT PITFALLS

In the defensive structure of a character disorder, a veneer of hardness—sometimes cynicalness, sometimes craftiness—is employed to mask the accumulated psychiatric lesions of an underlyingly traumatized person. Such patients, though there are few things they hunger for more than acceptance, do everything they can to be disliked and rejected.

I recall one seventeen-year-old patient who took out a pen-knife to whittle on the edge of my desk as he spoke, another (a twenty-six-year-old man) who put his feet up, soles on the wall during his session following my having newly decorated the office, and two other patients of character disorder diagnosis one of whom (a fourteen-year-old) wrote "Fuck Dr. Hammer" in chalk on my outer door and the other (a woman, married and in graduate school) who scratched "Shit" in the paint of the wall of the elevator.

How are these acts dealt with? Sometimes by confrontation and prohibition, sometimes by interpretation, depending on, among other considerations (the patient's length of time in treatment and the quality of the relationship, his readiness for insight, the meaning of the act, etc.), the severity of the acting out. The first patient was directly and firmly told to put his knife away. *Then* we talked about it. I inquired of the second how he felt now about the office. What he was doing dawned on him, he took his feet down, and exploration led in the direction of his feelings that the office now reflected a higher status on my part, and from there to his denigrating reactivity to authority figures. With the third-mentioned patient, I recalled that he had come to the office accompanied by a fellow member of his delinquent gang. My patient had been moving into connecting with his treatment and into experiencing warm feelings toward me. After I discovered the writing on the door shortly after his session, I wondered if he had not felt called up to make a show of bravado, of toughness to hide his softer feelings developing toward me, of rejection to disguise his growing acceptance of his therapy, and thus save face with his friend in accord with the value system prevalent in their gang. As we talked about it the following session, the patient sheepishly confided this is what it was. The fourth-cited patient, having engaged in several previous acts of the same nature against the property in my office or the apartment building, was categorically told that my practice was an outpatient one for functioning individuals and if she could not muster sufficient controls I would have to disqualify my situation as suitable for her. Our work up to that point had convinced me that it was not that she *couldn't* control her actions of this type, but that she *wouldn't*. That confrontation worked.

Patients of character disorder symptoms are often those who have retreated from the disappointments of insufficient parental affection into a narcissistic shell—whereby they hope to give themselves the love they feel they cannot receive from others. The emotional attrition they experienced in childhood frequently laid down a core of suspiciousness that warmth or interest from others are not genuine but have ulterior motives.

Those who have treated patients whose symptomatology is essentially that of a character disorder, may well ask whether these patients are capable of perceiving the therapist and his actual attitudes. To a degree, such patients do perceive them, even from the beginning, although, to be sure, their perception here is mostly peripheral and unsure. The patient may sense a friendly feeling from the therapist, an interest and a caring, but he is frightened of giving it credence. Caught between his perceptions and his cynical doubts, he sets about testing the therapist's genuineness: his concern, his perceptiveness, his interest, his integrity, his reliableness, his honesty, his frankness, his tolerance, his strength in the face of criticism, his susceptibility to flattery, his capacity for firmness, his ability to set limits or to take a stand. And underneath, running through all of it—can he be trusted?

The patient is not readily convinced, and he has many and varied means to put in the service of dismissing what he sees. If the therapist is well meaning, he is a fool. If he is ethical, he is square. If he is kind, he is weak; if tender, sissified.

What is the therapist to do?

I think of one patient, an ex-military officer, who early took a commanding stance to communicate that it was he who was in charge of the sessions. He would grandly inquire at points if I had any questions or any interpretations to make. He would announce, a moment before I would move to, when the session was up. His attitude was superior, controlling, and cynical. He knew all the answers. Modesty, caring, or consideration, although theoretically commendable, would if practiced or felt by him, deprive him of the dominant role over others due his worth. In his sessions he was quick to criticize my ability, my sincerity, and taste in clothes and art in my office. He wanted me to know he thought little of me in part and in whole.

His arrogance was muscled in his tossing an ashtray up and down in his hands as he spoke. As he verbally (and physically) strutted in seemingly so self-satisfied a way, the task before me was to hold his oneupmanship up to eye level so that it could be shown, not shown-up. As this was done, he then moved to a new phase, the infant under the "ballsy" front. He would try to suck excessively upon me in his requirements for my absorption in him, my friendship, my time, my energy and the loan of my books. What I did was gratify little and interpret much. To have gratified more would have been to be seen by him as manipulated, weak, and a fool.

One confrontation was particularly important. A short number of sessions after he was willing to use the couch in the treatment, he suddenly introduced the issue that he felt uncomfortable if I was watching him as he lay there. After attempting, without much success, to explore his underlying feelings here, I assured him I could lean back in my chair and just listen without looking. After awhile he came back to this with the idea that he would be more comfortable if he used the floor so that my desk shielded him from view. To see how this played itself out, I agreed and he took that position. Then he wanted to take the pillows from off the chairs and the couch and build a further barricade to my vision. After he did this, he then stretched out behind it and soon asked, "Can you see me?" When I replied that I could not, he then introduced the complication, "How can I believe you?"

I had gotten the feeling, by this point, that this was not predominantly a paranoid reaction so much as it was a means of testing me and testing the limits. Following on my feeling that his actions were more provocative than genuine, I merely replied, "Well, if you cannot trust me on the simple level of accepting my word as to whether I can see you, how can you trust me with the intimacies necessary for our treatment collaboration to work? If you can't trust me on this, our working together would make little sense." He got up from his barricade, smiled an I've-been-caught-with-my-fingers-in-the-cookie-jar look, put the pillows back where they belonged and lay down on the couch.

Only when I had "proven" myself in the face of his onslaught, was he ready to go on to a focus on what brought him to therapy— his exhibitionism, an offense for which he had been arrested and placed on probation, an act precipitated by his retirement from the service.

Another patient, a man who suffered impotency symptoms with his wife and acted out perversions and Don Juanism with numerous other women, joined with a friend of his in making arrangements with a black woman they picked up to take a hotel room for the afternoon. While he was having sex with her, she asked him to withdraw before his orgasm and pleaded she did not want a white baby. He reassured her that he would; but then he did not. She understandably went into a fury at him.

He went downstairs for a drink in the bar while his friend had his turn, and later came up thinking to jolly her out of her mood and have another turn. When she would not be "jollied," he could not understand it. "Put yourself in her shoes!" I oriented him. With such types of character disorder conditions, what is required and what proves helpful is to stretch the patient's capacity to identify with the other person's needs.

One technique tailored for work with character disorder patients whose pattern takes a delinquent direction is one which, for want of a better term, I'll designate "topping the patient." This refers to that intervention which serves to demonstrate to the patient that it is not that you, the therapist, don't function antisocially because you *can't,* but because you *won't.* Somewhere, early in the treatment, this type of patient must learn that what makes for the difference in your respective ways of life is not that you are not as clever as he, but are wiser.

Until that happens, the therapist is disqualified as someone to learn from, disqualified as a potential identification figure. I recall one patient, a young man who among other things would resort to dealing in marijuana. He came in upset one day and told of an incident in which he had just almost been knifed. Someone had phoned him and made arrangements for him to bring some "pot" to the hallway of an upper, infrequented floor of an apartment building where they would meet under the stairs to negotiate the business. When he arrived, there were two youths there who asked to see the merchandise. My patient asked to be paid first. They answered by drawing knives and laughed at the notion that they were going to give him money. When he protested and began to edge out, they slashed his skin to show they meant business.

As we got into various feelings and aspects of the above, the writer was struck with the awareness that not only was the patient showing no disposition to give up "dealing," but seemed at a loss as to how to "deal" differently. I stated that I saw that he was not by any means close to considering the basic issues and underlying meanings, and so let us at least consider for the time being how he might proceed with less danger. Rather than open doors for him to peer through, rather than merely guide him to see what he did not yet see of how he might "deal" more safely next time, *I* shaped up practical alternative ways for him to consider. He would raise objections, and I would reshape the alternative procedures to meet his objections. He ended the session viewing me with a beginning respect.*

Such patients have to be convinced that the therapist can function as well as they, or better, in their shoes. The patient has to begin to entertain the idea that it is not that the therapist couldn't live in the "jungle" or "live by his brains" as the former glamourizes he does, but that the therapist knows better ways.

The psychotherapist in this regard functions a bit like the Street Worker who integrates with a gang, first joining them at the edge of their values. Only if one can connect with them where they are at, can one begin to work at leading them out.

When I have presented this technique at training seminars,

---

* Harold Greenwald has arrived at the same technique. He told a patient of his, a procurer, something to the effect of, "Harry, you're such a schmuck, I live off call girls too, but I don't get into trouble and I gain considerably. I treat them for a fat fee, I wrote a book, *The Call Girl,* about them, I got my doctoral thesis from it, and it was made into a movie. You end up roughed up or arrested."

there has frequently been someone who would react with, "But aren't you collaborating with the patient in his criminal behavior?" I, too, have raised this issue for myself in a bit of soul searching. I think, however, that if one's good-citizen-middle-class "morality" as a therapist does not allow one to take off the kid gloves for fear of dirtying one's hands, these patients cannot be worked with. The therapist who remains straight-laced in language and moralistic in stance, who is squeamish or prim, will perhaps be more helped by these patients than help them.

To assist a patient to not get knifed while delivering marijuana, while he is not yet ready to address the issues of the drug dealing itself, does not make you a cohort in the crime. By providing practical concern, it sets the stage for later psychotherapeutic collaboration. It, furthermore—and this, of course, outweighs all else—may be of direct influence in saving his life.

In the eventuality then that he persists in doing things the more dangerous way, when a safer *modus operandi* has been focused, then at least it has served to unearth the masochistic (or whatever else it unfolds to be) dynamics beneath for therapeutic work.

With the younger of these patients, those who are in adolescence or young adulthood, it is helpful to know their speech: "Down rapping myself," "up tight," "turning on," "turning off," "my bag," and all of the colloquialisms of their own language. As the therapist speaks their tongue and as he steps closer to their value system, the initial thrust of the treatment does not properly address itself to a reversal of the deviant symptoms. Focus is instead on the more promising impetus for change in the long run, a close and positive relationship with the therapist with the goal of some identification, ultimately, with him. But the therapist must first become a meaningful person in order to be admitted into the patient's life.

Following this, corrective emotional experiences may then become actualized, experiences in which caring for the therapist, and caring for his caring for them, become associated with new ways on the patients' part. This process is facilitated by decreasing the feeling of identification-distance which the patient feels towards representatives from the establishment. In his developmental years, authority figures have generally been equated with criticalness, or rejection, or harshness. In our efforts to undo this feeling, the writer joins with Wexler,[11] in his finding that "It becomes crucial to de-emphasize the therapist's role as a professional and as someone difffferent from the patient. Joining the patient as far as possible at his level of interests and concerns —whether they be comic books, movies, TV, sex talk—in order to get closer to what is comfortable for him, to lessen his anxiety about what the outside world is going to again expect from him, becomes essential for a positive relationship." In this manner, the patient's ready reactivity *against*, rather than *with*, authority representatives may be reduced to manageable proportions.

USE OF GROUP THERAPY

Group therapy, for the character disorder patient, is particularly helpful. It can provide a wider world of people against which to appraise oneself and one's pattern, an experience to expand one's perspective and reappraise one's values.

I think of the patient, a gambler, who defended his pattern with, "But everyone gambles, my brother-in-law, my cousin, all my friends are down at the track all the time." In essence, then, the one who stands as normatively out of line is me, not him.

If the neurotic's range of vision is restricted, the character disorder individual all the more wears blinders. In group therapy he starts dispensing with these blinders as he is asked to try on what other people see: about him, but also about each other. His constricted aperture may be widened to take in the fuller horizon. The polyannish can now recognize a little of the previously overlooked "negative" range of life's spectrum; the prim recognize the psychosexual aspects; the practical, hard-headed, nonpsychologically minded recognize the gentler feelings; the grimly somber recognize the lightness others allow; the shallow gain some awareness of deeper matters, and so on.

From the group, the person may acquire a larger domain in which he may be able to, first, see; next learn to function; and, finally, gain a sense of feeling at home in the more expanded terrain.

From the group, as from the therapist, the type of patient we are discussing may learn to no longer value "beating around the bush" but instead respect "calling a spade a spade." Getting to know the self within, submerged below the surface maneuverings, if it is to occur at all, must be preceded and motivated by a glimpse of what could be: if one were to live one's life with more directness, "straight" as the vernacular puts it. Perhaps the most immediate place to learn this, before sensing his *own* potential for living, is from tuning in on (1) (hopefully) the analyst's sense of satisfaction in living, and (2) the group members' where their methods of pursuing their goals have not been as twisted out of shape as are those generally of individuals with character disorders.

Following a struggle against it, the patient arrives at a beginning shift in his values, one which I've found coincides with an identification with the therapist (and sometimes varied group members) and his (their) more humanist outlook, one no longer dismissed as appropriate to a "square," a "fag" or a "fool."

THE ROLE OF CONFRONTATION

The initial task (and it is to this that I continually return as the fulcrum of this paper) is to facilitate the patient discovering how pervasively his hampered mode of living is cheating him of much in life. His first courage in therapy is in being able to put aside the self-deception that aside from a specific complaint or so, he is pretty well off as he is. With the character disorders, treatment first really begins with the impact of the realization, as one patient put it, "My life is shit"—meaning that gratifications are counterfeit, any real meaning absent, and foundations built on the shaky sands of pseudo-values.

Preparing the patient for the deeper use of his treatment means setting the soil with a real *need* for new answers. This is established by crystallizing, via a proper use of *confrontations,* a genuine dissatisfaction with the old.

Confrontation is most central of those techniques directed at *preparing* a character disorder patient for change. Confrontation is essentially a form of *clarification,* one that is vigorous and direct and involves affect more than just intellect.

What, then, technically is a clarification? Ekstein[5] defines the distinction between *clarification* and *interpretation.* The former "assists the patient to reach a higher degree of self-awareness, self-differentiation, and clarity." The latter addresses "hidden meanings of behavior patterns, and their unconscious interconnections." After focusing their difference, he points out that *clarification* sets the stage for later *interpretation,* that it serves as a precursor of *interpretation* proper.

In all dynamic, uncovering therapies the concern remains the same: "who we are and why." Though there is overlap, *confrontation* addresses itself to the "who we are," and interpretation to the "why."

In the interests of the former, images, which register in the therapist's creative regions, i.e. his particular conception and experiencing of the patient, are especially effective. Images steer inward and strike, as they do in poetry and the other arts, at one's chest, or insides, or groin, or at some pocket in one's preconscious. And with few patients, as with those of character disorder structure, do confrontations have to be as vivid and effectively honed in order to connect with their more removed affective regions.

In treating them we may borrow tools from the most effective communicators we have among us. The poet, the novelist and the playwright teach us the power of imagery and of expressing the observable truth in this manner so that it brings communication into the gut, so it has teeth, effect, becomes a reality that has to be reacted to, dealt with.

Whether an interpretive lead comes alive for the patient depends on its content, and on its timing—that we well know. But, in truth, and this no one says much about, it also depends on the *way* it's put, on its style. The more usable interpretation has its own matter and its own manner, one which holds the patient both for what it says and for the way it says it. Being better attended to for the manner, it enables a fuller hearing of the matter.

To illustrate, I will borrow a few examples first from what I have elsewhere[7] presented on the use of images as a style of technique.

To quicken the process of assisting a patient to sense himself at and beneath his defenses, within his own skin, communication to the patient in the form of images offers the advantages of (1) economy of words, (2) directness of meaning, (3) basic pictorial expression, and (4) density of affect—the latter perhaps the most important of the four. To a masochist I once observed, "How nice to get a wound you can lick." "Wham! That connected," he said. I was struck with the degree to which this communication reached the patient as other more conventional interpretive explanations had not. Another patient, an intellectualized, obsessive-compulsive character disorder, "always," in his words, "told the 'truth' to everyone, no matter what!" I had earlier expressed to him the understanding that under the guise of truth he was often releasing hostility. He agreed from the top of his head only. One day when he was telling me a story of how he had just rather aggressively "told the truth" to a colleague about the other's faults, I commented, "with that one you hit him right on the jaw." At another time when he used the "truth" as a weapon, this time against his father, I commented, "That must have landed squarely *between his eyes*," suggesting the David and Goliath image in addition to the aggressive one. Images, we learn from the poet, have as their objective the production of an effect through *multi-layered communication.* These images, in two consecutive sessions, succeeded, where more conventionally expressed interpretation had not, in transposing the discussion of his underlying anger to the interior plane on which it raged. For the patient, the insight was then not in the nature of something *inferred* but something *experienced;* not merely cognitive, but affective. For the first time the patient could feel the anger, which had been deflected into his intellect, closer to home; as he reported, in his "muscles."

A colleague (my wife Lila) supplies another example of communication on multi-layered levels which images allow. She communicated to a female patient of the hysteric character disorder type, "You seem to comfort yourself by hugging your misery like a teddy bear " Images may do service, as the above one did, in referring in concentrated fashion to *both* the childishness and the woe of the patient as they were exploited for secondary gains. Such interpretations may be used also when the therapist wishes a comment to be either sobering or to possess some element of surprise, or both. It can be compelling, as can few other styles when a therapist feels a need for a mode of expression, to cut through the thicker defenses of a character disorder to connect with the emotional underside.

When the interpretive communication is shaped into a pictorial expression, an otherwise abstract or intellectual idea is given flesh by the concrete example. The image employed is not only a symbol, it is a more active participant than is regular verbalization in bringing the patient's affect to *felt* awareness.

The more defended character disorder patients can best be reached by an emotional encounter or, on an interpretive level, by a vivid, emotion-tinged image. Images are more *experienceable* than are other forms of communication. When the analyst can locate and employ an image umbilical to the patient's affect, then he moves the patient closer to his feelings. In images, thought and affect merge instead of staying separate. They help the patient to *think-feel* the interpretation.

Communication through the senses is via a more basic, elemental route than is communication through mere thought. The tactile may be called upon to join the visual as the sense addressed.

For example, a woman, twenty-eight years of age, was describing a situation I received and understood as wallowing in self-consoling gloom. She had told herself her boyfriend had forgotten her birthday, and she settled down for an evening of embracing her mood to her chest. Suddenly the doorbell rang and there was her boyfriend with flowers and a present under his arm. Instead of a sense of fulfillment, she experienced, "strangely," she said, "a feeling of deprivation."

"Why?" she turned to me, feeling at a loss. There seemed two directions in which to explore; one, the losing of her feeling of current *justification* for anger and, two, the disruption of her self-pampering masochistic feeling.

The second seemed closer to awareness, and I chose to address that aspect. But how could I most usably express my understanding of her reaction? "Could it be," I inquired, "that you had prepared a warm bath of unhappiness to soak in for the evening? . . . and Bill interrupted before you could get fully into the tub?" That worked. It served to draw out, and connect her with the subjective undercurrent of her experience. Then she knew, and felt, its emotional texture.

At the same time it served another goal. Patients early in the treatment enterprise need a response from the therapist to their unvoiced question: "Do you really know how I feel?" A patient worries himself with doubts over whether he will ever be able to convey to the therapist "This is how I felt," or to find out, "Do you hear my heartbeat, or silent laughter; can you sense my fear, or the tears behind my eyes?" An empathic image, formed within the therapist and shared with the patient, serves as one form of demonstration in response to the patient's needs. It facilitates the treatment moving toward that empathically necessary uniqueness each therapeutic encounter must become, if it is to be anything at all.

An affectively textured, discrete image of the patient's inner reality actually initiates a two-way movement: it helps the patient connect with the therapist as he extends a vivid communication; and it helps the patient connect with himself within. Thus, in furthering the patient's connections in two directions, interpersonally to the therapist reaching out to him and intrapsychically deepening down into his own feelings, the effect is to enable him to emerge from constriction—to stretch himself, to experience himself simultaneously more outwardly and more inwardly, in essence, *to expand.*

Of the advantages offered by an imaginal approach, one is central. An awareness must be actually felt, emotionally savored as it were, before it can be really used in therapy and mastered under the control of the ego. An image which reflects the patient's inner self provides much more of an affective experiencing of it than does the interpretation in just words.

Angyal[1], in his work which Abraham Maslow has referred to as "that jewel of a book," makes the point: "Whatever else the therapist does, he must see to it that the sessions do not drag and become humdrum; there is nothing worse than a sleepy therapist listening to a sleepy patient. A sense of vitality should pervade the therapeutic hour . . . and it is up to the therapist not to let the patient remain neutral."

"The langauge one uses is an important factor," he continues, "it should be pictorial, the more concrete the better. One must give pictures, because the unconscious speaks in pictures and will most readily respond to its own idiom. Discussions conducted in generalized, abstract terms are more apt to kill feelings than to evoke them. (The therapist must) help the patient recapture the sense of the true drama of being alive, of which his neurosis has robbed him."

An image whose affect is alive charges an interpretation with significance; is less apt to fall flat as an intervention. Images contribute leverage to the patient's reaching after the feelings inside, and depend for their evocative power on truth, but backing truth up, on their form.

After examining material ranging from that of the philosophers through that from psychological laboratory experiments, work on the perception of children, and the coming about of scientific contributions in physics and in astronomy, Arnheim in his monumental *Visual Thinking*[2] draws the conclusion that *all* thinking is basically visual-perceptual in nature. This is true from the usual garden-variety thinking of everyday life to problem-solving in the arts and imagery in the thought-models of science. Building from this, Professor Arnheim asserts the advantage of visual training for all fields of learning and, we might add, for communicating. The significance of images in thought and perception is not relegated, by Arnheim, to childhood but is seen as an equally basic component of adult logical and creative activity.

One point of clarification: a patient should, of course, not be inundated with images. This type of interpretive style should be used judiciously. Generally, the proper quality of the analysts' responses are *simple,* and I would join with Menninger[10] that of "quiet observers, listeners, and occasionally commentators." Against this backdrop, however, the occasional image which might occur to the analyst in reference to any single patient remains infrequent, and as such has the additional advantages of (1) a change of pace and (2) an enlivening quality.

To come back now to the patient of character disorder integration, in contrast to an essentially neurotic state, within the former condition the real person is more deeply buried beneath thicker layers of defense. The task in therapy is to exhume him, to connect with his authenticity, so that he can experience, under his sham, the reality of himself.

A patient recently described the beginning arrival of this end result. "Sometimes I jump now; if I'm in a restaurant, or on a walk, or something, as my head is becoming free for old things to slide forward. I come across something in my mind that startles . . . or hurts. But my life is returning to me."

Once confrontations, imaginal and other, effectively have clarified the characterological problem for the patient, and have elicited motivation to change, the next steps are as follows:

1. To indicate as frequently as necessary each instance of acting out which appears, bringing it always to the patient's attention.

2. Move to locate and bring up front the fantasies lying behind the acting out. (Elaboration of this must be reserved for a subsequent paper.)

DISCUSSION

Laing, of *The Divided Self* fame, in his work *The Politics of the Family*[9] continues to display his skill for deftly penetrating problems: "A simple way to get someone to do what you want, is to give an order. To get someone to be what one wants him to be . . . the best way is . . . not to tell him what to be, but to tell him what he is." Confrontation, essentially, is just this technique.

In another recent, equally attention-deserving work, *Beyond Counselling and Therapy*,[4] there is frequent reference to the therapist as a "whole person," meaning that he is expressively himself, engaging in an encounter with the client as another person. Aside from empathy, genuineness, and concreteness, the dominant technique utilized is confrontation. "The therapist is the enemy of the client's self-destructive tendencies," and he persists in attacking defenses which interfere with the client's full and direct contact with himself as an experiencing and behaving individual.

This emphasis is consistent with the contemporary trend in therapy toward directness, activity, and therapist involvement, emphasized also by Perls, Pollens and Robertiello, Ellis, Greenwald, Holt, Laing, and others. Gertrude Blanck[3] also speaks of the therapist constituting himself a real object who offers understanding, advice, hopefully wisdom, and indispensably objectivity. This is in the interest of enabling the patient to recognize the price he inevitably pays for his behavior pattern and attitudes. This element of technique is again "confrontation": "Analytically, confrontation has a . . . technical intent—to help the observing part of the ego 'look at' the experiencing part and (in this) confront itself intrasystemically. . . . The most valuable aspect of confrontation . . . is that it is in and of itself therapeutic because it promotes the ego's capacity *via exercise of function*. . . . Structural change comes about because the ego comes to occupy a stronger position in relation to id and superego; energy is freed from deployment, resulting in more conflict-free adaptation."

The therapeutic stance, with patients of character disorder problems, is first confrontative and the therapist proving himself someone for the patient to learn from. His stance can next become more traditional and the patient then be treated by interpretation.

Only in this latter phase of the treatment, when impeded development has been designated and confronted, is the patient motivated to change, to attain object relations and to make identification with the therapist. At such point, there is a willingness on the patient's part, it should be said frankly, to please the therapist; and real object relations may begin to become meaningful. Following this, the capacity to identify with others, in addition to with the therapist, grows feasible.

In structural terms, therapy moves to produce a favorable change in the imbalance of the patient's wish-defense system with which he comes to treatment, a change allowing not only better balance and control, but as previously stated, a less costly outcome. In addressing this wish-defense system in treatment, since we cannot much influence the biologically rooted wishes-impulses we therefore seek to effect the desired change in the defense, i.e. the ego side. This helps in terms of (1) what ego psychology designates as *binding*, and (2) the discharge mechanisms, notably capacity for sublimations.

This latter is particularly important. As drives are analyzed, their intensity and insatiability are a *bit* reduced. What remains is more capable of redirection into channels of sublimation. I think of an adolescent patient who was arrested and placed on probation for mugging. He was referred for treatment and I found him to be a passive-aggressive, aggressive type character disorder with many antisocial activities as part of his pattern of behavior. Toward the end of his treatment, as the frequency of his engaging in delinquent activities was dwindling, he found himself a part-time job after school. It was one of special relevance to his psychic economy—a job in a poultry market as a chicken killer. He enjoyed the work, perhaps because his "heart was in it," did it well and earned recognition, status and raises there. His aggressive, delinquent actions dropped out of his behavior; and in the years since then these symptoms have not reappeared.

Whitman[12] discusses a similar case in which treatment was successful with a narcissistic, exhibitionistic individual who was referred for therapy after being picked up by the police for exposing his penis in the subway. During the course of his therapy he decided to convert his amateur golf status to a professional one and he went on the circuit. He expressed the sublimation effect in his observation to the therapist: "When I was on the putting green holding my putter tightly with the huge gallery watching every move I made with it, I felt I wouldn't get into trouble anymore."

Another striking example is the patient who came into treatment with me because of his concern about his fire-setting proclivities. Sublimation and reaction-formation blended in his later becoming a fireman.

SUMMARY

These are the approaches—the use of images, "topping" the patient, clarification and confrontation, as well as the resource of group therapy—I have found helpful in converting a character disorder into more simply a straightforward neurotic condition. The resistances of character disorders are quite stubborn, and repeated clarification and confrontation are necessary before the therapeutic work can get under way. Once that is accomplished, the more conventional procedures of treating individuals suffering neurotic problems can then be more advantageously utilized.

REFERENCES

1. Angyal, A.: *Neurosis and Treatment: A Holistic Theory.* New York, John Wiley & Sons, 1965.
2. Arnheim, R.: *Visual Thinking.* Berkeley, University of California, 1969.
3. Blanck, G.: Crossroads in the technique of psychotherapy. *Psychoanal. Rev., 56*:498-510, 1969-1970.
4. Carkhuff, R. R., and Berenson, B. G.: *Beyond Counseling and Therapy.* New York, Holt, Rinehart & Winston, 1967.
5. Ekstein, R.: Thoughts concerning the nature of the interpretive process. In M. Levitt (Ed.): *Readings in Psychoanalytic Psychology.* New York, Appleton-Century-Crofts, 1959.
6. Hammer, E. F.: Symptoms of sexual deviation: dynamics and etiology. *Psychoanal. Rev., 55*:5-27, 1968.
7. Hammer, E. F.: *Use of Interpretation in Treatment.* New York, Grune & Stratton, 1968.
8. Kubie, L.: The concept of normality and neurosis. In M. Heimer (Ed.): *Psychoanalysis and Social Work.* New York, International Universities Press, 1953.
9. Laing, R. D.: *The Politics of the Family.* Toronto, CBC Publ., 1969.
10. Menninger, K.: *Theory of Psychoanalytic Technique.* New York, Basic Books, 1958, p. 129.
11. Wexler, F.: The antiachiever. *Psychoanal. Rev., 56*:461-467, 1969.
12. Whitman, R. M.: Psychoanalytic speculations about play: tennis—the duel. *Psychoanal. Rev., 56*:197-214, 1969.

D̲ʀ. Mɪʟᴛᴏɴ S. Gᴜʀᴠɪᴛᴢ, a practicing psychoanalyst and member of the Adelphi University Postdoctoral Program faculty, has long been interested in psychopathology as it is manifested within the framework of society.

Dr. Gurvitz begins his paper by exploring his theory that a great deal of psychopathy is rewarded and encouraged by society and that these rewards are largely anti-therapeutic and harmful in nature. He supports this with a presentation of several brief cases from his own practice which provide strong evidence for his premise. A more involved case history of one of his patients whose obsessive interest in sexual fantasizing was financially rewarded by society via dealing in pornographic literature follows. The study of this patient is particularly relevant, as the insights into this man's personality disorder are valid for our permissive society in general. The chapter concludes on an extremely provocative note: our society with its emphasis on freedom and permissiveness, particularly in regard to sex, may offer many opportunities for creativity; however, it also provides many channels for regressive and destructive forces.

In this substantive chapter, Dr. Gurvitz does not only expand our knowledge of acting out, but he gives us some provocative thoughts on the role of society in reinforcing psychopathy.

D.S.M.
G.D.G.

Chapter 8

Socially Rewarded Pathology

MILTON S. GURVITZ

C LINICIANS AND PSYCHOTHERAPISTS are accustomed to meeting in their practice individuals whose neurotic or schizophrenic symptoms are sufficiently uncomfortable to themselves to drive them into therapy. Others demonstrate behavior which is so disturbing to their families and friends that they are persuaded into therapy. And there are still others who come in conflict with society and are forced by legal pressures into at least verbally accepting the concept that they need help.

In working with children, I became quickly aware that there was a causal relationship between the child's behavior and the home and family in which he lived. Indeed I soon realized that in many instances the bringing of the child into therapy was a thin excuse for the parent (usually the mother) seeking help. While these are not particularly new ideas, the full realization of their implications often escaped me until I began to conceptualize the idea and to consider the possibilities in every case.

Partly as the result of rethinking some of my adult cases and because of extensive consultation experience, and increasing interest in psychohistory and ego psychology, I am becoming increasingly persuaded of the following:

1. That it is not the most neurotic person in the family or group situation that is driven into therapy.

2. That power is very often the independent variable which determines who goes into therapy and/or who suffers more.

3. That society, or more specifically our society, rewards certain types of pathology and punishes others.

A few brief cases may serve to illustrate these points. Attempted suicide is a way of expressing a person's feeling of

125

weakness, inability to be angry at the real person who is oppressing them and at the same time revenge on those who are close and yet are felt to be hurtful, all by turning the anger against oneself. It is also, in my experience, a call for justice, especially when this occurs during therapy. This is not to say that it is a neurotic call for justice and that there might be better ways, but we have to accept the fact that for this person at this time it is the only possible way. I use suicide as my first example because it is the one symptom which quite understandably panics most therapists and alienates them from the patient.

This situation was brought home forcibly to me some years ago by a patient who realized she needed psychotherapy but was too afraid of her husband to tell him because he considered neurosis weakness and psychotherapy beneath contempt. She tried psychotherapy for some months and paid for it out of her household money. Despite some improvement she still could not find the strength to tell her husband and suddenly one night, without any prior warning, she took enough sleeping pills to send her to the hospital. Obviously the situation was now out into the open and the husband accepted with good grace his wife's need for psychotherapy. Once he did so, however, he was confronted by two different recommendations. I felt that there was no further danger of suicide and that outpatient therapy could be resumed on a more intensive basis. Psychiatric consultation advised a period of hospitalization and possibly shock therapy because the woman did not admit that she was wrong and did not regret her act. It is indeed interesting that the husband understood his role and opted for continuation of outpatient therapy. Had this woman been hospitalized and perhaps given ECT she would have been punished for her act of courage and I think created a situation where further suicidal measures would have been considered. I might mention in passing that her therapy was quite successful and that she has since gone on to do graduate work and to become a member of an allied profession.

In another more recent case, a mother found herself caught between a seductive, inadequate husband and an acting-out sexually provocative daughter. Both, and especially the husband, made extreme demands on her. The husband demanded that this high school senior not only be thrown out of the house, but that in addition she could not stay with a relative since that would be rewarding and not punishing her. Therefore, the mother should find some place for the daughter to stay which should on the one hand be unpleasant and on the other hand controlling. After threatening suicide to the husband and being ignored, as she had been in the past, the mother took enough tranquilizers to constitute a serious suicidal threat which led this time to public knowledge. Similarly she was not repentant and indicated that unless things changed she would do it again. Her therapist was alarmed and wished to hospitalize her. I spoke to the husband and wife in consultation and found that they had not really talked alone and that the husband, for the first time had not only changed his views but also his emotional tone. He said, "Now that I know she is really serious, I have to go along with her, I *have* to change." They were then able to have a long and emotional existential encounter which has apparently changed the balance, at least for the present. The therapist was persuaded, with great reluctance, not to insist on hospitalization. Again, if hospitalization had occurred, the husband, who is the most neurotic of the trio in my opinion, would have come out on top and it would have been the wife who was the sick one. It was essential to her new-found integrity that she not deny the reality and justice of her act.

What is this woman's reality? How neurotic was her way out? Does it lead to an examination of the thesis that society rewards some pathology and punishes others? What were this woman's alternatives?

She is an attractive woman in her early forties, but her attractiveness is marred by severe strabismus in her left eye. She has three children and she is a trained decorator with a part-time clientele. She is also very much in love with her husband who is physically a handsome man and a generally attractive person outside of his neurotic involvements with his daughter. If she had taken the alternative of standing up to her husband and if her husband had left her, society offers her the additional punishments of (1) making do on much less money, (2) complete responsibility for the children, and (3) loneliness and isolation certainly in the initial stages and a highly competitive situation in finding other suitable male relationships. The husband, on the other hand, finds himself freed of the direct obligation for the household and children. While he suffers from financial restrictions, in general he operates in a wide open social field and a buyers market when it comes to feminine companionship and relationships.

I would agree that the basis of this woman's relationship with her husband is neurotic and there were other less neurotic solutions. But I do submit that faced with this kind of reality the choosing of less neurotic solutions becomes infinitely more difficult.

At this point I would like to advance the working hypothesis that socially rewarded pathology means that society tolerates and encourages the persistence of immature and infantile behavior in some situations and punishes analogous behavior in other situations. As we can see in the previous case the husband's threat to pick up his marbles and leave if he doesn't get his way is socially rewarded. It takes a great deal more ego strength for a woman to stand up to a man in this kind of marital situation than it does for a man to do so.

For contrast let's look at a completely different kind of situation. What comes to mind are two patients who both attempted to capitalize on their immature dependence on their skill at games as a way of making a living. Both are equally skilled and equally accomplished. The professional golfer commands high prestige and makes an excellent living at both playing and teaching. The professional chess player commands very low prestige and makes only a very marginal livelihood. Indeed, he is often driven to other sources of making a living with attendant frustration, hostility, and resentment. Both have strikingly similar problems in that they suffer from sexual inadequacy and intense anxiety and both have a child who is strongly in need of psychological therapy. On the one hand it demonstrates the power of personal psychodynamics to transcend reality considerations since the socially successful patient suffers anxiety as severely as the socially unsuccessful patient. On the other hand the professional golfer has adequate means to procure analysis and therapy for himself and his son while the chess player can barely scrape together a living; the golfer has to deal primarily with his psychological problems while the chess player has to not only deal with his impotency and anxiety but also with establishing a new vocational adjustment, plus his wife's continual crying "if only you hadn't decided to become a chess bum."

Inferentially one would expect that the golfer would deal more successfully with his problems. Actually, the reverse was true. The chess player under the most adverse circumstances has struggled successfully to deal with both his vocational and his sexual problems and the strengthened home has helped the child to deal with his deep pathology. The golfer, despite intensive analysis, did not do well, broke his therapy to favor his golf and solved his sexual problem by divorcing his wife and marrying a more complacent and passive woman who is content with fellatio and sixty-nine and prefers the social whirl to having children. At present he disdains personal therapy, refuses to contribute to his son's therapy, but gives promise of having a severe problem over alcohol in the coming future.

Another point to be made, then, is that while society rewards some pathology, the rewards are measured by money and power and social success and these are often anti-therapeutic and destructive to the family and close associates of the seemingly favored but deeply flawed "success." One is reminded of Oscar Wilde's quip, "Nothing fails like success."

Society like fortune is often fickle, and its varying fortunes have often unexpected effects upon the individual and our psychotherapeutic efforts. A long-term patient of mine came to me originally because he had been involved with the authorities as a dealer in pornography. Actually, the legal charge was mail fraud since he promised more than he could deliver. Mr. L. had supported his family in a very modest way from the proceeds of his mail order firm which specialized in pornographic books, magazines and films. He was constantly skirting the edge of prosecution and was continually involved with making his products sound attractive to his customers and yet stay within the law. He had been attracted to this business because of his lifelong preoccupation with sexual fantasies going back as far as he could remember. At first he used these fantasies as ruminations from which he would select the most appropriate and stimulating to use for masturbation. He would spend endless hours in daydreaming to construct these fantasies involving, even as a child, sadomasochistic and perverse themes. In early adolescence he discovered the world of written pornography and began to expand and write down his fantasies for his personal pleasure. After dropping out of college because his sexual ruminations interfered with his studies, he drifted into the pornography business. At about the same time, he married the first girl he went out with seriously and found that his sexual ruminations decreased markedly since he was able to establish regular sex with his wife. Mr. L. was able to separate his sexual life from his fantasy life, and this in a sense had to be so because while his wife was an interested and active sexual partner, after some initial experimentation she rejected oral and anal sex and he was never bold enough to suggest sadomasochistic sexual behavior. He thus carried on a dual sex life functioning normally and quite actively with his wife but at times drifting off into masturbation with his sexual fantasies, especially when there was some interruption in natural sex, such as during his wife's menstrual period, pregnancy, etc. At times when a new and interesting theme would seize upon him he would have masturbation continuously, but apparently he was able to keep them in quite logic tight compartments and he reports quite convincingly that during intercourse with his wife he did not have his sexual fantasies. Most of his masturbation after he was married was confined to his place of business.

A crisis came when he was apprehended and given a suspended sentence on condition that he continue the therapy that he began when he was arrested. He took another job in the publishing field and began to work hard at his therapy. His wife accepted his explanation that his involvement with pornography was simply a business arrangement. As he was otherwise a good husband and excellent father to his three children the family continued unbroken. In analysis we began to trace out the dynamics of his fantasies and his involvement in pornography.

These formulations were especially interesting to me because they appear to be valid not only for Mr. L. but also, as he so gleefully often pointed out, seemed valid for pornography in general, and the public's great interest in this kind of material while at the same time having the conscious need to repress and deny it. This man's fantasies were projections into adulthood of his infantile view of sex. They were infantile because:

1. There was a complete preoccupation with sex as the only activity in life and never getting tired or bored.

2. Sexual satisfaction was on a polymorphous-perverse level.

3. Despite great sexual activity no one ever got pregnant without taking precautions unless in some special way this was part of the sexual fantasy.

4. Figures in the sexual fantasies were always instantly aroused and always ready for sex.

5. Sex was without guilt and always accompanied by orgasm.

6. There was usually a strong, omnipotent figure who somehow dominated and controlled the situation.

Further he recognized that he had to constantly invent newer more ingenious or outrageous forms of sexual fantasies to stimulate his interest and that his interest in pornographic books, pictures and movies was an attempt by him to force the world to share his fantasies and either to accept them or to punish him. Actually he realized that his constant flirting with the law was a direct expression of this last idea.

Mr. L's therapy coincided with the beginning of the current legalization of what had once been pornography. Previously his business had consisted primarily of books and pictures which were attractively titled or sexually famous but actually quite tame and innocuous in order to keep within the law. When his term of probation was over he decided to go back to the business now that it was legal.

At this point his sexual fantasies had greatly diminished and he felt that he had learned so much from his therapy that he could now handle it as a business and not as a sexual preoccupation. As far as his wife, who was quite a simple person, was concerned, he was simply going back into the publishing business.

Mr. L. and his new firms were an instant success. His own dynamics and fantasies and his psychological knowledge appear to give him a very sensitive gauge as to what the public wanted and would accept. He was also clever enough in view of his previous difficulties and his wife's wariness to keep in the background and to use other people to front for him. Money began to quickly roll in, and Mr. L. who had always made a marginal living found himself suddenly affluent. In addition he began to circulate in an entirely new social milieu. Previously he had always moved in rather straight-laced social circles generally selected by his wife. Now he began to move in a much wealthier, sophisticated group in which he felt comfortable but where his wife was no longer comfortable.

After several years Mr. and Mrs. L. requested an immediate consultation and presented their urgent problem. Almost as if it were a great revelation it had suddenly dawned on Mr. L. a few weeks before that some of the things that he had been fantasying and dreaming about were not only possible but were actually being engaged in by people of outward respectability. He now began to make sexual demands on his wife which reflected his fantasies particularly on a sadomasochistic level but which were completely unacceptable to her. She had tried making some accommodations but the more she tried to go along with him, the greater his demands became. He also "discovered" that there was more than one attractive young lady who was willing to gratify his demands. Mr. L. gave his wife an ultimatum that either she would accede to his sexual demands or that she allow him to have an extramarital love life with no questions asked. Mr. L. did not modify his position and they were soon divorced. In the process he was completely alienated from his children.

About a year ago he came to see me again. His business was still successful but he had a new problem. At first he was delighted with his newfound sexual freedom. As he began to act out his fantasies he found his ability to enjoy sex decreasing more and more. Sadomasochistic acting out resulted only in greater boredom and less interest; and he became completely impotent. There was no satisfaction in any kind of sex or even in his previous masturbation fantasies. He approached his former wife for a reconciliation, but she was quite cold and rejecting. Deeply depressed, he could allay his anxiety only with alcohol and amphetamines. Since then he has decided to divorce himself from his various pornographic enterprises and is attempting to establish a completely different business and to painfully effect reconciliation with his family.

As long as Mr. L. felt that society would not accept his childhood fantasies he was able to make a reasonably successful adjustment with life. While he suffered privately and had a brush with the law he was able to function as a husband and father and for a while in other areas too. When society began to reward him for the very fantasies which he knew to be infantile and regressive, his superego could no longer maintain the conflict. While his infantile sexual fantasies were given free rein they fit in so poorly with reality that his sexual satisfactions actually diminished. His superego could not limit his behavior directly but enough guilt was engendered so that he became impotent and he could at best become an observer; a voyeur, which reduced him to the position of being again the child.

A free and more open society, while it offers more possibilities for creativity and genius, also gives freedom for destructive and regressive forces as well. Every period of freedom such as ours has always been accompanied by excesses which has led to a puritan reaction. It remains to be seen whether our society will be wiser and self-curing.

D<small>R</small>. H<small>AROLD</small> G<small>REENWALD</small>, a psychoanalyst who is an expert on feminine sexual behavior, has combined these two areas of expertise in this study of one form of sexual acting out—promiscuity.

In today's permissive society the definition of promiscuity is somewhat ambiguous. Citing from his experience with patients, Dr. Greenwald describes his major criteria for labelling behavior as such: the patient's self-image and the degree of compulsiveness exhibited by the woman in her sexual acting out. Emphasizing the importance of the therapist's realization and comprehension of his own attitudes and values, Dr. Greenwald turns to a discussion of treatment procedures. In examples taken from his practice, he indicates how treatment methods must vary according to the variety of promiscuity exhibited. Throughout, Dr. Greenwald stresses his belief that in order for treatment to be successful, reasons for the acting-out behavior must be discovered. The chapter concludes with a discussion of factors he has found to be causal.

In this very lucid and pragmatic paper, Dr. Greenwald gives us his formulations concerning sexual acting out and outlines treatment methods for effectively handling feminine sexual promiscuity.

D.S.M.
G.D.G.

Chapter 9

Definition and Treatment of Female Promiscuity

HAROLD GREENWALD

I WANT TO LOOK at a disorder which may, in fact, not be a disorder, and that is the whole problem of female promiscuity. However, in planning this paper, I realized that I had one serious problem. I could no longer really define promiscuity in today's world. When I started my practice, over twenty years ago, a young lady who had five or six affairs before marriage might consider herself promiscuous. Today, most of the young women I meet aged twenty-three or older, who had only five or six affairs, would consider themselves sexually deprived. So that it certainly becomes very difficult to pick a number and state that below this number one is just experimenting and that beyond this number one is promiscuous.

Last year I spoke to a woman who had had at least fifty affairs that she remembered. She said not one of them was casual and did not consider herself at all promiscuous because there was always a relationship. She was thirty-eight and had started having affairs at eighteen. In twenty years she had had 2.5 affairs per year, and with such a small annual yield, felt she could not possibly be considered promiscuous.

Now the question is often asked, "Isn't the promiscuous relationship one in which there is no "real" relationship?" This question is no longer in the realm of science but rather in the realm of morality. Then the problem becomes one of defining what is meant by a "real" relationship. How many months does one have to know somebody before it becomes a "real" relationship and one is permitted to go to bed with him? One patient became very indignant when members of her therapy group called her promiscuous because she had slept with seventy-five men the year before. Her answer was "I'm not at all promiscuous. I never go to bed with a man on the first date." Her definition of a "real" relationship was more than one date. When a "real" relationship is defined as one which sanctions an affair without marriage, a moral judgment is being made. After all, who is to say that a casual pleasurable relationship is worse (even if it is only once) than a long-standing dreary marriage in which the wife permits the husband to use her only to insure her economic security?

In addition to the individual's perception of promiscuity, there is also the societal one. Now when we say "society," we have to specify what country and what special reference group we are referring to. In a small Midwest town the definition of promiscuity might be quite different from that in New York. Even within the same city there would also be differences depending on the reference or subgroup.

In view of the difficulties in defining promiscuity, I have attempted to find other ways of looking at the problem and have come up with two provisional approaches.

The first is the question of self-image. When someone comes for therapy and says "My problem is that I am promiscuous," she is promiscuous. At least she has such an image of herself as a person. Such a girl would be different from someone else who might think "How lucky I am to be so popular. I have a lot of men who want me." She would not consider sleeping with many men a problem. Of course such girls do not come for therapy unless they happen to be psychologists or psychiatrists. Therefore my first criteria is the patient's self-image.

Second and closely related to the first is the compulsive nature of the promiscuity. By the way, I am discussing females not because of any invidious or uncomplimentary distinction between promiscuous males and promiscuous females; I just happen to find promiscuous females more interesting. An example of compulsive promiscuity would be if the girl feels she has no choice; when she finds herself in bed and involved sexually with men whom she believes she does not really want; when she cannot understand why this happens to her again and again and feels that she has no control over the situation. I think with such persons there is frequently a felt problem. What I am suggesting is that there has to be a problem that the patient feels, not one that the therapist alone is defining, before we can call it promiscuity and before it becomes treatable. As a matter of fact we might consider whether promiscuity is ever more than a moral problem. Perhaps all we are doing is making a judgment based on certain moral principles. There could be a society which would regard compulsive monogamy as reprehensible as a great many persons in our society regard compulsive promiscuity. I am reminded of the error a young Egyptian lady made in discussing the coming reform of the marriage laws of Egypt whereby polygamy would no longer be permitted. She asked a visiting American professor, "How do you get along with monotony?" She meant, of course, "monogamy." So the question remains, Is promiscuity a problem that requires treatment or is it just a moral question?

I think it requires treatment under the following conditions: when the behavior is painful to the person involved; when she feels worthless because of such behavior. The worthlessness may be the result of the patient's having incorporated the social disfavor of the group and she experiences pain because of such social pressure. A second condition for treatment is when it is very difficult for the person to have the kind of relationship she would find rewarding. I am not discussing what I or what Erich Fromm would find rewarding, but only what the particular person involved finds more rewarding. She might find that promiscuity makes this impossible.

I remember a patient who was twenty-nine years, eight months of age and she was concerned that she would be thirty soon and still unmarried. Now until this time she was not particularly concerned that she had slept with a great many men. She thought it was fun. I told her that if she wanted to get married, she had better stop sleeping with so many men. She did not listen to my advice, explaining that she thought this a good technique for interviewing prospective husbands. The method did not work so well even though it was an unstructured interview. When she did give up her promiscuity for a month or so, she got married. It was a poor marriage and she was better off before but that does not matter. Promiscuity does sometimes interfere with the possibility of establishing the type of relationship which a person finds more rewarding.

One of the unfortunate results of compulsive promiscuity for some persons is that it destroys the possibility of sexual pleasure. One of my patients was kind enough to label as Greenwald's Law a statement I had made to her that "Bad sex drives out good sex." By "bad sex" I mean compulsive sex which is not pleasurable. After my patient stopped being promiscuous for a short time she told me, "You know, a new man every night is always the same; the same man every night is always different." I don't know if she was trying to please me with a moralistic statement, but that was how she felt about it. This type of relationship and this kind of sex had been impossible for her as long as she was acting out by going to bed with every man who asked her.

Now that I have said something about the problem of defining promiscuity and what to look for, let me turn to the question of treatment. As in almost every other kind of therapy, the first and most important requirement to deal effectively with this problem is the attitudes and value system of the therapist. This does not mean that a therapist must have no values or that his attitudes have to be compatible with that of his patients. This is obviously impossible. But the therapist must be aware of his attitudes and, if necessary, be willing to make such awareness explicit in the therapeutic relationship. Recently when one of my patients complained how guilty and pained he feels when he thinks of being unfaithful to his wife, I told him I did not share his attitude but would try to help him nevertheless.

Another point in treatment, and this is closely related to the above, is to be as nonjudgmental as possible about the patient who may be acting in ways that are different from the therapist's and based on a different value system. It is important to recognize that many of us have very strict sexual standards for the *opposite* sex. Many men think that women should not be promiscuous; many women think that men should not be promiscuous. Therefore, if you are faced with a patient of the opposite sex who is acting promiscuously and you feel it is terrible, you still have to be able to separate the behavior from the person who may have this problem and recognize that she is still a worthwhile human being.

It is also important to recognize and understand generational differences. A friend of mine, a psychoanalyst, took her daughter who was hemorrhaging to a gynecologist. After the examination was over, the gynecologist came out to the mother and asked, "Is it possible that your daughter is pregnant?" My friend replied, "No, I don't think so. She hasn't been out on a date for months." The gynecologist said, "It looks to me like she might be having a miscarriage. Please ask her if she could be pregnant." The mother then went out and asked her daughter, "Have you had intercourse since your last period?" And the daughter answered, "Oh, yes." The mother continued, "But you haven't dated for months." The daughter explained, "That's the difference between our generations, Mother. You think you have to date to have intercourse."

In treatment it is also important to understand the different types of promiscuous women. Therapists should not label all persons who show similar behavior as being the same. They are not. For example, some girls whom I have met professionally have an uncomplicated and free sex life. They like pleasure! As one girl recently told me, "I like to fuck; that's all." So that sex to such persons may be uncomplicated and they just enjoy the experience. Their behavior is no problem to them. Such an attitude could be interpreted as pure pursuit of the pleasure principle much to the anguish of the puritanical attitude many therapists adopt for their patients. A great painter loves to show his paintings; a great poet often loves to read his poetry and some girls who have been told they are great in bed feel the same about demonstrating their virtuosity.

A beautiful Scandinavian friend of mine explained when we were discussing the whole question of sex, "You see when I was young I was very generous." For some attractive women sexual activity is a sign of generosity. Here are all these men who want them, would like the pleasure of their company, so why should they hold back. However, in discussing treatment we are dealing with persons for whom the behavior is more painful and compulsive.

In my experience as a therapist I have found that one of the reasons some people engage in promiscuous behavior is that they are afraid of serious involvement. It is much easier for them to be superficially involved with many persons than to be involved with one. An extreme example of such an attitude, and it does seem extreme to me, is the statement made by a few of my patients, explaining "You say 'goodnight' and then he says 'oh, come on, why don't you let me?' You don't want to get involved in a long conversation as to why you won't. So it's easier to go to bed with him." To these patients it seems less involving to go to bed and "get it over with" than to engage in a long conversation. There are people who are pathologically afraid of deep involvement and find it easier to go to bed right away.

There are others who have a tremendous need for physical contact. Some day I would like to revise the theory of psychosexual stages in order to emphasize the role of skin erotism, i.e. the need for physical contact. I think it would be possible to look at oral, anal and genital stages as specialized types of skin erotism. I think the need for physical contact even precedes the psychosexual stages. Many women are promiscuous because they have tremendous physical craving for contact either because very early they are deprived of such contact or, more often in my experience, it was suddenly withdrawn when they still needed it. They do not really want sex; they would prefer merely to be held closely but are willing to pay the price of intercourse to feed their contact hunger if necessary.

Another kind of woman who becomes promiscuous is one who is very lonely and believes she knows no other way of getting companionship. As one girl told me, "Before I started putting out I was unpopular. As soon as all the boys in the neighborhood found that I was ready to hop into bed with them, wow, did I become popular! My phone didn't stop ringing." Unfortunately all too often they find that these kinds of physical contacts do not help solve the loneliness problem for them.

With some women sex is used as a source of power. It used to be that men would boast about how many women they had. Now with greater equality and perhaps thanks to the works of women's liberation, women too want to show how many men they can get into bed. In the Adlerian sense you could call this "masculine protest." I think it may be simply a matter of demonstrating the power of great attractiveness. At another level, however, as shown in patients' dream material, there are women who cannot bear an erect penis and wish to destroy such erection. If they cannot get rid of it by a verbal attack, they get the men into bed. This is the fastest way of getting rid of the erect penis.

A more common type is the frigid promiscuous woman. It is sometimes very hard to determine which is the cause and which is the effect, because with some women having sex with a great many men makes them frigid. With others, being frigid and yet being very exciteable, they will search for man after man hoping that finally they will find the one with the magic penis with whom they will be able to achieve the much-desired orgasm. Achieving an orgasm is unlike achieving in other ways, for the more you look for it, the harder you search, the less possibility there is of attaining it. Frequently all they have to do is relax and enjoy it. However, these women cannot relax so they keep frantically searching for the right man. In this behavior, too, there may be a challenge, an unverbalized message, i.e. "You think you're the one that's going to be able to do it. I'll show you. It won't happen."

There is another kind of woman who still feels guilty about having sex but will not assume responsibility for her actions. I had such a patient who kept telling me the same story session after session: "I went out with this man and he asked me to come to this party and before I knew what was happening, I was in bed with him." She was frequently involved in situations with men where she described feeling "powerless." She would never take responsibility for her behavior.

Sometimes the problem of hostility to parental figures, whoever it was that said "thou shalt not" is involved in promiscuous behavior. So often when parents say "If you do this you will be a bad girl," they are in a sense showing their daughter the best way to punish them. Simultaneously they are often asking their daughters to act out their own sexual fantasies.

In treating those who are compulsively promiscuous out of rebellion to parental injunctions, I have often pointed out that while they thought they were being independent, what they were really doing all these years was acting out of defiance to mother. Therefore they were still really tied to mom. "If mother says 'A' and you do 'B' then you are really still following mother and she is just as much in charge as though you did everything she asked. In effect, you are doing everything she does *not* want you to do."

Once they see this point very clearly, then I sometimes reverse my statements, saying, "But actually you are only acting out your mother's wishes. She has known you for twenty years; for eighteen of these years you have always done exactly what she told you *not* to do. If she still is continuing in the same way, then this must be what she really wants you to do. Frequently patients become depressed after such an interpretation. However, I will advise them to go home and tell mother that they have really been very good girls doing just what mother wanted them to do. Often there is a real change in the behavior when patients recognize that they have really been blindly obeying a parent's unavowed wish.

The interpretation most frequently presented is that promiscuity is a defense against homosexuality. Many girls engage in a whole string of compulsively heterosexual acts when they begin to feel an unconscious attraction to some woman. I am not at all sure how often this is true, and I want to point out that in our field we frequently make this interpretation about promiscuity being an act of hostility or a defense against homosexuality not because it is necessarily correct, but because we are often offended by the promiscuous behavior. We then attempt to control the behavior with such an interpretation. Many psychoanalysts, because they are morally outraged, make such interpretations without the evidence. It is unfortunate because the evidence may be there, and if it is, this interpretation might be helpful. But to make such interpretation without information from the patient is again substituting moral judgment for understanding. Treatment, to be effective, has to be specific to the individual with whom we are dealing.

The next step is to help the patient distinguish between the social attitude about her sexual behavior and her own value system. It is more mature to operate according to one's own value system rather than to accept the one imposed by society. For example, I have known young girls who were involved in groups where promiscuity was the norm. They felt they had to go along with such behavior even if it was not what they wanted. Either way you have to make it clear that the patient has the right to choose what she would like to do. Frequently, the causes of promiscuity are complex. If, for example, patients report a tremendous feeling of worthlessness and inadequacy, you do not treat the promiscuity alone; that is the symptom. You have to then deal with the entire character of which promiscuity is one small part. Sometimes dealing with the symptom and showing the patient that she can handle the problem may make her feel less worthless. If this is one example of the many ways which cause the patient to consider herself worthless, then this will be the problem to which you will have to address yourself.

The simplest way I find in dealing with most behavioral difficulties is to first determine whether the patient wants to change. I try to show her that up to now she has been promiscuous because this has been her choice; this is what she wants. Once I can make it clear that this life style is the one she has chosen, I will then proceed and tell her, "Look, there are many benefits from this life. You go to good restaurants; you receive expensive presents; you meet interesting people. You do find it enjoyable in certain cases. Are you sure you want to give it up?" If the patient still insists that she wants to give it up, then I ask her to make the commitment to change.

But you cannot ask for such a decision without the preliminary steps of pointing out the payoff for the past behavior. Once the patient agrees that she wants to give it up, I will test her control by asking questions like "What's the hurry; why now?" or "You've tried to get me in bed for a long time; do you want to now?" If she has really made the decision, she will stick to it. If she weakens, then we have more work to do in arriving at a decision which she can keep.

A great deal of working through takes place when the patient makes a decision she cannot keep. Now when she acts out, it is with full awareness and it is much easier to understand the reasons for the acting out.

One last caution: though I have indicated many possible reasons for compulsive promiscuity, in this as in all behavior disorders, it is crucial to discover the reasons for the behavior in the individual patient rather than to take for granted a reason. Only then will the patient feel understood and ready to change.

D RS. RALPH GUNDLACH and Bernard Riess each possess a rare combination of talent in that they are well-trained, experienced psychoanalysts and good experimental psychologists. They have used these attributes to explore systematically and formally one form of sexual and social acting out, that of lesbianism.

Gundlach and Riess' extensive study of female homosexuals clearly demonstrates that the behavior of lesbians is unequivocally different from that of male homosexuals in terms of early socialization, family interrelationships and present love relationships. Their data were drawn from questionnaires and their own clinical studies and are presented in tabular form; additionally, two case studies are offered to enrich clinically their research-oriented presentation. This is followed by a summary of their findings.

In this well-documented research and clinical study, Drs. Gundlach and Riess present us with a great deal of interesting data on the etiology and experience of lesbianism. We are grateful for this stimulating and scholarly paper.

D.S.M.
G.D.G.

Chapter 10

The Range of Problems in the Treatment of Lesbians

RALPH H. GUNDLACH AND BERNARD F. RIESS

IN TODAY'S WORLD OF frustration, action, reaction and repression, the various aspects of the act, actor, action and acting assume more than ordinary importance. In the mental health professions, we find ourselves constantly involved in making both distinctions and judgments among the many parameters of the active verb and noun. We try to have patients "translate insight into action." This has a positive valence. However, we do not like unplanned and thoughtless action unless it is "spontaneous." In encounter groups we ask people to feel sensuous and sexual but not to act it, especially out or in.

It is therefore essential to define the most negatively perceived form of acting, namely out. We propose thereafter to ask whether *female* homosexuality is a form of acting out or in. In answering this query we deal with two issues: first, we will present data to show that female homosexuality is not a mirror image of the male; second, that it is not a unitary form of behavior descriptive of and having the same origin in all women who choose a like-sexed love partner; finally, we will point to the relevance of data from our own study for the treatment of some female homosexuals.

Information on female homosexuality is far less satisfactory than about men. West's 1968 book[19] is very general, although it has some material on women. Cory's book[2] on women homosexuals (1964), even though endorsed by Albert Ellis, is a male homosexual's description of the lesbian. Magee[14] (1966) is a short, good layman's account of the problem.

As for frequency of lesbianism as contrasted to male homophile behavior, most authorities claim it to be far less. Among subhuman primates no exclusive female-female patterns have been seen; no orgasm results from the infrequent behavior; and homosexual arousal is much less frequent than with males. In primitive peoples, Ford and Beach[4] report far fewer cases. Only among the Mohave Indians was such behavior openly sanctioned and its existence was documented in only twenty-seven of the seventy-six groups studied by the authors. Dr. Kenyon,[11] an English authority, believes, on the basis of "guess-timate" that lesbianism occurs "in the order of one to forty-five of adult women." Kinsey's figures[12] show 13 percent of his sample to have had some homosexual experience but his total study population was heavily loaded with unmarried females (58.2% of the total). Thus the literature on female homosexuality is not productive of answers to our initial questions.

We find that there are good and numerous illustrations of acting out by male homosexuals. For instance, the compulsive exposure of genitals, both actual and suggested by the tight clothing, the compulsive cruising for one-night stands, the public toilet quickies, the established patterning of the other participant as often, father or brother images.[1, 6, 10] In our study and in the case reports in the analytic literature, we find very few instances of any of these behavior patterns among lesbians. Even, as in the California study of female prisoners convicted of felonies[18] where 75 to 80 percent of the women engaged in homosexual activity, only 7 to 10 percent were lesbians outside of jail, and again, even here, the female pattern is different from the male.

In our study[6, 7] we have found that lesbianism is less dependent and less explicable on the basis of libidinal organization and gender establishment than on social factors, particularly male-dominated beliefs and male-organized expectations and attitudes. These social factors operate to define the adequate "characteristics" of women. One need only point to the emphasis in early life on the boy's becoming a "man," showing his aggressiveness of his penis. Only recently have women been deemed educable and they still live in the "Valley of the Dolls" as toys to be manipulated. Our scientific vocabulary speaks of penis-envy and refuses to recognize the clitoris. We have castrating women but no word for the defeminizing male—perhaps because all males look at women in this way.

A second kind of difference emerges from the studies of birth order in relationship to the homosexual pattern. Gundlach and Riess[6] found that, in small families, the lesbian was more frequently the first born whereas in large families—four or more sibs—more homosexual women came from the later offspring. This suggests a bivalent process. The girl, not having the social value of a male child, is a disappointment to parents and bears the burden of the double-bind, namely, act as if you were the boy we want and also be the girl you are. In large families, the end person, literally low on the totem pole, may be unattended to and neglected. Hence, to attract attention, she acts in a masculine way or, failing in that, relates only to her second-class companions, the girls.

The relevance of developmental stages must also be taken into account. Until about the age of nine to ten, the girl identifies and is identified by society with boy-like behavior and goals. Then comes menstruation: and parental expectations change to the goals of sexual submissiveness, marriage and children. The implicit choice becomes marriage or a job, a choice which reaches a crucial level at seventeen to twenty.

It appears then, that biology in itself[17] does little to determine what the pattern of sexual development will be, whether homosexual, heterosexual, monosexual, polygamous or monogamous, polyandrous or any other choice of love partner. These behaviors are resultants of multivariate factors, especially the teachings and the patterns of the institutions and folkways of the society. Sexual relationships are adult interpersonal relationships and are subject to the same developmental processes as any other relationship.

In the United States, the man-dominated society sets up patterns of behavior in the social and economic spheres which influence the whole structure of family life. Like other overdetermined functions, there may be some compensatory reactions. So we feel empathy for the "henpecked" husband as well as for the kitchen and child imprisoned woman.

In concluding this section, we make a final distinction between the satisfaction of the need to achieve orgasm (certainly more characteristic of male than of female homosexuals) and the need for affection, companionship, belongingness, bodily contact and long-continuing love relationships (more frequent in woman homosexuals than man). There has been so much recent research on orgasmic behavior that we can no longer subscribe unthinkingly to the alleged superiority of vaginal over clitoral orgasm or of the analog nature of the clitoris. The evidence reverses the older view; today we have data to show that all embryos are female for the first six weeks of life, that the penis is an overdeveloped clitoris, that women's passivity and satiability in sex is a function of attitude and societal expectation rather than a biological given.

It is a technological assumption that the penis and vagina exist for each other. In ethology, Lorenz and Tinbergen have shown that ducklings "naturally" will follow the experimenter rather than the mother of their species. So, the choice of a love-partner or love-"object" is determined by experience broadly defined and not by nature, drive or instinct.

What then is pathological about adult sexual interrelationships? What is acting out sexually? Certainly where guilt is attached to behavior, behavior enforced by societal demands, the result can be pathological. Where society demands that males prove their manliness by sexual exploits, the pressures may produce maladjustive behavior. Women in our world do not have to prove their femininity by sexual actions. They are, however, not so readily encouraged to be accomplishing individuals, nor accepted if they are as independent as their male counterparts. This builds up a sense of low self-esteem which may lead to pathologic acting out.

Now let us turn to some factual evidence regarding lesbians—acting out or not—which may be of use to psychotherapists. Our data include both questionnaire studies of a large sample of women and clinical cases of women who have both responded to this questionnaire and been in therapy with a colleague or ourselves.

We[6] obtained answers from 226 middle-class lesbians and from about the same number of middle-class non-lesbians, all from the United States and Canada to an elaborate questionnaire of 450 items.*

We have prepared a set of tables from which to project certain important generalizations which will constitute the ground-work for our approach to the problems of therapy with lesbians.

Table 10-I presents some items of general interest about our populations. Here the total set of respondents is divided into

TABLE 10-I

BACKGROUND INFORMATION ON COMPARISON (C) AND
HOMOSEXUAL (H) WOMEN WITH AND WITHOUT THERAPY
(In Percentages)

	N =	C no ther. (131)	C ther. (98)	H no ther. (136)	H ther. (90)
1. Age: 18-25		29	14	18	30
31-40		21	39	40	34
46-60		20	12	11	9
2. Were parents from USA? Yes, both.		65	58	74	74
3. How far did you go in school?					
a) HS graduate or less		20	21	41	26
b) 1-3 yrs. coll. or bus. sch.		31	27	24	30
c) 4 yrs. coll./some grad. sch.		44	39	30	24
d) professional degree		14	22	13	26
4. Age when received psychotherapy					
a) under 20			13		31
b) over 20 (some more than once)			94		74
5. Number of sessions: over 100			48		31
6. Was therapy successful?			44		20
Very unsuccessful.			3		20
7. Present living arrangement: (H: lesbian relationship; C: with spouse)		66	52	60	42
Live alone		11	22	24	28
8. Separated or divorced		11	17	21	20
9. Parents' religion?					
a) Catholic		4	9	19	13
b) Jewish		20	38	8	26
c) Protestant		52	42	57	50

* We are gratefully indebted to Daughters of Bilitis whose officials, especially Florence Conrad, sanctioned the research and aided in the formulation of the questions, assisted in the collection of the completed instruments by encouraging members and friends of D.O.B. to return questionnaires, and by taking responsibility (in the interest of preserving anonymity of respondents) of mailing the material to willing participants and being the intermediary in correspondence.

four categories: two groups of non-homosexuals ("comparisons"), those reporting no psychotherapy, and those with psychotherapy; two groups of homosexual women, those not having and those having had psychotherapy. We obtained as large a population of lesbians as possible within a given time and, as the incoming numbers began to decrease, started the collection of non-lesbians through the good offices of our friends and associates. The comparison group matched, approximately, the overall lesbian group with regard to age, education, residence (East, Midwest and West) and also to size of community of residence. We wanted some in each group to be in therapy and had assistance of therapists† who collected lesbians and non-lesbians from their private practice. They also filled out separate answer sheets regarding these patients, including materials on life histories and dynamics. Obviously, then, the proportion of respondents among H or C who had psychotherapy provides no basis for speculations as to the percentage in therapy in the United States at large.

Note that question 2 (Were your parents born in the U.S.A.?) reveals that about three-fourths of lesbians, whether having had therapy or not, had both parents born in the U.S.A., but fewer C and fewest C with therapy had both American-born parents. Speculations that may relate these facts to question 9, parents' religion, and to the location of the research team in New York City are intriguing, but lead to no clear-cut answers.

Questions 4, 5 and 6 deal with the therapeutic experience. Significantly more lesbians had therapy before they were twenty (some had therapy both before and after they were twenty). Fewer lesbians found the therapeutic experience satisfactory; more found it not very successful. From comments on the questionnaire returns, many lesbians felt that their therapist did *not* understand them or have sympathy with their problems, had a different objective in therapy than they had, and tried to push it upon them.

---

† We are very grateful to many colleagues for their assistance in getting respondents for us, especially, Fred Marcuse, Keith Sward, Robert Challman, Mary Jane Hungerford and fifteen staff members of the Postgraduate Center for Mental Health.

Question 7 (What is your present living arrangement?) was treated in a special way. We combined those cases living with a spouse and those living in a lesbian relationship. The difference, 66 percent for C and 60 percent for H not in therapy, is not significant. The answer "living alone" occurs in about 25 percent of three subgroups while in the C no-therapy group only 11 percent so answered.

Question 8 reveals that more lesbians were separated or divorced than non-lesbians; over 20 percent. Obviously more than 20 percent of the lesbians are or have been married.

The major issue at this point is the assumption that female homosexuality is, by definition, evidence of psychological or emotional disorder, a personality disorder, as listed by the American Psychiatric Association's Diagnostic and Statistical Manual. Among professionals, probably Evelyn Hooker[8] is best known as tentatively holding the opposite view, based upon her study of a group of male homosexuals who could not be distinguished on the basis of projective test results evaluated by top experts from a group of heterosexuals, nor were so-called pathological signs found in many of the protocols.

Table 10-II contains samples of items on which there were significant differences between those who did and those who did not have therapy—and where there were no significant differences between H and C in therapy, nor between H and C *not* in therapy. About half the items deal with respondent's relation to her mother, the others are about equally divided between respondent's relations with father, and relation between the parents.

All answers are consistent in that the "no therapy" group has better conditions for healthy growth, and the therapy group is generally in a less favorable situation since there tend to be worse relationships with and between parents, and between parents and child. Yet we know that half of the group with no therapy (we do not dare say "normal" group) is made up of lesbians. In the Bieber study[1] of male homosexuals and comparisons all in analysis, many of these same questions appear, with the H being worse off in contrast to the comparison group.

TABLE 10-II

ITEMS ON WHICH PRIMARY DIFFERENCE IS BETWEEN THOSE
HAVING THERAPY AND THOSE NOT, AND WHERE
HOMOSEXUAL (H) AND COMPARISON (C)
IN EACH GROUP ARE SIMILAR
(In Percentages)

	No Therapy H & C (267)	Therapy H & C (186)
1. How far did you go in school? Professional degree.	14	24*
2. There was love and affection between parents.	44	22**
3. Did one parent frequently humiliate or show:		
a) contempt for other? No	61	36**
b) each attacked other and was contemptuous	11	22**
4. Did one parent frequently try to undermine other? No	68	40**
5. Did either parent use you against the other? No	81	61**
6. Did mother have a least favored child? No	58	42**
7. a) Was mother dominating with you? No	56	37**
b) Yes	35	54**
8. Did your mother "baby" you? No	74	54**
9. Were you excessively dependent on mother? No	76	65**
10. a) Did mother understand and accept your feelings? Yes	30	11**
b) No	29	46**
11. Afraid of mother? No	68	53**
12. a) Attitude towards mother? Respect	54	27**
b) Hatred and contempt	9	17*
c) Fear	14	28**
d) Defiance	18	31**
e) Yearning for affection	19	39**
13. Was mother a good parent? Yes, better than average.	45	23**
14. Was mother a good wife?	43	31*
15. Anyone in family you didn't want to be like? Mother	28	47**
16. Did father understand and accept your feelings? Yes	30	13**
17. a) Were you afraid of him? Extremely	5	16**
b) More than most girls my age.	5	13*
18. How did he enforce discipline? He was fair.	38	14**
19. a) Was he a good husband? Yes, better than average.	41	28**
b) No	21	39**

---

* = Sig. c .05
** = Sig. c .01

But here, with the women, H equals C, whether we consider the therapy group or the non-therapy group.

Table 10-III presents a sample of those items in which the lesbians as a group differ from the non-lesbians and where there are no significant differences due to the presence or absence of therapy.

Because of the restrictions, one cannot use this table to get a total picture of H vs. C. However, it does appear that a larger proportion of the H group than C have mothers who tended to be younger and to be indifferent to this child. More of these H

TABLE 10-III

ITEMS IN WHICH PRIMARY DIFFERENCE IS BETWEEN HOMOSEXUAL
(H) AND COMPARISON (C) TOTALS, AND WHERE THERAPY
AND NO THERAPY TOTALS ARE SIMILAR
(In Percentages)

		H(262)	C(229)
1.	How far did you go in school? College and some grad. wk.	28	39**
2.	Father's education? Graduate work and Prof. degree.	9	21**
3.	a) Mother's age when you were born? Under 30	71	59**
	b) 30-39	22	35**
4.	a) Mother discouraged masculine attitudes in you.	30	19**
	b) Neither encouraged or discouraged.	50	69**
5.	How did mother usually punish? Withdraw privileges	37	24**
6.	Mother's attitude toward you? Indifference	21	9**
7.	Attitude toward Mother? Love	54	64*
8.	Was mother a good wife? No	21	32**
9.	Did father have a favorite child? I was an only child.	20	13*
10.	Who was father's favorite child? Younger sister.	8	3*
11.	Who was father's least favorite child? I was.	11	5*
12.	Father let it be known he preferred a son.	8	3*
13.	a) Played mostly with girls, childhood to menstru.	25	43**
	b) Played mostly with boys	31	9**
14.	a) Who were your real friends? Girls	58	76**
	b) Boys	15	7**
15.	Were you well known as a tomboy? Yes	55	14**
16.	Did you enjoy the reputation? Yes	50	25**
17.	Before menstruation, did you want very much to be a boy? Yes	48	16**
18.	a) Anyone you idolized and wanted to be like? Sister	5	17*
	b) Female teacher	35	16**
	c) Girlfriend	12	19*
19.	As a child, do you recall any sexual attraction to a woman? No, don't remember.	39	83**
20.	Female most attracted to:		
	a) mother, sister, cousin, aunt	15	2**
	b) teacher	26	4**
	c) classmate	29	9**
	d) other	18	5**

* = Sig. c .05
** = Sig. c .01

girls (significantly more being only children) felt their fathers preferred another sib and seemed indifferent to her. And, in the face of a situation that may have seemed cold and unresponsive, the impression is that the young girl felt isolated, tried to be assertive and a tomboy, engaged in athletics, played with boys, had few real friends, and more desired to be like some female teacher, perhaps a mother-substitute.

Table 10-IV collects some of the items in which there are differences both between H and C, and also between no-therapy and therapy, and where the direction of difference between H

TABLE 10-IV

ITEMS ON WHICH HOMOSEXUAL (H) DIFFERS FROM COMPARISON
(C) AND THERAPY FROM NON-THERAPY GROUPS
(In Percentages)

		C		H		Significance of Diffs.	
		No Ther.	*Ther.*	*No Ther.*	*Ther.*	*Cols.*	*Cols.*
		(131)	*(98)*	*(136)*	*(90)*	*1,2*	*1,3*
						vs	*vs*
		col. 1	*col. 2*	*col. 3*	*col. 4*	*3,4*	*2,4*
1.	Parents' religion? Jewish	20	**38	8	**26	**	**
2.	Did either parent undermine you with the other? No	82	*68	77	**59	**	**
3.	Parents' attitude toward you as a girl?						
	a) Both accepted me	89	**68	75	**50	**	**
	b) Other	2	* 9	8	*19	**	**
4.	Was mother sexually seductive? No	95	**81	84	76	**	**
	b) seductive but unaware	1	6	5	12	*	*
5.	Mother usually let me do what I wanted if reasonable.	75	**50	63	*48	**	*
6.	Response to mother's requests or pressures? Usually comply	51	39	42	**23	**	**
7.	How did mother usually punish? Withdrawal	13	**34	10	**21	**	**
8.	Did father have a favorite child? No	52	*37	33	27	*	**
9.	Did father have a least favored child? No	66	*51	57	*40	**	*
10.	Did father encourage feminine attitudes in you? Neither	53	46	66	53	*	*
11.	Father was warm, loving, affectionate.	56	**33	41	30	**	*
12.	Attitude toward father?						
	a) Respect	63	50	50	*32	**	**
	b) Love	78	**53	56	46	**	**
13.	Father a good parent? Yes, better than avg.	49	**22	35	**18	**	*
14.	Brother or sister seductive before first menstruation? No	78	66	65	56	*	**
15.	Recall attraction to male before menstruation? No	31	*15	54	42	**	**

* = .05 level of significance.
** = .01 level of significance.

and C is the same as between no-therapy and therapy. One sees a general progression from most favorable, C with no therapy, to least favorable, H with therapy with the exception of numbers 1, 7, 10 and 15. The two middle columns vary around a midpoint. It would seem that there is some equivalence between the comparisons-who-have-therapy and the lesbians-not-having therapy, in regard to these items.

Differences within the H group that are significant, or within the C group are marked within their column. The last two columns of the table show the significance level of the differences: column 5 between total H and C; and column 6 between no-therapy and therapy subgroups.

At least one major conclusion may be reached from these tables. No simple picture of the relationships between women in or not in therapy and homosexuality has emerged, or is likely to emerge. It also does not support the hypothesis that all lesbians are emotionally disturbed.

Because of the complexity of the relationships revealed by the straightforward tallies of questionnaire data, we used a new statistical approach to our data. In addition to filling out the questionnaire, about two hundred respondents had also answered a semantic-differential test in which the task was to characterize, by thirty-two pairs of adjectives attitudes toward four classes of persons: mother, father, woman and man. Obviously these evaluations were independent and unrelated in the testing to the process of filling out the questionnaire which had been done many months previously.

The strategy involved a two-stage computer operation; the first was to combine the answers to the four semantic differentials into "one test" for each respondent; then to compute a factor analysis of the interrelations of attitudes. A set of fourteen significant factors emerged. What those factors were is, at the moment, not our focus. The second step was to perform an operation in which the population could be grouped according to the similarities between them on the S-D test factors rather than on whether they were lesbians or non-lesbians.

In this way, using data independent of the questionnaire or any knowledge about these women other than their responses to the Semantic Differential form, there were generated six subgroups of women. One included about 25 percent of the entire population, four groups each included about 16 percent of the group, and the smallest group only 5 percent of the population. Each group is defined in terms of extreme scores on one or more of the fourteen factors, deviating in each factor from the answers of the rest of the population.

TABLE 10-V

ITEMS ILLUSTRATING SOME DIFFERENCES AMONG Q-GROUPS OF WOMEN
(In Percentages)

		Q-1 13 H / 37 C		Q-2 12 H / 22 C		Q-3 22 H / 10 C		Q-4 34 H / 1 C		Q-5 10 H / 24 C		Q-6 2 H / 8 C	
Number of factor loadings which express positive or negative attitudes toward:	**N =**	**+**	**−**	**+**	**−**	**+**	**−**	**+**	**−**	**+**	**−**	**+**	**−**
Mother		2	1									2	1
Father		3							3		1		
Woman		3							2				
Man		3	1		2		2		1		4		

Questionnaire Items:

Item	Answer	Q-1	Q-2	Q-3	Q-4	Q-5	Q-6
1. There was love and affection between parents	No	56	21	19	46	47	
	Yes	72	26	28	66	62	
2. Does one parent humiliate other?	Mother humiliates father	8	56	25	14	21	
3. With which parent did you side most frequently in childhood?	Mother humiliates father	20	15	59	32		
4. You felt closest to which parent?	Mother	14	41	19			
	Father	38	56	9	20	59	
	Neither	18	12	13	54	71	
5. Was mother domineering?	Father	68	44	44	60	62	
	No	76	26	56	43	15	
6. Mother usually let you do what you wanted		80		16	17	15	
7. Mother's attitude toward you in childhood?	Love	8	44	22	66	59	
	Satisfaction	72	21	38	34	53	
	Disapproval	72	18	63			
8. Your attitude toward mother?	Love	26	24	91	68		
9. Mother's attitude to self?	Acceptance	74	34	63	29		
10. Was father physically demonstrative?	No	28	26	13	46		
11. Was father domineering?	Yes		9	34	0		
12. Was he accepting and interested in your feelings?	No						41
13. Father let you do what you wanted							
14. Father: arbitrary/unfair disciplinarian							
15. Your attitude to father:	Love	68	68	28	71	68	
16. Father satisfied with self?	Accepting	16	15	47	17	12	
17. Whom did you *not* want to be like?	No	10	76	31	29	44	
	Mother	38	12		49	12	
18. Female H.S. teachers: Had *crush* on some		24	53	13	14	47	
19. Sex with penetration? AGES:	17-20	38	0		34		
	21-25	8					
	No Intercourse						

Note: Each item listed differs significantly from at least one other in that row.

This will be much more understandable if we turn to Table 10-V and see the meaning in specific terms.

The top legend in the table indicates the number of H and C present in each group. Note that about one-fourth of the Q-1 group are homosexual, that in groups Q-2, Q-3 and Q-5, the minority numbers 10-12 and the majority is 22 to 24. Only one group, Q-4, has a marked predominance of women of one sexual orientation. Thus, the way these women actually cluster into homogeneous groups as regards their expressed attitudes toward Mother, Father, Woman and Man is not primarily related to whether or not they are lesbians, nor further, is it related to whether or not they were ever in therapy. Actually, Q-5 had the fewest in psychotherapy (24%) while about 46 to 48% of those in Q-1, Q-2 and Q-4 were in therapy. The next entries state the number of factors which identify each group, with either positive or negative directions, as regards Mother, Father, Man and Woman.

Entries in the body of Table 10-V are made only in cases where the percentage differs significantly (.05 or better) from that of one or several other Q-groups. Thus, the blank spaces indicate a clutter of intermediate numbers.

Q-1, the first and largest group with 13 H and 37 C, is composed of women with positive feelings toward Mother, Father, Woman and Man. They are distinguished from the rest of the population on twelve of the fourteen factors, having "good" feelings toward parents and good family relations. When we look at sample questions in Table 10-V, the Q-1 group turns out to have the highest percentages with "good" and the lowest percentages with negative answers.

The group most similar to Q-1 is Q-4, made up almost exclusively of lesbians. These two groups include most of the women with positive attitudes to Mother, Father and Woman, and together they have as many or more H than C. As in Table 10-V, Q-1 and Q-4 groups are on the same end of the spectrum in sixteen of the nineteen items, and at opposite poles on only three (items 9, 19).

In sharpest contrast to the "good" conventional patterns expressed in common by Q-1 and Q-4, Q-2 and Q-3 have factorleadings all negative in tone. Q-2 with 35% H, is defined by two factors, both anti-mother. Q-3 with nearly 70% H by six factors, two anti-mother, two anti-father and two anti-man.

These two groups (Q-2 and Q-3) from data not presented here seem characterized by mismatched parents as expressed in conflicts showing little love and affection but rather contempt for the mate, undermining the other, regarding the other as inferior and using the child against the mate. As a consequence, few respondents have love for mother, and about a majority find neither mother nor father good as wife or as husband, and 77% would *not* like a marriage like their parents marriage.

The two groups differ in that more of Q-2 are Jewish (41% to 6%) and more of Q-3 are Protestant (32% to 66%). Q-2 women tend to side with father, Q-3 with mother. Q-2 find it easier with father around, and Q-3 find him fear-invoking, but they in turn, complain to him or are angry and rebellious.

It must be noted that the proportions of H and C in these two groups seem reversed: (Q-2 has 12H and 22C; Q-3 has 22H and 10C). Further there turn out to be a number of items in which the Comparisons of Q-2 are like the Homosexuals of Q-3, and the reverse!

The remaining group, Q-5 has this characterization. The fathers are generally seen as strong, active, powerful, dominant. and the mothers weak, powerless and unattractive. They may have projected the consequent animosity onto the image of women with negative scores on all four factors.

We present these statistical findings to undermine any simplistic notions that may pervade our field regarding the familial and social backgrounds of lesbians in our society, and to make clear that any single case presentation or even several cases could in no sense be any more definitive of "the" lesbian background than one case presentation could define the course of development in a heterosexual woman. In fact, for any lesbian's case history, one can find a heterosexual or an asexual woman's story which is confusingly similar. Often one could not tell that the person would move to homosexuality until she did, something which might not occur until the mid-twenties.

Our approach, obviously, does not consider homosexual

practice in females to be in itself a diagnosis: it is a description of the gender of the currently preferred partner and may or may not be symptomatic of something else.

Our data confirm the findings of Jenkin and Vroegh[9] that masculinity and femininity are not extremes on one dimension but are qualitatively different. We attribute this to the functionally important sexual factors such as musculature, child-bearing, and glandular-metabolic functioning, and to the culturally determined roles and life pattern available by society to its men and women.

The data presented here, and in Gundlach and Riess,[6] indicate that women's efforts to solve their role and identity problems certainly do not parallel or reciprocate those of males with their additional value on aggressiveness, competition, sexual prowess and hard-headed practicality as proof of manliness. The primary problems for women are their human worth and significant functioning and role in an industrial, male-dominated society, the expected meek acceptance of the superior status of boys and inferior status of girls, marriage as a career, or a combination of both with the appropriate accidents of the right man and circumstances. These problems are not so much the preoccupation and tasks of the years of infancy but of later times, with increasing maturity and awareness of the wider world. The playtime of childhood with the mixed message of equal to but different from boys, the tomboy, anti-sissy period, is abruptly terminated with the onset of menstruation. The alternatives, the real choices for life's role now confront them, and again come to a climax in the late teens. Women seem not so concerned with being female. They take that for granted, nor do many seek sexual potency which seems so much an aspect of penis-functioning. Their primary needs are more related to *not* being alone, the need for companionship, warmth, closeness, tenderness and love.

We start with a case that is not usually seen in private practice, nor is she a person who could fill out our questionnaire. In terms of stages of ego development, she centers around the impulsive and the defensive, exploitive stages (Loevinger[12]). She was induced to come to a day treatment center by her homosexual partner and participated in the program for some weeks. At first the two most frequent words Patty used were shit and fuck. She would bitterly-kiddingly make baudy invitations and references as a way of getting attention and of disrupting any meeting or encounter. Soon it became known that her apartment was a salon often to youngsters, homosexual or bisexual, perhaps sadomasochistic, perhaps without money or apartment and happy to use pot or sometimes other drugs. She was tough and ruled the girls by offering goodies and by thrashing or beating some who didn't conform to her code of loyalty. Some in disfavor will stay in their rooms or sneak out fearing Patty would catch them on the street and beat them up.

For the first nine years of her life, she was the sixth child. She had one sister, the oldest, the only child to sleep in a room of her own. Four brothers and she slept in the same room in two sets of double bunks where she and the next youngest brother shared a top bunk bed. Her mother didn't clean the house; the older sister seemed to do a little prostitution. Sex, drinking and fighting kept the family together. Patty claims she was unhappy with the dirty style of life. She did, of course, have considerable sex play with her bedmate brother and was often teased and scapegoated by the boys and parents. When she was around twelve her father woke her up one day by feeling her growing breasts and pubic hair. She ran to mother who passed it off as of no importance. After father's second approach she ran away, still not getting mother's support. Instead she was put in a state home for two years. On her return she soon ran away again, and was sent to another "home." She was furious with the accusations made against her, and especially mother's abandoning her and siding with the rest. It was some triumph that a medical examination at age seventeen proved that she could hardly be a prostitute since she was still a virgin. So she found a man to marry. The experience was, she said, that "he put his joint in and then took it out" and that was all. She had a child. This life was hardly satisfactory to her and soon she left him. He did come back again, introduced this "member" once again, and again she conceived. Patty fought her parents and everybody else till she fell ill of a collapsed lung. Her mother again double-crossed her, cajoled her into giving up her children, signing them away to her now married oldest brother living upstate. Now what Patty wants to do is to get her children back and bring them up in her lesbian household, having them to love and care for. She is sure she could work and support them, and they could grow up better with her than she did with her family.

It would seem she was heterosexual till she faced male failures and found males harsh, egocentric, unfeeling, never satisfying. So Patty turned to women with whom she could find warmth and sexuality. However, even here she was suspicious of betrayal as from her mother and she was driven to control her scene.

With adequate care and learning situations, Patty can grow out of this immature state. She is not fixed rigidly as a lesbian or as impulse-dominated, but is responding simply to what is gratifying in her chaotic underworld. In the wider sense her problems stem from insecurity, economic dependency and immaturity as a person. She now responds, impulsively acting out her feelings and trying to manage her social environment as far as she can.

Low self-esteem in many "youngsters-come-adults" seems based on incorporating mother's or father's repeated characterizations of them. Slogans or labels become imprinted onto the child's inner tape recorder. An underlying conflict develops between living up to these instructions or asserting oneself against them with attendant guilt. The echo of childhood terror of abandonment or threat of being "wiped out" for being "bad," e.g. wilful, disobedient, nuisance, or expressing criticism or anger at the present reverberates in them. We list three varieties of the many variations in adult reactions to this underlying theme. All involve a form of acting out.

Some may be looking for a father or mother to replace the bad or inadequate parent to make up for a feeling of having been disappointed and never allowed to establish autonomy. Some of these women may be impulsive reactors who select a partner regardless of "its" sex since other aspects of the relationship may be paramount, e.g. being "needed."

A second stage for people with low self-esteem may be heterosexual orientation, but the negative self-image is so projected in social relations that they attract only unsatisfactory or inadequate men. They may then give up and retreat to mutual consolation with another woman in a clinging relationship. However, as their self-esteem and courage mount, they emit new social signals about themselves and their relatability and are quickly responded to by more compatible types, both males and females.

A more complicated acting-out program is revealed by women who have suffered a sequence of frantic, often disastrous relationships, all of which have something in common as though the relationship was following some ancient script or scenario.[3, 5] The woman typically is caught by the "chemistry" of someone who turns out to be a stand-in for one or more personages important in childhood with whom the relationship was not satisfactorily worked out. The aim seems to be to reenact the old scene, but with an effort to make the other person over, to require him (or her) to love, accept, confirm, acknowledge the heroine. These recapitulations are usually unsuccessful, but aim at releasing the struggling patient from self-imposed masochistically dependent relationships.

Fairly representative is the story of Eleanor, a quiet, soft-spoken, controlled and bashful (apologetic) person, modestly and tastefully dressed but so as to appear inconspicuous. Her mother was domineering and aggressive with Eleanor and the older sister, but terrified with the realization that her husband was sick and lingering on. She was a food fadist and forced Eleanor to eat father's health foods, a juice diet. Eleanor was very threatened by the competition with her older, pretty, bright and dutiful sister. She wanted care and love so much that she fought and screamed against going off to school. Father lingered ill till she was fourteen but she remembers nothing at all of him. She does recall mother's words: "It is easier to lose a child than to lose a husband." In her guilty worthlessness, she wishes that she could have died in place of father if only then mother would have loved her! So she is preoccupied with dislike for herself as being dumb, athletic (and a girl!) and ugly. She has no sense of self, no feeling that she can express her will. She always goes along with what others say and never did a thing on her own until college. There she allowed herself to get into a masochistic homosexual relationship which gave her some secondary gains. She wants a mother and mothering, seeks passively an exclusive relation with a domineering person like mother without the burden of the older favored sister or sick father.

Many women—lesbian, heterosexual, asexual—provide illustrations of variations on the theme of being nobody and compensate for this ego predicament by becoming effective helpers, the clean-uppers at parties, the good listeners, those who serve as a way of trying to earn the right to exist in the company of others.

Many patients have been brought up under severe restrictive, inhibiting, sterilizing and nonloving situations but may have adapted to this foundation for living in a variety of different ways. Many are burdened wth feelings of little self-worth, compounded with fright or suspicion of any kind of intimacy, especially sexual. Some allow themselves to seek closeness and affection with other "lost souls" (male or female) with mutual dependence and role-playing of mothering. Sexual caresses enter the pattern as easily as masturbation. Others manage to focus on the prohibitions so as to deny themselves any sexual feelings and regard their genital areas as remote, untouchable except in a mechanical way, unstimulable, but perhaps available as a concession to others.

SUMMARY

Acting out defined in the call for this conference seems to fit both neurotic and character disorders. It raises a number of significant questions regarding persons engaging in homosexual behaviors and faced also with problems of adjusting in this society with its strong prejudices and discriminative procedures against homosexuals. We find that lesbians differ from male homosexuals in our society in patterns of behavior and interrelations within the family and in early socialization. Our comments will be confined to findings about lesbians.

1. We find quite infrequently that homosexual behavior is a defense against heterosexual behavior with its overtone of incest.

2. We find that many of our middle-class women have a variety of disorders related to feelings of inferiority, low self-

esteem and character disorders from early unresolved inter-relationships fundamental to a sense of autonomy. All these could be considered acting-out behaviors. Homosexuality is only one possibility, for there are many parallel cases of heterosexuals caught up in similar predicaments.

3. Our findings are at variance with any labeling of lesbianism as "pathological character disorders" (see the A.P.A.'s Psychiatric Diagnostic Categories). To define illness in terms of the person with whom one has a love relationship compounds the confusion between mental "illness," social pressures and legal codes. Lesbianism may occur as one of the manifestations of disorders such as phobic reactions but, in and of itself, it cannot define pathology.

4. The search for a more complete understanding of female homosexuality has led into a wide and diffuse area. No statistical, logical nor physiological breakdown of our data isolated the homosexual women as pathological.

5. From our data, there are many lesbian relationships which seem as genuine as good heterosexual marriages, not based on defensive maneuvers, acting-out behaviors or substitutive selection of love partner.

6. Both the heterosexual and homosexual women are importantly faced with and affected by the changing life styles of American families and of factors within the childrearing complex.

REFERENCES

1. Bieber, I., et al.: *Homosexuality: A Psychoanalytic Study of Male Homosexuals.* New York, Basic Books, 1962.
2. Cory, D. W.: *The Lesbian in America.* New York, Citadel, 1964.
3. Eisenbud, R.: Masochism revisited. *Psychoanal. Rev.,* 54:561-582, 1967.
4. Ford, C. S., and Beach, F. A.: *Patterns of Sexual Behavior.* New York, Harper, 1951.
5. Gruen, A.: Autonomy and identification. *Int. J. Psychoanal.,* 49:648-655, 1968.
6. Gundlach, R. H., and Riess, B. F.: Birth order and sex of siblings in a sample of lesbians and non-lesbians. *Psychol. Reports,* 20:61-62, 1967.
7. Gundlach, R. H., and Riess, B. F.: Self and sexual identity in the

female: a study of female homosexuals. In B. F. Riess (Ed.): *New Directions in Mental Health.* New York, Grune and Stratton, 1968, Vol. I.

8. Hatterer, L. J.: *Changing Homosexuality in the Male.* New York, McGraw-Hill, 1970.

9. Hooker, E.: The adjustment of the male overt homosexual. In H. M. Ruitenbeek (Ed.): *The Problem of Homosexuality in Modern Society.* New York, E. P. Dutton, 1963.

10. Jenkin, N., and Vroegh, K.: Contemporary concepts of masculinity and femininity. *Psychol. Reports, 25:*679-697, 1969.

11. Kenyon, F. E.: Studies in female homosexuality. *Acta Psychiatrica, 44:*224-237, 1968.

12. Kinsey, A. C.; Pomeroy, W. B.; Martin, C. E., and Gebhard, P. H.: *Sexual Behavior in the Human Female.* Philadelphia, W. B. Saunders, 1953.

13. Loevinger, J., and Wessler, R.: *Measuring Ego Development.* San Francisco, Jossey-Bass, 1970.

14. Magee, B.: *One in Twenty.* New York, Stein and Day, 1966.

15. Ovesey, L.: *Homosexuality and Pseudohomosexuality.* New York, Science House, 1969.

16. Rycroft, C.: *A Critical Dictionary of Psychoanalysis.* New York, Basic Books, 1968.

17. Stoller, R. J.: *Sex and Gender.* New York, Science House, 1968.

18. Ward, D. A., and Kassebaum, G. G.: *Women's Prison; Sex and Social Structure.* Chicago, Aldin, 1965.

19. West, D. J.: *Homosexuality.* Chicago, Aldin, 1968.

Dr. Lawrence I. Hatterer, in the course of his twenty years of doing psychotherapy, probably has treated more male homosexuals than most other American psychiatrists. With this rich fund of specialized information and knowledge and his well-rounded theoretical background, Dr. Hatterer is an authoritative source of elucidation on the acting out of the homoerotic impulses in males.

Dr. Hatterer explains why a multidimensional approach is necessary to the understanding and treatment of homosexuality in men. Through his extensive work with homosexuals, Hatterer cites evidence that family dynamics are not solely responsible for a man's homosexuality, as is often believed. His discussion of trigger mechanisms that lead to homosexual behavior sheds light on causal factors other than familial interactions. A recognition of the importance of these trigger mechanisms, which differ in strength and subtlety for each individual, is necessary to broaden and, thereby, increase the success of therapy techniques with homosexuals. Dr. Hatterer includes a discussion of the psychological needs of the homosexual and an examination of the relationship between the homosexual male and what the author terms the homosexophylic woman.

The acting out of male homosexuality is one example of the multiplicity of character problems covered in this volume. Dr. Hatterer's well-documented and original contribution to this field offers new insights toward understanding and treating this disturbance.

D.S.M.
G.D.G.

171

Chapter 11

The Many Dimensions of Male Homosexuality

LAWRENCE J. HATTERER

HOMOSEXUALITY HAS MANY roots and many motivations. Homosexuality can be born out of child or adolescent curiosity, sexual experimentation, or love, nonsexual motivations, partial or total blockage in erotic and/or social relatedness to women. The etiologic and motivational factors in the evolution of homosexual phenomenae are vast. Current views on these factors can best be reviewed by referring to the bibliography.

The common and most prevelant psychodynamics of homosexual acting out have their roots in constitutional deficiencies, distortions in intrafamilal interpersonal and peer relationships, disturbed gender and/or erotic identifications and the resolution of nonerotic goal and conflict. For some, homoerotic practice brings neither total sexual gratification, or resolution of conflict nor a realization of the ultimate nonsexual goal. They represent elements of a homosexual act that characterize that act as a form of acting out. The causes and perpetuation of homosexuality in every male have many dimensions during different periods of his life and at any point in time that he experiences homosexual impulses, phantasies and/or engages in overt acts.

The author has diagnostically evaluated eight hundred males and treated from three months to fifteen years two hundred of them who were troubled by their homosexuality. The vast majority revealed innumerable combinations of distortion in their past and present family histories with varying degrees of impairment in their ability to establish and to sustain a satisfactory social, erotic and/or gender identity. Some degree of malfunction in their relatedness to peers and authority accompanied by a

173

defect in their capacity to perceive and appropriately express assertive, aggressive and hostile affects or to cope with the excesses of their passive, dependent and power-oriented behavior was evident. Current writings document and detail these causes of male homosexuality. However, they often stress only a few dimensions: the disturbed family with the frequently stereotyped mother and father and sons constellation and their interactions along with the consequent impairment in male identity in one or several spheres, erotophobic reaction to women and the presence of a variety of accompanying distortions in character. The application of these few sets of dynamic dimensions fail to account for the multifaceted nature of the evolution, persistence and growth of the untold forms of homosexuality that are currently appearing in the millions of males in our culture.

Hence, it is necessary for a therapist to have a *many-dimensioned approach* to the understanding and treatment of homosexuality in men, one that not only encompasses the genetic and transference dynamics that produce and sustain a man's homosexuality but also other factors that contribute to perpetuating the slow or rapid growth of his homosexual consciousness and activity once it is seeded in his conscious and unconscious life. The author's clinical observation and therapeutic experience have taught him that *more* than an exploration and exposure of family dynamics, working through of Oedipal and castration complexes, and transference and character distortion is required to arrest, modify or alter the ongoing and frequently rapid growth of a male's daily, weekly or periodic homosexual consciousness and behavior.

As yet there is no scientific documentation of anything other than the prevalent family constellations and interactions.[1] We are on the threshhold of uncovering etiologies and dynamics from adaptational, motivational, sociologic and environmental vantage points. Over the past ten years, the author has tape-recorded every session of the short- and long-term therapies and the initial diagnostic interviews of 105 patients who have homosexual problems. He has studied thousands of hours of taped records microscopically and macroscopically for a period of nine years. This study demonstrated that every male's homosexual activity is not solely derived from specific family dynamics, but can emerge and grow because of other factors. Significantly, *the persistence and growth of a male's homosexuality is many-dimensioned and ultimately can be totally removed from familial origins.*

A common phenomenon of all males troubled by homosexuality is "hypersexualized consciousness." That is, all of the male's life practices and total identity becomes sexualized. Life is seen in terms of homosexual practice and/or interaction. Nonsexual interpersonal interactions and life's problems can be reduced to and resolved by homosexual phantasy and/or activity. Hypersexualized consciousness usually appears in adolescence, continuing in some persons to the point of addiction. Until a patient is aware of his oversexed consciousness and of the many determinants that induce and trigger his homosexuality, controlling, altering or inhibiting his homosexual habituation is not possible. Genetic reconstruction and insight cannot dissipate his hypersexualized consciousness and life style.

Hence, it is vital for the patient to become conscious of and explore each homosexual attraction, phantasy or impulse that leads to an overt homosexual action so that he can understand the *one* or *many* mechanisms that trigger his particular form of homosexuality.

The author learned that each patient harbors within him a *variety* of *trigger mechanisms,* which set into motion his particular phantasy which inevitably leads to an erotic response involving his mind and body. In working with tape-recorded histories of patients who demonstrated the varieties of trigger mechanisms it was evident that each patient tended to be particularly susceptible to one or more specific trigger mechanisms in varying combinations under differing circumstances and time periods. The trigger mechanisms discussed below are described in accordance with their prevalence in this author's patient population. They rarely occur alone but invariably overlap each other. They also occur with different intensities, depending upon the patient's age, past and present homosexual history, and immediate environment.

Trigger Mechanism 1.   Homosexual Imagery and Environmental Stimuli

The most far-reaching of all the trigger mechanisms is homosexual imagery, mental or physical, internalized or externalized, coupled with homosexual environmental stimuli. The most common environmental stimuli are (1) overt, practicing homosexual friends and homosexual social milieus such as bars, public meeting places, movies, lavoratories and cruising grounds; (2) suggestive homosexual literature, magazines, books, plays or movies; (3) imagery of past homosexual contacts or dreams during or preceding masturbation.

Trigger Mechanism 2.   Biological Drive

The rhythms of a person's biologic sexual appetite, unrelated to specific external stimuli, have to be taken into account as triggering homosexual responsiveness. All men have periodic urges for sexual activity unrelated to specific people or environments. Not uncommonly in the spring, or other predictable times, a person can experience a spontaneous surge of sexual drive.

Sometimes a patient has a recurrence of homoerotic urge based on biologic rhythms established in his past. Hence, each patient has to become conscious of the ebb and flow of his sexual appetites particularly when in a sexual void. A strong erotic physical appetite can loom as a frequent trigger to his homosexuality if blocked to all other outlets.

Trigger Mechanism 3.   The Search for Maleness

Another prime trigger mechanism can be a patient's constant need to attain one form or another of maleness that he feels he lacks. The maleness desired usually is physical, such as genital adequacy, muscularity, size of body, sexual virility and/or an ability to be aggressive, dominant and convey stereotyped male attitude and behavior. He attempts to identify with and possess, most often erotically, and/or divest the desired male, or idealized male, of his maleness. He often embarks on an endless search in phantasy and/or practice for the male qualities desired in each idealized male he encounters.

The methods he uses to attain maleness can include erotic,

emotional or intellectual seduction and any way he can get a male to acknowledge *his* maleness. Subtleties and/or overt attempts at erotic domination or submission or manipulation of men are also used. When responded to erotically or possessive of the man erotically he has the illusion of having acquired the other's desired maleness for himself. Sometimes even the slightest suggestion of a man's emotional interest is invertedly interpreted as having made the other male give up his maleness to him. The most frequent form of literal or symbolic acting out of his need for maleness is acquiring, by looking at, masturbating manually, orally or anally the man's penis and inducing him to orgasm. For some, then and only then, does he feel in possession of that man's maleness. For others, it is more removed and it is the wish to possess other portions of the male's body or his total being.

Sometimes the psychological need to control, aggress or dominate the male who possesses the desired maleness is more important and erotically arousing to him than the sexual activity. The hunt and conquest becomes more vital than the homosexual orgasm as evidence of having attained another man's maleness. These secondary satisfactions can become self-perpetuating and ends in and of themselves. The effect of his search for maleness or the degree of homosexual activity triggered depends on the extent to which the patient, usually from adolescence, has habituated himself to specific homoerotic imagery via looking at males in books, magazines, films, etc. A therapist has to make clear to the patient that in *homoerotizing his search for maleness,* he in turn *habitually homosexualizes his identification.* In fact, he ultimately feels less rather than more male when he has induced orgasm in, or been brought to orgasm by another male.

His search for maleness was his way of reaching out for nonerotic affection and recognition from a man. A patient might discover that what initially was an attempt to get close to and identify with a man later became erotized and subverted to pleasureable erotic experience. Unknowingly, he found himself in a frustrating, dead-ended, contradictory cycle of a search for an ideal male to be close to, who when found, was no longer ideal because he had become unmanned by their mutual homosexual practice. Inevitably, feeling less manly, he then becomes compelled to move on to still another man for "maleness."

Trigger Mechanism 4.   Rejection and Failure

A most common mechanism that can be observed in all patients is that any form of *rejection* by another human being and/or failure at any undertaking triggers homoerotic impulse, phantasy and act. This trigger mechanism is the one most frequently discovered by the patient on his own prior to entering therapy. A subtler form of rejection about which a patient is frequently unaware is the *"triangular power play,"* i.e. a life situation or interpersonal intanglement in which the patient is minimized or emasculated by one person in the presence of another, being most damaging if an intimate such as a mother, father, surrogate figure, mentor or valued male has minimized him. These emasculations do not necessarily have gender or sexual connotations. They can relate to other activities that connote maleness. However, when they do relate to gender and/or male sexual adequacy, they are *the most damaging* to the patient and can most rapidly trigger his homosexuality. His greatest perceptual distortions with regard to rejection take place in his relationship to women.

Trigger Mechanism 5.   Competition and Comparison

Competition is also a most significant trigger mechanism leading to homosexuality. Here again, the element of male adequacy plays a predominant role. The most common competitive reaction is for a patient to compare his maleness in physical terms: face, height, weight, muscular structure, ability to perform sexually, aggressive actions, voice and all other forms of physical appearance or behavior that connote maleness. Such comparisons can become obsessive, as in "cruising" and "crotch gazing" for their own sakes or in an addiction to magazines of male physique photographs.

All unfavorable comparisons which the patient makes of himself with others can trigger his homosexuality. He can engage in mentally masochistic flagellation of his ego because of daily, unconscious comparisons with every adequate male he meets, both in sexual and in nonsexual areas. He thus finds himself in an endless succession of cul de sacs in his work and social contacts.

Trigger Mechanism 6. Phobic Reaction to Women

Binding, hostile, demanding, aggressive, overprotective, or emasculating women can trigger a patient's homosexuality. Premature traumatic seductions or erotically aggressive women can also provoke the patient's homosexuality. Traumatic, hostile, demeaning, emasculating or direct rejections by women, particularly when the patient is making his first attempts at heterosexual contact or when he has initiated an asexual relationship can trigger a high degree of homosexuality. Increased homosexual practice is triggered by women whose own *sexual* identifications are ambiguous. They make the patient overly conscious of his sexual adequacy and role. He can become defeatingly defensive as in the relationship and the woman might unconsciously feminize him by assuming an assertive and dominant "male" role which rightfully should be his.

A large number of patients in the group were on one level frightened and on another level attracted and submissive to the competitive aggressive and demanding woman. Typical names given to these women are "fag hag," "faggot moll," or what the author terms the *homosexophylic woman, i.e. the woman who is both attracted to the homosexual male and to whom many homosexual males are attracted.* However, these relationships with homosexophylic women are amongst the most highly provocative of the male's homosexuality. The homosexophylic woman parallels the traits of the homosexual's mother. The patient becomes caught in the classic Oedipal relationship. He feels comfort and familiarity in his attachment but is completely unaware how provocative it is of his homosexuality. His first involvements with women can often be *the* most damaging and inciteful to his homosexuality, particularly where the contact is initiated and sustained by a woman. He is less triggered to homosexual behavior when he himself initiates and sustains the contact and is aware of his and her interactions and character.

Some patients withdraw from aggressive women who initiate

relationships by vigorously returning to a homosexual practice. If in a relationship with an aggressive woman for a long time he can be unaware that that very relationship provoked his homosexuality. Similarly he can be unaware of how his own hostility to such a woman, which he does not openly express because he is afraid of hurting her or of her retaliation, also triggered ongoing homosexuality. Being unable to confront the woman directly with his hostility inevitably triggers his homosexuality. Almost all patients were not able initially to identify the degrees of a woman's aggressive and hostile behavior. This inevitable blind spot results in either a denial of the woman's total nature or a belief that the woman is a totally accommodating and unhostile person.

A feminine woman with the desire to be dependent and passive also can threaten him because he fears the responsibilities in such a relationship. Premature attempts at relationships with dependent women who demand more of him than he feels capable of giving can trigger his homosexuality. Many homosexual men prior to entering treatment, who were engaged or hastily married such a woman, found themselves *more* homosexually driven than in their past.

Subtle and Least Obvious Trigger Mechanisms

There are a host of trigger mechanisms which are less identifiable yet can be frequent in occurrence and as important as the ones heretofore mentioned:

1. Fatigue and lowered resistance.
2. A need for reward or pleasure in the absence of both.
3. A need to share success.
4. Alcohol and drugs.
5. Unfamiliar locales.
6. Asexual transition period.
7. Pressures from the therapist.
8. Homosexual work identity.

The clinical evidence of the above multidimensional dynamics supports the necessity to broaden the view of the etiology and ultimate treatment of men troubled by their homosexuality or by their homosexual life styles.

SUMMARY

The causes of male homosexuality and the reasons for its continuance, lie beyond the family dynamics and other aspects of past history emphasized by most researchers. Therapy of patients troubled by homosexuality who desire to alter their behavior requires an understanding of present factors that produce homosexual impulses, phantasies or acts.

Males habituated to homosexuality develop a "hypersexualized consciousness" through which they see every aspect of their lives in sexual terms. The patient must recognize not only this oversexed consciousness, but also the "trigger mechanisms" that induce his homosexuality. These "trigger mechanisms" operate in various combinations. The major ones observed and discussed are (1) homosexual imagery and environmental stimuli, (2) biological drive, (3) the search for maleness, (4) rejection and failure, (5) competition and comparison, and (6) phobic reaction to women. Others include fatigue, alcohol and drugs, and unfamiliar locales. These findings emerged from a fifteen-year study of over eight hundred males troubled and untroubled by their homosexuality of whom over two hundred were treated for periods ranging from three months to fifteen years intermittently.

REFERENCES

1. Bieber, I., et al.: *Homosexuality: A Psychoanalytic Study.* New York, Basic Books, 1962.
2. Hatterer, L. J.: *Changing Homosexuality in the Male—Treatment for Men Troubled by Homosexuality.* New York, McGraw-Hill, 1970.
3. Hooker, E.: Male homosexuals and their worlds. In J. Marmor (Ed.): *Sexual Inversion: The Multiple Roots of Homosexuality.* New York, Basic Books, 1965.
4. Hooker, E.: The adjustment of the male overt homosexual. In H. M. Ruitenbeek (Ed.): *The Problem of Homosexuality in Modern Society.* New York, E. P. Dutton, 1963.
5. Hooker, E.: Male homosexuality. In N. L. Baberow (Ed.): *Taboo Topics.* New York, Atherton, 1963.
6. Marmor, J. (Ed.): *Sexual Inversion: The Multiple Roots of Homosexuality.* New York, Basic Books, 1965.

7. Ovesey, L.: *Homosexuality and Pseudohomosexuality.* New York, Science House, 1969.

8. Ruitenbeek, H. M., et al. (Eds.): *The Problem of Homosexuality in Modern Society.* New York, E. P. Dutton, 1963.

9. Schofield, M.: *Sociological Aspects of Homosexuality.* Boston, Little, Brown, 1965.

10. Socarides, C.: *The Overt Homosexual.* New York, Grune and Stratton, 1968.

LAURA DEFREITAS, an old friend, student, and associate of the late Henry Guze, wrote this very personally meaningful paper from notes available after the untimely death of Dr. Guze which occurred a month after he presented a paper at the Adelphi University conference. Henry Guze was one of the country's foremost experts on sexuality and was particularly interested in the acting-out phenomena found in transsexuals.

In this paper, Laura deFreitas discusses Guze's concepts of transsexual behavior and the constitutional and cultural concomitants associated with the syndrome. Factors in the patient's background which may be responsible for transsexualism and the behavior patterns typical of both male and female transsexuals are presented from samples of Dr. Guze's cases.

Henry Guze and Laura deFreitas view transsexual behavior as a distortion of self-perception and provide two brief case studies that are illustrative of this point. Following this, she discusses causality and provides data from relevant primate studies that have been done concerning gender role. She concludes by suggesting that learning processes may, in fact, be factors in the adoption of transsexual acting-out behavior.

Miss deFreitas has faithfully recreated Henry Guze's ideas synthesized from many years of close collaboration. Her paper is a worthy memorial to Dr. Henry Guze offering an exciting and provocative formulation of his ideas on the acting-out behavior of transsexuals.

D.S.M.
G.D.G.

Chapter 12

The Transsexual Phenomenon: A Problem in Body Image with Specific Reference to the Expression of Violence

Henry Guze and Laura deFreitas

T HE TRANSSEXUAL PATIENT has challenged the observer to search for meaningful hypotheses with reference to the etiology of the transsexual syndrome. Benjamin,[3] in his now classic first volume on the subject, has laid the groundwork for a recognition of the constitutional components often associated with this condition. Unfortunately, his position has been confounded by the suggestion that the patients under study were also severely disordered psychiatrically. In the data presented herein, based on a sample of fifty-three cases, it appeared that many of the patients evidenced schizophrenic-like reaction patterns, masked by the specificity of the transsexual syndrome. Although there has been considerable dispute with reference to this diagnostic description, the problem of diagnosis must not be lost in the verbiage of the nature-nurture controversy. Eysenck[7] has pointed out, perhaps correctly, that multiple diagnoses are generally more useful in nosological studies than single designations. The latter type of diagnosis frequently attempts to push the patient into a forced category, a Procrustean bed which may or may not fit. Thus, an effort is made in this paper to use a multidiagnostic approach and to present categories which describe the transsexual patient in a variety of ways. While there may be considerable overlap in descriptions of homosexual, transsexual, and transvestite patients, there are numerous distinguishing features which may be outlined. In the description of the transsexual subjects

examined in this investigation, the following two major characteristics have emerged as significant parts of the gestalt.

First, the patient cannot accept his self-image as belonging
to his designated sex. This has appeared to be a problem in
self-perception.[9] We may ask ourselves why a fertile, successful
humanoid male insists that he has been cheated and that his
body and "soul" are of disparate genders. Typically, the patient
informs the therapist that he is imprisoned, imprisoned in
himself, since he is "really a woman in the body of a man."
This phenomenon is striking even to the seasoned psychotherapist.
Immediately, a series of problems are brought to the fore,
particularly those relating to the nature of masculinity and
femininity. Herein lies a complicated riddle. How does one
know his sexual designation? Perhaps the plight of uncertainty,
where it exists, is a basis for a split in the personality dynamics.
Such a question is hardly different from the standard question
asked by schizophrenic patients, "How do I know that I am I?"

Second, there appears to be a strong compulsion on the part
of most male transsexuals to escape from the "disgusting business
of violence." When there is not an evasion of violence, there
is a peculiar feeling of fear and curiosity. One wonders whether
this is not a limited type of reaction formation. (In the small
number of female transsexuals examined in our study, the pattern
seems to be reversed. The female patients have participated
often in aggressive physical encounters. In one case, the young
woman had fractured the leg of the girl friend's father after a
mild disagreement.)

It would appear that a profitable approach to the understanding of the transsexual syndrome must include an examination
of the human being from the standpoint of ethology, i.e. man as
an animal in the field. Perhaps a look, therefore, at research on
other primates may be illuminating at this point. (It is not
suggested, however, that we merely take the data from lower
primates and transpose them to man.) There are a number of
primate studies which demonstrate that some animals are dominant over others and that, under certain circumstances, within a
given social structure, agonistic behavior comes to the surface.
Dominance-submission hierarchies are established, and the

"defeated" animals are often mounted by the victors. Thus, a defeated male primate typically presents quarters[1] instead of committing suicide as do some vanquished male humans.

We should like to argue that, at the human level, the male transsexual is a person participating in a hierarchy as a subordinate. He is, for some reason, conspicuously different from his peers, and he is unable, perhaps terrified, to fight his way against other males. (Occasionally, one sees compensatory aggressive behavior expressed in verbal hostility. Some of the forms this may take are intense spitefulness or resentment toward the diety and authority.) This pattern is completely reversed for the aggressive female transsexual. Can it be argued that, at the human level, the subservient role leads to identification with the female whereas the aggressive or dominant role leads to the opposite? The constitutional predilection to be defeated in a world that emphasizes power and equates it with masculinity often leads to accentuation of the gender crisis. Thus, "I am afraid to be a man" becomes equated with feelings of persecution and the idea that one is more safely seen as a woman. Physical prowess is emphasized, and there is a worship of the masculine image which the patient feels he cannot attain.

It is not yet clear whether the converse is true for the female transsexual as our sample of females is much too small. However, we do know that women who seek a sex change are aggressively oriented. It would appear that they have been companions of vigorous (perhaps hostile) fathers. Strangely enough, they seem to be involved in a reverse masculine protest. "If you can't beat them, join them." Is the fear of being a woman tantamount to the fear of being suppressed by the male?

Probably the transsexual person is forced to his decision by the cognitive awareness that he is different. Why is he an ugly duckling? Bieber[4] has suggested for the male homosexual that the child feels assaulted as a male and thus builds defensive maneuvers and identifies with the female. For the transsexual, the answer to what the senior author calls the "ugly duckling syndrome" may lie in the range of constitutional variables that are present between the extreme masculine and the extreme feminine. These may be manifested in the sense of outer appearance, either physical or behavioral, as well as in the endocrine mechanisms. Indeed, the work of Barraclough and Gorski[2] and that of Gorski and Whalen[8] demonstrates the homeostatic quality of brain endocrine relations and the existence of brain mechanisms which are masculine and feminine. Nonetheless, not all effeminate men desire to become women or think that they *are* women imprisoned in men's bodies. If they do so desire, such feeling is maintained in a controlled fashion and is not accompanied by the desperate decision that one has been sexually cheated at birth.

Does this problem become serious only in a culture that dictates the meaning of gender? There are two aspects to the definition: (1) gender as a physical framework and (2) gender as a psychosocial posture involving the performance of behavior acceptable to the given role (including what is *believed* to be acceptable). A provocative question might, indeed, be, "How does it feel to be a girl?" or "How does it feel to be a boy?" We may ask ourselves, "How do I know that what I am experiencing is commensurate and appropriate for my gender position?" There is hardly any research which proposes to answer these questions. Margaret Mead[13] has pointed out that, "In any human group, it is possible to arrange men and women on a scale in such a way that between a most masculine group and a most feminine group there will be others who seem to fall in the middle, to display fewer of the pronounced physical features that are more characteristic of one sex than of the other." Sexual role is obviously influenced by the biological and cultural frameworks within which it takes place, but, as yet, there are few data relating to the self-image and its implications for sexual role.

Some societies have provided for the range of sexual identification from masculinity to femininity by accepting the *berdache*, the man who dressed and lived as a woman (or pseudo-woman). There are no data to indicate whether the *berdache* was a happy human being nor can it be said that the *berdache* was the result of environment as such. Did the *berdache* think of himself as a man, as a woman, or as a member of a third sex? What is the relationship of the *berdache* to "acting-out" behavior? Although our culture provides earlier opportunity for the girl child to identify with the female,[10] we do have the uncertain female, the perpetual tomboy. Very little is known about her and her role in any society.

In the sample of patients under discussion, we have become increasingly attuned to the existence of a problem in self-perception. As has been pointed out elsewhere,[9] male patients who seek corrective gender surgery experience themselves as being men but perceive themselves as women imprisoned in male bodies. What a dilemma! How do they know they are women? They cannot have clear knowledge of what a woman feels like since they can only gain such data by inference. Therefore, the problem revolves around self-image. The person who cannot participate as he understands the requirements for his given role sees himself as a *misfit*. In confusion and despair, he may seek another role commensurate with his level of performance as a person, a role that seems more conducive to survival. It is at this point that the phenomenon which has been labelled "acting out" may emerge. It is my contention that acting out is a threshold phenomenon. In other words, we have the potential within us to act out a variety of positions, many of which may be, at least, partially inimicable to our thinking but many of which we could enact if the threshold for it were sufficiently reduced. Since it may be said that the transsexual has been "imprinted" with a fear of violence and with subservient patterns of response, he cannot fulfill the requirements, as he sees them, for masculinity. These involve a fantasy (often romantic) of a powerful, hyper-masculine male, usually a kind of man the patient has never known. This cognitive patterning is a phylogenetic development. While it is possible to influence the gender role of infrahuman primates, it is unlikely that they would "want" to be sexually changed even though their behavior might be atypical for their sex role. Perhaps the phylogenetic development of awareness of sexual dymorphism has led to additional cognitive conflicts about what constitutes adequate definition of masculinity and femininity.

The following thumbnail sketches are presented to illustrate some of the behavior that may appear in transsexual patients.

It is not clear, however, whether such behavior is indigenous to the transsexual syndrome alone and sufficient to distinguish it from other gender identity problems.

1. T.R. is a forty-year-old male who served in the Army during World War II. At present, his body is that of an obese, soft male reflecting, no doubt, the effect of estrogen hormonal therapy. (It should be noted that many of the males who want to be women begin to take estrogen as soon as they can.) The patient admires men who are dressed in military clothes and are mounted on horses. One detects a fetishistic component in much of his behavior. He is an extremely subservient person who has been considerably "pushed around" by both men and women. He is terrified of being hurt and yet desires to be operated upon. The contradiction in someone who is frightened of physical violence and yet seeking drastic surgery is compelling.

2. O.G. is a forty-year-old successful engineer who is also a colonel in the Army Reserve. He is tall and of normal masculine habitus. He is presently married and the father of two legitimate children (in addition to others he has fathered unofficially). He has a history of being found attractive by women and has been regarded as a good sex partner. At the age of sixteen, he decided he was a woman. In spite of this self-perception, he did well at some "masculine" activities and became, among other things, a tennis champion. One day, after an argument with a girl friend, he performed self-surgery as a preliminary step to achieving the total freedom he had been seeking. This patient's history reveals nothing especially dramatic except for the presence of dominant parents and a dominant sister.

In these cases, as in many others, there seems to be a constitutionally effeminate and passive person who feels that he cannot compete. He is forced to be a "man," but he has established the idea that women are less persecuted. He believes he can escape persecution if he "poses" as a girl which he feels he actually is anyhow. There would then be a consistency between the image and the appearance since the self-image is already that of a female. The patient, in Pygmalion-like fashion, creates a female character who becomes a consistent rival—ultimately to his very existence.[10] It is important to emphasize that there has been usually a multiple causality in the transsexual's search for gender identity:

1. For some reason, he has a history of being passive or pacified as a little boy. (Perhaps his masculinity was suppressed in ways which have been indicated by Bieber and his co-workers[4] with reference to homosexuals. We do know, however, that some boys have been suppressed, but still do not want to be women.)

2. He does not know how to counterattack, and he has adopted the role of subservience or submission which, at the human level, has been cognitively that of the female.

3. The patient now feels that he must fulfill the demands of the role of female.

It is interesting to note that an ape in the same circumstances would not be in the same dilemma. Male apes can act passively and effeminately and not be split as to gender role. The constitutional delimitation may affect gender, but the human definitions are verbal. Unlike the animal, the person is directed by the limits of the word. Perhaps the Sapir-Whorf hypothesis is applicable and operating here, and a male believes he is expected to behave in accordance with the meaning of the word "man."

If the transsexual phenomenon depended solely upon an error in gender orientation related to the level of brain functioning, it seems unlikely that the animal "human being" would be concerned with surgical intervention. He would not know what a male should be like. It must be remembered that the transsexual person is embedded in a culture which emphasizes his condition. He is alert to his being an anomaly and feels out of place—more often, it would seem, because of his feelings rather than because of his morphology. His ideation suggests that a given system of feelings—in this case, masculinity—is accompanied normally by a specific morphology. Herein lies the complicated body image problem of the transsexual. Personal behavior is a function of the "image of the body that one has in his mind."[15] At the moment, there is no clarity as to how the brain is involved in gender orientation. MacLean[12] has, however, described some somatosensory aspects of genital function (points between the caudal thalamus and the medulla which, upon stimulation, result in bodily or genital scratching and, sometimes, genital discharge with motile spermatozoa.)

Perhaps of more immediate value to the concepts dealt with in this paper are the studies describing the display of penile erections among squirrel monkeys. "In the case of two males, the displaying animal utilizes the display as a means of exerting and establishing dominance. If the recipient does not remain quiet and submissive to the display, it may be violently assaulted."[14] One of the monkeys referred to herein was Caspar, the dominant male in his group. He displayed to all other males, but none, in turn, displayed to him. Edgar, the lowest male in the colony, displayed to none of the other males but was displayed to by everyone else. (Apparently, Edgar's display was only to the investigators.) During display, the behavior of monkeys is similar to that of two dogs smelling each other's genitals, but in the former case there is more emphasis on visual cues.

Let us return to the significance of these data in the study of the transsexual. We maintain, on the basis of interviews with such patients, that they are persons who, in the case of the male, have assumed extremely subordinate or passive attitudes. They have self-images of inadequacy regardless of their talents and accomplishments. Their thinking reveals that they experience themselves at the bottom of the ladder for masculinity. Furthermore, they receive stimuli from other males which are either dominating or sexual. We do not know how this phenomenon comes about.

Stoller's work[16] suggests some clues. He reports cases of excessive mothering of the male as a cause of this disorder. Typically, the male child has been overprotected and maintained almost inseparably from the maternal body. In addition, there are psychodynamic factors in the maternal history which, however, do not preclude susceptibility on a constitutional level for the child's transsexual response. There are clear indications in the research of Doorbar[6] that the transsexual candidates are narcissistic and depict on the TAT cards a history of an "unhappy childhood when they were rejected by girls because they were boys and by boys because they were 'sissies' or in some other way effeminate." Here again is a particular image of the self accompanied by the denial of masculinity. Is this a fear response? To all of the persons interviewed, there seems to be an ultimate safety in the female role and in female clothing, the latter presenting a good place in which to hide. We have never seen a transsexual male in anything but dresses or skirts when he is in his female role. The transsexual person will go to an extreme to appear as a female—an ultra feminine female preferably. Is this to reduce the likelihood of an aggressive encounter? A woman does have some privilege—even today—and, although, she may be sought after sexually, she is usually not involved in hand-to-hand fighting. (At least, we do not see it as frequently.)

Stoller[16] has suggested the following characteristics as distinguishing the transsexual young boy from those having other gender identity problems:

1. The boys desire to be anatomically female and find the presence of the penis disgusting. (This tendency may be manifested at a very young age. In New York, there are cases in treatment between the ages of four and eight.)

2. The mothers of these boys need to keep the infant boys close to their bodies for a very long time.

3. The mothers tend to show excessive permissiveness of whatever the boys want.

4. The mothers have a history of bisexuality and of acting like masculine boys in childhood.

5. The mothers have a sense of emptiness in their marriages, and they reproduce with their husbands the earlier relationships they had with their own mothers. They generally had early close relationships with their fathers which ended when they became old enough to assume biologically female roles, and, in some ways, the mothers use the little boys as a kind of "good" father substitute.

6. The mothers of these mothers were remembered as extremely distant and angry.

7. The fathers are passive and distant, almost never seen by

their sons, and they do not actively stop the feminizing process. The above data are unquestionably of significance. However, a serious problem lies in the fact that there are no controls. Are there boys with similar or even identical histories who do not become transsexual? Can we say that the above characteristics distinguish the potential male transsexual from other children who later develop serious gender identity problems? While their presence seems to lead to a passive male, it is not clear why there is a sudden decision that one is a woman. The onset of the decision seems to come about almost in a cognitive fashion while later maintenance becomes rooted in drive. Thus, the patient may find, in seeking for some means of adaptation to a threatening environment, that he can function more easily and safely in the feminine role. Somewhere, there must, indeed, be a period of critical conflict. We do not know when. How early in life does the child experience a gender confrontation? How can it decide whether it is a male or a female? Currently, genetics cannot account for the behavioral direction.

Kupperman[11] has pointed out further that "there is no demonstrable clue as to the identification of a possible endocrine dysfunction in the etiology of the transsexual." He adds, ". . . since the libidinous drive of both the normal male and female is enhanced with androgens, sex orientation is not dependent upon a specific endocrine or chromatin pattern but is an attribute primarily based upon the psychological direction of the patient himself." However, Diamond[5] has suggested that the dual capacity of individuals to be boys or girls must depend somewhere upon some disorder in the neuroendocrine mechanism. It is possible that there are constitutional or personality components whose study have been neglected. People do differ in spite of the fact that many psychoanalysts do not wish to recognize those differences. Pavlov showed that there were various ways in which the nervous systems of different dogs could work. There were weak (or cowardly) dogs, and there were strong (or courageous) dogs. The latter divided into "equilibrated" and "nonequilibrated." The "equilibrated" were further still divided into "mobile" and "inert." From these types,

Pavlov developed a series of human types (melancholic, choleric, phlegmatic, and sanguine).

Whether one accepts Pavlov's categories or not, human beings *do* differ from each other temperamentally. This, we believe, is the key to the transsexual phenomenon. A number of highly sensitive genetic males are unable to adapt to the masculine role and are "afraid" of the demands of the environment and particularly of the presence of violence. These persons then become phobic in the sense of feeling out of place and unable to establish a niche as a male. The female transsexual, conversely, is "afraid" of being a female and aggressively resists the position.

We would propose that masculinity and femininity form multidimensional continua and that all persons are in fluctuation between masculine and feminine aspects of behavior. Each individual has his own threshold as to the dominant aspect of his behavior, and the acting out of the opposite sexual pattern is, theoretically, possible for all persons. In addition, the culture sets demands for behavior appropriate to a given sexual role. (More often, in the case of transsexuals, the patient himself in his mini-culture has set demands.) If the patient fails or is unable to meet these demands, he may perceive himself as being sexually misplaced and assume he would be more comfortable in the role of the opposite sex.

The phylogenetic picture of sex behavior shows more and more dependence upon aspects of learning as one approaches the level of man. The human response becomes increasingly, it would appear, dependent upon learning factors acting upon individual differences in temperament and self-perception. A very sensitive male or female may develop uncertainty about his experienced image as related to his perceived image. When this occurs, the inconsistency and disparity in the self-image creates an urgency for correction. The potential transsexual is functionally split, and he cannot be at peace until there is unity.

REFERENCES

1. Altman, S. A.: *Social Communications Among Primates.* Chicago, University of Chicago, 1967.
2. Barraclough, C. A., and Gorski, R. A.: Evidence that the hypothalamus

is responsible for androgen-induced sterility in the female rat. *Endocrinology,* 68:68-79, 1961.

3. Benjamin, H.: *The Transsexual Phenomenon.* New York, The Julian Press, 1966.

4. Bieber, I.; Dain, H. J.; Dince, P. R.; Drellich, M. G.; Grand, H. C.; Gundlach, R. H.; Kremer, M. W.; Rifkin, A. H.; Wilbur, C. C., and Bieber, T. B.: *Homosexuality.* New York, Basic Books, 1962.

5. Diamond, M.: A critical evaluation of the ontogeny of human sexual behavior. *Quart. Rev. Biol.,* 40:147-175, 1965.

6. Doorbar, R. R.: Psychological testing of transsexuals. A brief report of results from the Wechsler Adult Intelligence Scale, the Thematic Apperception Test, and the House-Tree-Person test. *Trans. N. Y. Acad. Sci.* (Series II), 29:455-462, 1967.

7. Eysenck, H.: Classification and the problem of diagnosis. In H. J. Eysenck (Ed.): *Handbook of Abnormal Psychology.* New York, Basic Books, 1960.

8. Gorski, R. A., and Whalen, R. E. (Eds.): *Brain and Behavior: Vol. III, The Brain and Gonadal Function.* Berkeley and Los Angeles, University of California, 1967.

9. Guze, H.: The transsexual patient: a problem in self perception. *Trans. N. Y. Acad. Sci.* (Series II), 29:464-468, 1967.

10. Guze, H.: Psychosocial adjustment of transsexuals: an evaluation and theoretical formulation. In R. Green and J. Money (Eds.): *Transsexualism and Sex Reassignment.* Baltimore, Johns Hopkins, 1969.

11. Kupperman, H. S.: The endocrine status of the transsexual. *Trans. N. Y. Acad. Sci.* (Series II), 29:434-440.

12. MacLean, P. D.: Studies on the cerebral representation of certain basic sexual functions. In R. A. Gorski and R. E. Whalen (Eds.): *Brain and Behaviors Vol. III, The Brain and Gonadal Function.* Berkeley and Los Angeles, University of California, 1967.

13. Mead, M.: *Male and Female.* New York, William Morrow, 1949.

14. Ploog, D. W., and MacLean, P. D.: Penile display in the squirrel monkey (Saimiri sciureus). *Animal Behavior,* 11:32-39, 1963.

15. Schilder, P.: *The Image and Appearance of the Human Body.* London, Kegan Paul, Trench, Trubner, and Co., 1935.

16. Stoller, R. J.: Etiological factors in male transsexualism. *Trans. N. Y. Acad. Sci.* (Series II), 29:431-433, 1967.

17. Teplov, B. M.: Problems in the study of general types of higher nervous activity in man and animals. In J. A. Gray (Ed.): *Pavlov's Typology.* New York, Macmillan, 1964.

18. Whorf, B. L.: *Language, Thought, and Reality.* Cambridge, Massachusetts Institute of Technology, 1956.

D R. DANIEL CASRIEL has probably worked more extensively and more creatively with drug addicts than any other psychiatrist on the current scene. In this comprehensive presentation, he integrates his theoretical system of personality with his practical and useful treatment method for drug addicts. The resultant paper provides a vivid understanding of the Daytop Village program, a therapeutic community for the rehabilitation of drug addicts. Dr. Casriel clarifies how drug addiction (an example of acting out) is treated according to the Daytop plan, thus giving us the roots of his present, widely heralded methodology with other character disorders—the Casriel "encounter" and "marathon" format.

Dr. Casriel begins his chapter with a theoretical discussion of character disorders. Included is a brief review of the literature on the subject along with speculations as to why some therapists are hesitant to treat people with acting-out problems. Drug addiction is explained as a defense mechanism which facilitates the individual's withdrawal from reality. Following a discussion of psychodynamics, Dr. Casriel gives a thorough account of the procedures at Daytop. The entering addict's sequence of rehabilitative stages is recounted, along with a description of Daytop treatment techniques.

Dr. Casriel shares with us the origins of his unique group process treatment method offering new insights into one of the most flagrantly acted-out character problems of our time—drug addiction.

D.S.M.
G.D.G.

Chapter 13

The Acting Out Neurosis of Our Times

DANIEL CASRIEL

IN THIS PRESENTATION I will describe the theoretical framework and therapeutic approach that I have evolved in my work with one segment of the acting-out psychiatric population—the drug addict. Since the terms *acting-out neuroses* and *character neurosis* are interchangeable today, and since in my opinion the drug addict is one of the more flagrant examples of this pathology, this paper hopefully will, in talking about the addict, add to our understanding of acting out and therapy with character disorders.

As is well known, the rehabilitation and successful psychiatric treatment of the antisocial character disorder has lagged far behind and beyond the treatment of the neurotic as well as of the psychotic. That subgroup of character disorders called drug addiction has been least successfully treated. During the past fifty years, as other forms of psychopathology have melted in the sunlight of psychiatric knowledge, various psychodynamic theories expounded to explain addiction have not helped to cure the patient.

The clinician has been aware of this fact. He has absented himself from confrontation with the problem. His knowledge that the addict is incurable in theory and in practice has allowed him to excuse himself. He has sent his addicted patients through

This chapter is based on a paper presented at the annual meeting of the American Psychiatric Association, May, 1966, and was published in part in *Physician's Panorama*, Oct., 1966.

Daytop and AREBA are therapeutic communities for the rehabilitation of drug addicts. Daytop is a nonprofit organization funded by government agencies. AREBA is a private corporation funded by patient fees. Daytop is geared for the lower and middle class, and AREBA for the upper middle class.

the doors of Lexington, Fort Worth, and, more recently the scores of newer addiction centers located within our finest medical centers. Of course a few courageous physicians have continued to attempt to understand and treat the addict. Some professionals also have used methadone as the treatment for heroin in a manner reminiscent of the way heroin was employed in the treatment for morphine at the close of the last century.

Society in its desperate battle to protect itself from the addict has passed more and more laws with harsher and harsher penalties. But the threat of long prison sentences has not attenuated the progress of this malady which is reaching epidemic proportions in some sections of our cities. Hospitals, jails, prisons and penitentiaries are filled, and stand in mute testimony to society's failure with the problem. Almost forty years ago August Aichhorn in *Wayward Youth* complained:

> It is . . . pain which makes the neurotic aware of his illness and ready for treatment. The fact that the delinquent does not suffer discomfort from his symptom constitutes one of the chief difficulties in the analytic treatment of delinquents.[1]

The addict is only one type of character disorder who has much in common with his brother, the nonaddictive delinquent.

Aichhorn went on to say that "The remedial treatment of the individual can begin only when the transference is established." "It was evident that we were dealing with human beings who had been deprived of the affection necessary for their normal development." Because of severe love deprivation the libido returned to the ego, with a resultant severe narcissistic state. Later emergence of the libido from the narcissistic state proceeded via a narcissistic rather than an anaclitic type of object-choice relationship. But those disposed toward a narcissistic object-choice loved only themselves, could not establish a transference, and therefore were refractory to psychoanalytic treatment (Freud in discussing schizophrenia, homosexuality and delinquency). Aware of this fact, Aichhorn indicated "first we had to compensate for the great lack of love and then gradually and with great caution begin to make demands upon the children.[1] No pressure that could be avoided was brought to bear on them . . . [The workers] intervened in fights and brawls only to prevent injuries, without taking sides in the altercation. . . . [As expected] as a direct result of our attitude, their aggressive acts became more frequent and more violent until practically all the furniture in the building was destroyed, the window panes broken, the doors nearly kicked to pieces." Finally the aggressive subsides. "We conceive of the process as corresponding to that outlined in Freud's 'Group Psychology and the Analysis of the Ego' in that a strong emotional tie to the worker developed after the period of the greatest aggression. This intense object relationship to the common leader paved the way for identification with him and in turn led to an emotional relationship to each other (i.e. peers)." The libidinal energy, freed through explosions of affect, could now be turned toward normal goals. "Self control (of the therapist) requires a great deal of training . . . it is not easy to keep one's temper when several boys stay in bed all morning." . . . break up all the furniture, or provoke one in countless ways. Using this therapeutic concept as a basis for successful treatment it is no wonder that few therapists were willing to dedicate their lives to the treatment of adolescent delinquents.

Aichhorn was describing twelve youths, aged fourteen through eighteen, as his aggressive group. Compared to the potential and proven violence of today's delinquents, his boys were rebellious *little* boys.

Sandor Rado in his paper "The Psychoanalysis of Drug Addiction"[6] ten years later gave a theoretical formulation of the addictive disorders which, unfortunately, offered no new hope or help in their rehabilitation of the addicted.

And for the past thirty-five years, though theories have been modified, reformulated, and rephrased, the successful treatment of the addict has failed to materialize.[2] Noyes and Kolb even went so far as to say "group psychotherapy is not successful."[5]

As in many cases of pure and applied science, treatment is sometimes stumbled upon before the etiology has been fully uncovered. Paradoxically then, we sometimes understand the nature of the illness, the nature of the maladaption, only after rehabilitation has been established; occasionally by accident rather than by design. Since we, as professionals, did not have a practical theoretical technique of effective treatment, it is no wonder that relatively few of us ventured into this area as therapists.

For over ten years this reporter has been observing the results of treating addicts with techniques originating in Synanon.[3] Dederich, the founder of Synanon and a nonprofessional man, not governed by nor limited to the framework of our thinking, evolved a promising method for productive engagements and rehabilitation of the addict. This method was greatly modified in Daytop Lodge and Village by this reporter. It is my opinion that a successful amalgamation between the professional and paraprofessional has taken place at Daytop which has resulted in a therapeutic climate which appears to be very promising of probable rehabilitation and possibly even cure of the addict—on an effective, efficient, inexpensive basis.

Since this reporter was more familiar with adaptational psychodynamic theory it was to this theory that he looked, to organize and explain the apparent success of this new treatment technique.

To recapitulate part of the adaptational theory which immediately concerns us, adaptational as well as Freudian psychodynamics stated that the basic motivational forces of human behavior is purposeful and goal directed. In general, behavior is designed to avoid pain and gain pleasure. The adaptive responses in situations of danger (which is an anticipation of pain) is either flight and/or fight. "Flight is integrated through a perception of danger, the emotion of fear, and escape from the source of danger; fight is integrated through a perception of danger, the emotion of rage, and the intent to destroy the source of danger. The unconscious mechanisms of defense utilized by the ego (the executive apparatus) are based upon this integration of emergency functioning. They are attempts to protect the ego against anticipated danger by mental operations which alter perception, distort the effective emergency signal, and change the appropriate action in a variety of ways. The end result is reinforcement of repression and substitution of behavior which is acceptable to the ego. These ego functions, in turn, are molded by interpersonal experiences unique of each individual in his particular culture."[4]

Guilt was evolved as a fearful emotional reaction, an anticipation of punishment for the danger one feels toward a loved object when the individual feels he is hurting or doing something against the wishes of a loved object. It was felt that when love was absent or strongly attenuated in early childhood and infancy there was a resultant defect in the guilt mechanism, and as a result a very poorly controlled personality (impulse-ridden) developed who could very easily be asocial or antisocial. Where there is nothing to be gained by conformance, an individual would not conform. It was thus felt that people who were delinquent or asocial were so because of the defective guilt mechanism which is evolved from a lack of parental love and that not much could be done with this type of personality. They would have to be controlled from the outside because they could not control themselves from within. This was dramatically born out to this writer several years ago: while working as a court psychiatrist, a habitual severe aggressive delinquent was asked if he ever felt any guilt over his misdeeds, which included robbery, knifing and shooting. The closest he could come in understanding the emotion was to answer "Yeah—when the judge got the goods on you and he asks you if you're innocent or guilty."

In the same clinic, Freudian theory or narcissistic object-choice was validated when, after months of "therapy" one of the very few delinquents who occasionally showed up for an appointment said, "You know, Doc, you're a pretty all right guy for a square—do you need any free tires for your car?"

This observer would modify adaptational psychodynamic theory to state that there are three major mechanisms of defense used in coping with danger. Already accounted for are two mechanisms of defense called flight and fight, using the emotions of fear and rage. This reporter proposes a third major, perhaps more primary, mechanism is one which avoids danger or pain. This mechanism is neither fight nor flight. It uses neither the emotions of fear nor rage and may be called detachment using the nonpainful "emotion" of withdrawal. Just as a turtle puts his head into a shell, so do some people withdraw from the pain of awareness, the pain of reality; what they experience as the danger of everyday functioning by withdrawing unto themselves. Although the mechanism of fear might have originally stimulated the turtle to put its head into the shell, once its head is in the shell, the turtle presumably feels secure without experiencing anxiety or anger. The turtle has succeeded in effectively cutting himself off from contact with the rest of the world, for a period of time that he, the turtle, chooses. Indeed this mechanism of defense can be lifesaving at times, such as the case of the turtle when a dangerous animal is present, also as the case of human beings when the best means of coping with danger is to withdraw. Those individuals who are lost at sea survive best if they can withdraw their feelings and emotionally detach themselves from the pain of reality. Those human beings who cannot successfully do so and who react to the danger of a situation through fear or rage are more vulnerable to destruction because there is no place to run and fighting is futile. However, the mechanism of detachment using withdrawal can also be a pathological defense under certain conditions. Thus, the turtle who puts his head into the shell at the approach of a truck runs the risk of having himself destroyed if the truck should run over his shell.

In a similar and analogous way, human beings also attempt to withdraw from pain and the anticipation of pain that they realistically or neurotically encounter in everyday living. It is now theorized that *those people whose primary mechanism of defense is detachment are those who fit into the psychiatric classification of character disorder.*

By successfully removing themselves from the pain of reacting to stress, they have detached themselves and spend their energy reinforcing, by encapsulating, their isolation to a nonpainful state of functioning. Like its sister defense mechanisms of fight and flight, the psychodynamic defense of detachment may have been a very realistic one in the individual's early experience. Once patterned and ingrained, detachment very frequently becomes an intrapsychic fortress of one's own making. The patient has taken flight without fear into a fortress in which he feels secure, but realistically in which he is quite isolated, incapacitated, and imprisoned. His original fortress has become his stockade. The longer the individual stays in his own jail, the thicker the walls become by secondary encapsulation, with the result that the individual is less and less able to cope with the problems of everyday living.

Once this intrapsychic world with relatively little tension is evolved, the individual will overtly or covertly fight anyone who attempts to remove him from his prison-fortress—from his encapsulated shell of detachment. Once the adaptational mechanism of withdrawal and detachment is evolved and becomes a primary mechanism, the standard psychoanalytic techniques using introspection and observation are useless. The individual patient, though he hears, cannot be reached—though he knows, he will not change. He will avoid the truth with or without outright lies. Though he may pay lip service to treatment, he spends conscious and/or unconscious psychic energy in reinforcing his defensive detachment by a secondary encapsulation. A pastime which has in addition a pleasurable component—the encapsulative shell can be made out of alcohol, drugs, narcotics, homosexuality, delinquency, or just a quiet emotional detachment from all meaningful emotional relationships without necessarily being asocial or antisocial. As a matter of fact, encapsulation could be socially productive; the shell can be reading in the library every spare minute, up in the attic with a stamp collection, down in cellar with the tool chest, out at the links with the golf clubs, or in the office with the patients. The detached person identifies with others with the same shells, which gives him pleasurable reassurance and reinforcement.

If we forcefully remove one means of encapsulation—one shell—such as narcotics, the individual will seek a substitute encapsulation such as alcohol or drugs. To paraphrase Berne, this is the shell game many people play.

Feelings such as fear, anger, guilt, and depression are painful to experience and therefore motivate the affected person to attempt to ameliorate the pain. These feelings may become so painful that they may prevent the neurotic person from functioning; but even if rendered helpless, the person remains in tremendous pain.

On the other hand, people classified as character disorders

are usually suffering no intense pain even though their functioning in many areas is defective, deficient, or absent.

A neurotic, like a person with a toothache, because of severe pain, seeks professional help to alleviate his suffering. He will do anything and everything the professional commands to alleviate the pain. The character disorder, on the other hand, like a person with rotten teeth, feels no pain. Although his personality or teeth are decaying and although he runs the risk of losing all his teeth (or all his functioning) he does not race to the professional, be it doctor or dentist, and frequently, when forced to go for an appointment others made for him, he fails to keep it. He knows his teeth are bad, and he also knows he should go to the dentist, but he fears the dentist will hurt and he knows his teeth don't hurt now. He uses all kinds of rationalizations and excuses for not going to the dentist today, and says, "Perhaps I'll go tomorrow." Of course tomorrow never comes. He occasionally develops an acute toothache and comes running, screaming at the dentist to do something about the pain. When the pain is alleviated, he fails to keep the next appointment to do something for his rotten teeth. If a little pain remains he may take pills or alcohol until the pain goes away in preference to returning to the dentist.

The character disorder, and especially the drug addict, like people with rotten teeth, have little if any internal motivation to seek help. Thus, as Aichhorn observed, this is what we, as professionals, have been up against in the treatment of the character disorder, and the problem is how they can be treated efficiently and successfully psychotherapeutically.

When one uses the primary mechanism of detachment and the secondary mechanism of encapsulation as a defense early; and the more completely these mechanisms are used, the more immature and defective the emotional level and the personality development. A human personality, like a flower, cannot grow in a closed box. When an individual utilizes withdrawal early in life or when an individual even later in life uses withdrawal into emotional detachment as a total defense mechanism, his personality and character stops growing, regresses, and atrophies.

The problem in treatment becomes obvious. To effectuate

treatment one must first remove the encapsulating shell and prevent the individual from withdrawing into detachment by acquiring or running into any other kind of encapsulating shell. Then, once exposed to the light of reality, powerless to isolate himself without his fortress-prison-stockade of an encapsulated shell, he is in a position to be taught how to grow up. For the primary[3] addict, also called the "street" addict—a full-time institutional therapeutic environment must be utilized to enable the individual to grow up and develop emotionally, socially, culturally, ethically, morally, sexually, vocationally, and educationally. This is no small undertaking, but nothing less will suffice; these principles underline our efforts and our treatment techniques at Daytop.

Empirical observations and research at Daytop has found that there are only two proscriptions needed for adequate treatment. They are simple. The proscriptions are (1) no physical violence and (2) no narcotics or other chemicals, and by inference no other shells under which to hide. By these two simple prohibitions we have successfully eliminated fight and withdrawal, two of the three ways an individual uses to cope with pain or danger. There is only one avenue open to him, one reaction open to him, only one mechanism of defense which he can utilize, and that is by reacting to real and imagined stresses and strains, real and imagined pains and dangers—by fear.

Motivated by fear, the addict can do one of two things. He can stay at Daytop and attempt to cope with his fears, or he can run out the door sometimes never to return, frequently to return again at some later date. From the records of our first five and one-half years of experience, we now anticipate that 30 percent of those who come to Daytop will sooner or later remain. We do not know what happens to the other 70 percent who will never return. Perhaps they are dead, perhaps they are in jails, perhaps they are in hospitals, perhaps they are still attempting to be drug addicts, perhaps they have stopped taking drugs themselves, perhaps they are on methadone, or in some other treatment facility. (Eighty percent remain to finish the program at Areba.)

Why does the addict voluntarily stay at Daytop? The key

word is overwhelming identification on the part of the entering addict, genuine love, responsible concern with controls and regulating boundaries on the part of the members. Even though the identification in Freudian terms is that of narcissistic object type, the addicts stay long enough to develop healthier bonds such as anaclitic identification and finally out of a positive transference to the group and facility. They do not do this on their violently destructive terms which poor Mr. Aichhorn had to endure, but on ours which forbid any physical expression of anger.

How does identification at Daytop evolve? First, the addict usually comes in as a last resort, his motivations apparently identical to those seen in the addicts applying for admission to any voluntary institution. There is no place else to go. Frequently, he wants to stay only until the "heat's off" on the outside, or because he is so physically ill and desperate that he needs a haven to rest and rehabilitate. None, early in the Daytop movement, and very few even now, come in with the hope or expectation of really being cured.

> The addict sees the members of Daytop, a few of whom he might have known or heard of on the street, who seem happy and functioning. At first he feels certain that they must be getting their drugs surreptitiously or that they are "conning" him for reasons not yet apparent. But the addict is too tired and sick to think about the reasons. He knows the first thing he has to do is to free himself of the physiological need. He is dismayed when he learns he has to do this without the aid of any drugs. As he stays at Daytop, he is surprised that he goes through "cold turkey" relatively painlessly in contrast to the unbearable pains he experienced while he was in jails, hospitals, and on the street. People about him are busy talking, eating, lecturing, working, ironing, listening to music. He finds himself being drawn into conversation or being a fourth for cards. If the pains get too severe, someone offers to massage his muscles, or take him down to the showers. It becomes a matter of personal pride to ignore the pains as much as possible. He is aware that everyone around him has gone through the same thing, and he doesn't want to be considered weak.[3]

This is just the opposite of what happens outside of Daytop, where the more he complains, the more sympathy he hopes to obtain and the higher his status for having been a "junky" with a large habit.

After a few days, the addict feels a little chagrined and very surprised at having "kicked" with comparatively little pain, discomfort, or exhibitionism. He feels the others have tricked him into diminishing his addiction and his pains. He feels rather helpless, because behavior patterns he used on the street in reference to kicking the habit had no chance of being utilized here. He feels unmasked in front of "ex-hypes" who seem to know his every thought, mood and feeling. They good-naturedly ridicule and laugh at any attempt he makes at "conning" the group into pitying or babying him. But they are not hostile to him, nor is he rejected by them. *It is as if he cannot communicate with the members of Daytop using his patterns of thinking, feeling, and behavior from the street. Only if he listens to them and does what he is told does he feel he is in communication.* He starts to plan to leave as soon as he's strong enough. He is surprised to find the group can read his mind. They good-naturedly laugh at him as one would who sees an infant struggling to walk. They tell him, "Wait till the three-month depression sets in." They play on his curiosity and challenge his manhood to stick it out. By this time, the new member begins to realize the older members are really off "junk" and they really are as happy and as well as they say they are.

A new awareness emerges. At this time, the addict begins to wonder what Daytop is all about. He asks questions. He starts to cooperate. He goes to work. He does what he is told to do. He accepts the statement, "The only thing a junky knows when he gets here is how to shoot dope." He accepts the criticism in his everyday relationships and the exaggerated ridicule and hostilities in the Daytop group encounters. He learns to think and communicate verbally in planned seminars and to talk out during organized public-speaking periods. He finds, and is surprised to see, that his behavior is changing. He gleefully "Daytops" the newer members. He is constantly reminded of his own sickness by seeing the newest members in their days of illness.

He becomes involved in a job-status system at Daytop. He

attempts to get off the dishpan and toilet details. His pathologically aggressive or seductive manipulative attempts to prove himself are picked up immediately by the group. Again, he is embarrassed, ridiculed, scolded, laughed at. By his new association and his new environment, his "code of the streets" values change. It is now a matter of honor to "squeal" on oneself and others. The Daytop law of being honest with yourself and others takes hold. No secret, no matter how personal, has any immunity —there is no pleading the Fifth Amendment. One's past and present behavior and thoughts are now opened to everyone's inspection.

At this point, after three to six months in Daytop, the second critical time of awareness is reached. The ninety-day "hump," as they call it, is the hour of departure for some, because they cannot take the pain of emerging emotional self-awareness. At last they are beginning to become aware that their manipulative behavior really cannot work; they begin to realize just how irresponsible they really are and what a mess they have made of their lives. As the repressed and unconscious feelings become conscious, the pain of depression, the panic of fear and the dread of strong guilt of greater or lesser intensity develops. Some awaken with frequent repetitive nightmares, just as people who were in concentration camps develop nightmares *after* they are freed from their imprisonment. Those who do leave Daytop are usually pleading to return within one week. On leaving, they may again take the narcotic way into a world of insensitivity to pain, but to their great surprise *and panic* they find the drugs no longer effective in the same way. They have become too aware of the real world to be lulled into a false sense of security by heroin. It is only through the constant understanding and support and examples in the environment that the members are able to weather the emotional storm.

Thus, in Daytop, the addicts find they are living through emotional pain they once thought impossible to bear without drugs. And they live through it without the help of drugs, alcohol, narcotics, or even tranquilizers.

This brings the addict to a third level of awareness, when he says to himself, "I *am* able to live in the stream of life without pills or narcotics." This new awareness, plus the senior members' statements that "this depression won't last" and the constructive work in which he is now engaged, gradually brings the addict out of his depression.

Entering then onto a fourth level of awareness, the addict now reevaluates everything that has gone on before. He is now a "missionary" in search of "gut-level" truth. This is a term used in Daytop to describe the purely emotional, resonant, honest feelings that are comparable with those of people in analysis who have finally felt their visceral affective feelings. The addict is no longer so afraid to face himself. This stage appears to last for about another year. During this time he is emotionally maturing. He has found a purpose and a positive direction in life. He reports his subjective feelings and attitudes, which he realizes are immature. He "cops out" spontaneously in the Daytop group therapy sessions called encounters. He attempts to become objectively critical of his own performance. He is surprised to be offered better jobs in Daytop, jobs that he may now feel unworthy to accept, but that six months before seemed beneath him. This feeling of unworthiness and inadequacy is now attacked by others in and out of the encounters as being neurotic. And so the process goes for another year. By the end of eighteen to twenty-four months a new personailty has emerged —one starkly different from that of the "dope fiend" who entered.

While he stays, the member is given two prescriptions which the boys at Daytop call (1) "Go through the motions and do the thing," and (2) "Act as if." By "going through the motions and doing the thing" they mean you have to do as you are told whether you like it or not, or sensible or not, or rational or not. As a matter of fact, Daytop doesn't care what the individual thinks or feels about it. They insist that the member do what he is told to do, and by so doing, he goes through the motions. When an individual complains that he doesn't exactly know how to do what he is told, he is then given prescription number 2. "Act as if."

Act as if you knew what to do.
Act as if you had the experience.

Act as if you are mature.
Act as if it's going to be successful.
Act as if you are going to grow up and get well.
Act as if you are already well and adult.

I've noticed that when people go through the motions of acting as if, they start thinking as if, and finally feeling as if. The time lag between acting as if one can get well, for instance, and feeling as if one could get well, takes about three to six months.

Treatment can also be understood and used as a communication and educational technique. An entering member is taught first to identify, understand, verbalize, and express his feelings in a comprehensible fashion. He is taught and made aware that those undifferentiated somatic painful feelings that he has experienced on a visceral and emotional level, those feelings that he has never allowed to emerge on a conscious intellectual level, are nothing more than fear, anger, guilt, and depression; emotions experienced by all humanity, and not some exclusive emotion which only the individual himself has a monopoly on. He later learns that these feelings are not exclusive to what he felt was the mystical, para-human called the drug addict. As his defensive tools, crutches, and weapons are removed, he becomes aware that there is no difference between himself and others like him, and there is no difference between others like him and the rest of humanity.

The tools of communication and education used at Daytop are as follows:

1. The encounter, which is a form of group therapy for the creation of aggressive and provocative interchange. They differ most from conventional group therapy by frequently becoming verbally violent and openly hostile though some of the group members are experienced in the techniques of the encounter. The encounters are basically focused on the "here and now" feelings of the individual.

2. The thirty-hour-plus continuous group therapy sessions called marathons.

3. The seminars.

4. Public speaking periods.

5. The psychodynamic probes, which are an attempt to have the individual understand his personality structures.

6. The community relations which are an essential part of Daytop.

7. The lectures.

8. The rituals and rites of passage, such as the intake process and indoctrination process, the entering of a regular membership after a month, the Daytop birthday celebration after a year's residency, and the primitive rituals to maintain discipline called the pull-up, the haircut, and the general meeting.

All these are communication techniques native to a therapeutic environment which is patterned as a highly organized, paternalistic, tribe-like family structure. The use of status and mobility are therapeutic tools used for growth and development, as is the total relationship between the members at work and at play.

The patriarchal structure gives approval for performance only. The individuals are constantly given achievable goals; all jobs are necessary and carry with them appropriate status. There is only one environment, and not the we/they environment seen in prisons and hospitals like we, the sick patients, and they, the well doctors; or we, the criminals and they, our jailers.[3]

Most recently this author has introduced still another group process radically different from any other. It is called the New Identity Group Process. A method has finally been evolved that markedly accelerates the emotional reeducation that all need.*

We have reviewed here the psychodynamic and theoretical foundations used as the basis of the approach along with some clinical comments and actual techniques used at Daytop,† as an illustration of one of the most flagrant caricatures of the acting-out personality, the drug addict.

---

* This will be described in detail in a book to be called *A Scream Away from Happiness,* to be published in Winter, 1972 by Grosset and Dunlap.

† A detailed study of Daytop appeared in a book by the author published by Hill and Wang in the Fall, 1971.

REFERENCES

1. Aichhorn, A.: *Wayward Youth.* New York, Meridian Books, 1935.
2. *American Handbook of Psychiatry.* New York, Basic Books, 1959, pp. 614-623.
3. Casriel, D. H.: *So Fair a House—The Story of Synanon.* Englewood Cliffs, N. J., Prentice Hall, 1963.
4. Kardiner, A.; Karush, A., and Ovesey, L.: A methodological study of Freudian theory: IV. the structural hypothesis, the problem of anxiety, and post-Freudian ego psychology. *J. Nerv. Ment. Dis.,* 129(4):354, 1959.
5. Noyes, A. P., and Kolb, L. C.: *Modern Clinical Psychiatry,* 5th ed. Philadelphia, Saunders, 1958, p. 57.
6. Rado, S.: The Psychoanalysis of pharmacothymia. *Psychoanal. Quart.,* 2:1-23, 1933.

D<small>R</small>. R<small>UTH</small> F<small>OX</small> is a physician who has achieved national prominence for her work with alcoholics. The acting out of the alcoholic is given a global perspective in that Dr. Fox comprehensively integrates the medical aspects with its psychological and social concomitants.

Dr. Fox begins her paper by presenting the etiology of alcoholism and describing the character traits she frequently found in the four thousand alcoholic patients she has treated. She includes a discussion of the short-term and long-term physiological effects of drinking on the body. Dr. Fox stresses that the focus and course of acting out is dependent upon the alcoholic's background and underlying personality structure. She then extends her elaboration beyond excessive drinking to other problematic areas in living for the alcoholic.

The next section of the paper is devoted to psychotherapeutic techniques that have been successful in treating alcoholics including the use of Alcoholics Anonymous, group therapy, psychodrama, drug therapy, marathons and encounters. Dr. Fox concludes with a brief summary of the alcoholic's symptoms and corresponding treatment methods.

Thus, Dr. Ruth Fox offers us a lucid and well-balanced understanding of the character structure and acting-out behavior of the alcoholic, indicating and elucidating a wide range of therapeutic possibilities.

D.S.M.
G.D.G.

Chapter 14

Overall Treatment of the Alcoholic

RUTH FOX

ALTHOUGH THE ORIGINAL title for this chapter was "Acting Out in the Alcoholic," after much thought I have taken the liberty of changing the title to "The Overall Treatment of the Alcoholic." The reason for this change is to give a more well-rounded perspective than the totally psychoanalytic one that the original title would imply. I believe the alcoholic to be an ill person with not only psychological and social problems but also an underlying chemical or metabolic disturbance which cannot be ignored. When one sees a severe alcoholic while he is drinking or in the severe withdrawal stage, which is characterized by a totally irresistible urge to continue drinking or may develop into delirium tremens or convulsive seizures, one is dealing with a serious *medical* emergency. Though he needs psychological understanding and much support and encouragement, conventional analytic psychotherapy *alone* is totally ineffective. The mortality rate in delirium tremens, if not properly treated medically, can reach 15 to 20 percent and probably much higher in the individual who never gets into a hospital for the medication he needs. At times like this the term "acting out" focuses on a relatively unimportant aspect of the total picture and since these complications nearly always occur *eventually* in the severe and untreated alcoholic, they cannot be overlooked. Unless the alcoholic is treated not only psychologically but medically, socially, and spiritually, the chances of recovery are extremely slim.

Of the many definitions of alcoholism one of the most satisfactory, I believe, is that of Morris Chafetz: "Alcoholism is a chronic behavioral disturbance which is manifested by undue preoccupation with alcohol to the detriment of physical and mental health, by a loss of control when drinking has begun, and by a self-destructive attitude in dealing with personal relationships and life situations."[9] But it is also an addiction.

Most psychiatrists look on alcoholism as primarily a form of neurosis and ignore the fact that it is primarily an addiction which has both physiologic and emotional components. As an individual finds that some drive is satisfied by alcohol, he tends to repeat the experience of drinking more and more often and becomes emotionally dependent upon it. Alcohol may gradually become his chief source of pleasure, as well as his chief tranquilizer. He may fail to use other avenues of self-expression, may not develop the skills of life through the trial and error techniques, and may avoid facing and dealing with his difficulties as they arise in a realistic manner. He may thus become dependent and addicted. This can readily happen to the shy, introverted, awkward, anxious, and conflicted adolescent or young person because alcohol at first seems to solve all his problems. Actually, his performance may begin to suffer early, by his dropping out of school, a poor work record, and unsatisfactory personal relationships. Underlying all this is an immature personality.[23]

Another adolescent or young adult may find surcease from the pain of a deep-seated neurosis showing itself in phobias, obsessive-compulsive behavior, or hysterical reactions. Alcohol may serve as a temporary solution for his feelings of inferiority, panic, conflicts, or sexual problems. Underlying his alcoholism is a neurotic constitution. He may rather quickly become addicted to alcohol.

Borderline or overt psychotics may also turn to alcohol and add addiction to alcohol rather quickly to their already excessive mental and emotional burdens. But there is another group of persons, not noticeably immature, neurotic, or psychotic, who also can become alcoholic. These are the excessive social drinkers whose drinking gradually increases over the years, although it may take ten to fifteen to twenty years of this excess before the addictive process takes over.[6] These individuals differ markedly from the immature or neurotic or psychotic alcoholic in that they have in the past used normal avenues of self-expression to which they can revert after giving up alcohol.[23]

As the addictive process grows, all alcoholics, no matter what their background, tend to become very much alike in their behavior. It is as though the disease of alcoholism molds them into a stereotyped reaction.[39] Starting off with merely a mild social or psychological dependence, a physiologic dependence is added. This shows itself by changes in tissue tolerance, adaptive cell metabolism, withdrawal symptoms, and the phenomenon of craving, all of which leads to a loss of control over drinking.[34]

Added to this emotional and physiologic dependence, there may develop certain organic diseases such as cirrhosis of the liver, polyneuropathy, chronic brain syndrome, Korsakoff's psychosis, and so forth, either as a result of the toxic effect of alcohol over many years or as a result of the unhygienic way the alcoholic lives, neglecting food, and rest, having frequent accidents, and so on. These diseases are not per se a part of the addictive process but are really a by-product or consequence of the addiction which may cause the individual to feel so ill that recovery is often difficult.[14]

The many psychologic studies on alcoholics have failed to reveal a specific prealcoholic personality. These studies, of course, have all been done on individuals who are already addicted and may reflect a regression in the personality due to the addictive process rather than the basic character structure of the individual. During an active addiction the addict is undoubtedly a seriously disturbed person unable to cope with the realities of life. As the addiction increasingly controls his life, the individual's behavior becomes grossly nonadaptive. To obtain more of the drug may be the most important thing in the world, so that responsibilities toward family, job, and society no longer matter. The lying, sneaking of drinks, and the use of household money are not, however, measures of the moral integrity of the alcoholic but are rather an indication of his great need to maintain his addiction and to prevent the almost unbearable withdrawal symptoms.[25] When sober, the alcoholic often feels trapped, afraid, alone, and deeply guilty—unless, of course, he is psychopathic. Convinced that he cannot live without alcohol, he builds up an elaborate defense system in which he denies that he is alcoholic and ill. rationalizes that he needs to drink for business or social reasons, and projects the blame for the trouble he is in on the persons nearest to him, usually the spouse, the family,[30] or the boss. The normal longings for recognition, prestige, and love become less and less attainable as the addiction advances, so that the alcoholic feels less and less worthy, less and less secure, and less and less loved. This downward spiral is intolerable to the alcoholic, so that he resorts to drinking again unless he can get the outside help he needs.

A battery of psychologic tests done on three hundred consecutive private patients showed gross disturbance in each case. Although not conforming to any one personality type, these patients showed markedly similar character traits. Characteristic of them all was low frustration tolerance and an inability to endure anxiety or tension. All showed depression, with emotional withdrawal, a sense of isolation, extremely low self-esteem, sensitiveness, and a masochistic type of self-punishing behavior. Dependency strivings were very marked, frustration of which led to depression or hostility and rage. Most showed impulsive repetitive acting out of conflicts on a superficial level. In all cases there was a marked hostility and rebellion with defiance against authority figures, and almost all showed problems in the sexual area. The tests were administered after a few weeks of sobriety and indicate either a fixation at an immature level or a regression to such a state. Many of these traits were markedly lessened after therapy.[22]

With such gross disturbance in the psyche each individual will need therapy of some sort, but what kind of therapy cannot be decided upon until sobriety has been attained and a personality assessment undertaken. Psychiatrists can then use their traditional skills with marked benefit to the patient, provided they also recognize and treat the addiction itself.

Psychotic alcoholics may need prolonged hospitalization, although borderline schizophrenics may often be carried successfully on an outpatient basis, provided they maintain sobriety. The neurotic alcoholic may need prolonged psychotherapy, often psychoanalysis. The immature alcoholic may need support for a long time as he matures, while the individual who has become addicted in later life, and has developed in the past a better integrated personality, may do extremely well with a minimum of therapy, provided he can be convinced that he is alcoholic and can therefore never drink again. Even in these cases, a few weeks or months of therapy may be needed while he is learning about his illness and adjusting to a life of sobriety.

Alcoholism has become a way of life which is no longer tenable, and therapy is largely that of helping the individual to find a new way to live. The prevailingly negative, fearful, and hostile feeling tone must be replaced by a more positive attitude with hope, self-confidence, courage, a faith in himself, and a feeling of belonging.

Because of the long years when drinking alcohol was pleasurable and rewarding, it will never be given up without a struggle. Glamorized by our society as the smart and sophisticated thing to do, drinking has become an integral part of our lives.[25] The alcoholic cannot understand why it has to be denied to him, why he has become addicted to it, when 90 percent of those who drink do not. Not until the consequences of his alcoholism force the alcoholic to give it up, will he even think of doing so. It usually takes a crisis such as the loss of a job or family or prestige or health to convince the alcoholic that he must give it up. He needs to suffer the consequences of his self-destructive way of life. Confronted with the crisis, he first tries to drink moderately and finds that he cannot. He next tries going on the wagon and finds this only of temporary relief. Finally, convinced that sobriety is his only answer, he despairs because he does not believe he can live without alcohol, and unless he can envision a life without alcohol as more rewarding than one with it, he will not give it up. The doctor must give him hope and encouragement.

As with any other long-time chronic disease, relapses are to be expected early in treatment and the doctor should show the same patience and understanding that he would if a patient with asthma or gastric ulcer relapses. A calm discussion as to why the relapse occurred can help in understanding the dynamics underlying the case. As therapy progresses, the relapses will occur less frequently and will be of shorter duration. We cannot force the alcoholic to stop drinking, but we can create a climate in which he can recover.

Attention must be paid to every aspect of the patient's life, and rehabilitation or "redirection" must be physical, psychologic, social, and spiritual, a task which is too great for any one person to undertake. It is for this reason that the team approach is often used in clinics and hospitals for alcoholics. Recovered alcoholics can be of invaluable assistance.[2]

It is difficult to understand the acting-out propensity of the alcoholic without first understanding something of the many and various underlying dynamisms involved.[16] It is a mistake to consider alcoholism as an entity since all kinds of persons who can tolerate alcohol at all can become addicted to it if they drink enough for a long enough period of time. Alcoholism is a disturbance of behavior with many determinants, some social, some psychological, and some physiochemical. As in all addictions, there is not only an emotional dependence on the drug but a physiological one as well, which partly, at least, accounts for the craving to continue drinking when the blood level of alcohol begins to fall. Alcohol is also an anesthetic, a poison which when taken in excessive amounts can grossly disorganize an individual's psychic processes, causing a temporary psychosis. By abolishing the inhibitory functions of the cortex, it causes all sorts of repressed and unacceptable impulses to be expressed which no more represent the basic personality of the individual than would the actions of a person emerging from the anesthetic effects of ether. No organ of the body escapes damage unless drinking is extremely moderate.[38]

Alcoholism cuts across all segments of the population, the rich, the poor, the bright, the stupid, the socially, artistically or intellectually gifted, as well as those not so well-endowed. Of the 6 to 8 million alcoholics in the United States, only 3 to 5 percent are on skid row. Another 20 to 30 percent may have a psychotic, psychopathic, or severely neurotic underlying condition as well as their addiction to alcohol. Many also show traits of an underlying depression, immaturity, character disorder, etc. Nevertheless, after sobriety is well-established, I believe that 70 to 80 percent function well in society, working in industry,[17, 49] the professions, the arts, living in a family setting, and carrying on as near a normal life as most of the rest of us. In the early stages they do not know that they are becoming dependent on alcohol and will vehemently deny that their drinking is any different from that of their often excessively drinking companions. Unfortunately for their drinking friends this all too often is true. It is not until they get into serious difficulties because of it, with threatened or actual loss of job, or family, or prestige, or reputation, or health, that they will admit they do have a problem. Many will "hit bottom" by losing fortunes, friends, social position, injuring themselves or others through accidents such as fires, drunken driving, fights, jail sentences, etc. As their disease progresses, their ostracism and isolation become progressively more painful and complete, until they finally feel completely shut out from participation in the normal activities of life. No alcoholic wishes to drink the way he does, and he keeps vainly hoping that he can recapture again the ability to drink moderately. We don't honestly know why he cannot—whether the defect is constitutional, either inborn or acquired, whether it is merely a learned or conditioned response,[26, 51] as the behaviorists would have us believe, or whether it is a blind, compulsive acting out of unconscious conflicts. In any event, it seems that an irreversible metabolic change has occurred so that the alcoholic can never return to normal social drinking. Of course, there are also psychological and social factors.[34]

Though most psychiatrists insist that alcoholism can occur only in the neurotic individual, I myself, after working with well over four thousand alcoholics in the past thirty-five years, believe that it is possible for even a reasonably well-adjusted individual to become addicted to alcohol merely through long years of daily heavy drinking. Having then become addicted, he shows all of the psychological, social, chemical, and physical deterioration of the individual who has been alcoholic for much of his adult life.*

Recent studies, especially those of Stanley Gitlow, show that

_____

* The pronoun "he" is used throughout, though there are in our large cities and suburbs about as many women alcoholics as men.[24]

there are profound chemical changes brought about by the action of alcohol on the central nervous system which profoundly affect behavior. Gitlow has pointed out that there is a double action of alcohol, a short period of relaxation of about two hours duration which masks a longer-acting increase in psychomotor activity. This shows itself in a markedly increasing tension, anxiety, and nervousness. If the drinking is heavy, this tension can be almost unbearable so that the patient resorts to more and more alcohol to gain an all too short respite from it.[28] As the effects of the excess of alcohol increase, the behavior becomes more and more disturbed and distorted. It is probably inaccurate to speak of this extremely regressive, drunken behavior as "acting out" in the usual psychoanalytic sense. Perhaps that term should be reserved for the behavior of the immature alcoholic when he is abstinent. Even then many of his actions and moods may be grossly influenced by the results of his recent drunken actions. Guilt, shame, frustration, anger, self-pity, a devastating loneliness, despair, isolation, and rejection may overwhelm him and he then may react to this by his acting out. His behavior represents immature methods of dealing with, to him, overly stressful situations.

As he gains sobriety of a more lasting nature, one may find a person who still has a great propensity to "act out"—or one may find a reasonable, fairly well-adjusted individual. After years of sobriety many alcoholics adjust to life very well. Others, who were immature or neurotic before their addiction set in, may need considerable therapy to attain maturity.

Addicted persons who have in childhood received the normal amount of both love and discipline from both parents are more apt to become addicted, if they do at all, later in life and though they frequently need support and guidance as they attain sobriety, their prognosis for permanent recovery is very good.

On the other hand, many alcoholics come from homes where there has been great emotional deprivation. Family life has been scarred by death, desertion, divorce, insanity, alcoholism, drug addiction, poverty, quarreling, etc. Some mothers have been unpredictable, harassed, and unhappy, at times overprotecting and at other times impatient, rejecting, and overcontrolling toward the child. Many of the fathers were passive, submissive to the dominating wife, indifferent to the children, and frequently or permanently absent from the home.* Some took out their own frustrations on the children, lashing out at them with severe and unjustified punishments. Other fathers were driving successes, egocentric, selfish, overbearing, tyrannical, and belittling to the wife and children. Frequently both parents expected perfect performance from their children while breaking rule after rule themselves.[19] Unsure of themselves, neither parent was able to set necessary limits for the child's behavior and was unable to transmit to the child the sense of responsibility needed to mature into an independent adult.[33] As role models neither parent could be considered satisfactory nor was the child ever taught consistently what his own role should be.[41]

It is significant that 52 percent of a large series of several thousand alcoholics had a father or mother or both who were alcoholic.[34] It has been estimated also that alcoholism will occur in some of the children of about 35 percent of alcoholics.[31] Thus, though alcoholism has not been proven to be genetically determined, it often "runs in families" and might be considered "contagious." Many factors, such as disturbed or inadequate family training, imitation or identification with the alcoholic parent, difficulty in adjusting to a frequently disturbed non-alcoholic parent, may all play determining roles in the future development of the child of the alcoholic. One sometimes feels that becoming an alcoholic may depend upon the presence of five factors: frequently an adverse childhood situation (with alcoholism in a parent being but *one* of various possible deviances); often the failure of a good psychological maturation in childhood; a *possible* biochemical abnormality which renders the individual addiction-prone; a currently existing psychological and/or social situation which leads to unhappiness; and lastly the availability of the drug alcohol and the association with heavily drinking companions who act as a constant push toward drinking. Of course the proportion each factor plays will vary

---

* McCord, Wm. and Joan: *Origins of Alcoholism.* Stanford University Press, 1960. This book gives an excellent study of the family backgrounds of adolescent boys who later became alcoholics.

greatly. One recent estimate is that about 58 percent of narcotic addicts are the products of alcoholic homes.[31]

Even children from a wealthy environment may be emotionally deprived and therefore vulnerable to delinquent, deviant, or alcoholic behavior. They enter adolescence heavily burdened with immature and neurotic traits, with low self-regard, shy, depressed, or with hostile, grandiose or rebellious attitudes. They are often uncertain of their sex roles, are anxious, and may act out by delinquent behavior which may show itself in heavy drinking, or drug taking, dropping out of school, stealing, rioting, running away, staying out all night, being defiant, etc., in an attempt to be "grown up," manly, and sophisticated. Many of these feelings can be carried on into adult life and tend to become fixed in the personality. Feeling insecure and frightened, these individuals may overcompensate, professing a bravado they do not feel. They may act arrogantly, overbearingly, see themselves as unique, special, and therefore justified in making inordinate demands on others which when thwarted, drive them into vindictive rages which threaten to overwhelm them. They are in deep conflict, have little sense of their real identity, have few long-term goals, are torn between a wish to be dependent and a wish to be independent. Some retreat into a fantasy world in which they feel omnipotent and will brook no interference. Beneath this front lies a frightened child, no matter what his or her chronological age may be.

Alcohol can temporarily dispel anxiety and conflict or raise the level of self-esteem, giving the alcoholic an exalted sense of his powers, a feeling of masculinity, and a sense of belonging. He sees himself as he would like to be—omnipotent, clever, brilliant, successful. Is it any wonder he drinks? The rewards are great and immediate, and there is little effort involved in getting these rewards. Alcohol temporarily seems to solve all his neurotic and existential problems so that his drinking can be looked on as an attempt at self-cure. The normal, well-adjusted social drinker derives pleasure from drinking, but he does not use it as a means of dealing with deep-seated emotional problems.

Behind what seems like a simple wish to drink, there is, however, in the alcoholic of any age, a whole complicated structure of dynamic factors underlying it which do not occur in the moderate social drinker. To understand his so-called "acting-out behavior" disturbances—and alcoholism is one of the most frequent—requires an understanding of psychoanalytic principles, especially as regards the phenomena of the unconscious determinants of behavior, the concept of transference, and the concept of resistance to change. Silverberg discusses acting out as follows:

> There is a type of patient who is forever acting out, both within the analytic situation and outside of it. By the term "acting out" I mean that the patient, instead of discussing a specific phase of his difficulties and attempting to understand it by means of verbal formulation, gives it vivid and graphic expression in a piece of behavior. He is impelled, by motives he does not understand, to behave in the specific way involved. Sometimes, particularly after frequent repetitions of the same piece of behavior, he is aware of its irrationality or he may at least have doubts of its complete rationality. For the most part, however, patients attempt to rationalize their acting out and often have little difficulty in producing rationalizations eminently satisfactory and convincing to themselves.[47]

Anyone working with alcoholics on either an individual basis or in a group setting has ample opportunity to see this type of rationalized acting out. To blame is a nagging wife, a sometimes true but often distorted "memory" of a rejecting parent, an unappreciative boss, a fancied slight, etc.[20]

The repetitiousness, the futility, the irrationality, the lack of any permanently pleasurable outcome, and the flimsy rationalizations all attest to the frequent transference nature of the alcoholic's actions. The alcoholic "transfers" to current situations and persons old attitudes, feelings, jealousies, hates, loves, and beliefs from the past. To accept the fact that there are realistic forces, both human and physical, over which we have no control, is an idea foreign to the alcoholic. Yet recovery cannot take place until he does concede this.[47, 48]

Acting out can be regarded as a way of avoiding by psychomotor behavior the anxiety caused by conflicts, both interpersonal and intrapsychic. The patient acts rather than thinks or plans. Delany states it well: "Acting out is bringing fantasy into real situations with people. It is a working out in the environment of an internal conscious or unconscious fantasy."[12] The alcoholic acts out not only through his uncontrolled and destructive drinking, but also in many areas of his life where he may have grossly distorted relations with his spouse, his children, his parents, his employer or employees, and in his social and civic contacts. Though held somewhat in check when sober, the acting out in relation to the therapeutic situation may show itself in arriving late, missing appointments without notice, coming in inebriated, arguing about nonessential matters, being rude, leaving in a huff, etc. How these situations are handled in therapy is important, for they generally denote a state of acute anxiety in the patient. A negative countertransference can drive the patient away for good. In a group setting these negative reactions are hopefully well-handled by the group itself.[20] Along with condemning the act, the group also gives the necessary emotional support. Members of the group can often spot the familiar defenses of the alcoholic: denial that he is suffering from the disease of alcoholism, or at least minimizing its importance; rationalizing that he *needs* to drink for any one of several reasons; and projecting the blame for the trouble he is in on someone else, often the person nearest to him—wife, husband, mother, employer, etc.[16]

The type and extent of acting out when drunk depend a great deal on the background of the intoxicated individual. With the middle and upper income group of educated people, the acting out is *generally* not so wild or violent as it is in those of the lower stratum of society. Women of the upper classes can often hide their alcoholism for a long time even from their husbands, and, because they are too ashamed to be seen drunk, do most of their drinking in their own bedrooms. As they progress in their illness, however, there is the inevitable lowering of standards, the sense of shame, loneliness, self-hate, depression, and frustration. When the husband becomes disgusted and begins to withdraw his emotional support, the wife not only becomes frightened that he will leave her but may become vindictive as well. One wife hacked up all the furniture in their apartment after the husband refused to kiss her in the morning after she had kept him awake all night with her drunken abuse. She then slashed to ribbons all of his suits, coats, and underwear with razor blades. After she sobered up, she was so deeply ashamed of this behavior, of which she had no memory, that she forthwith joined Alcoholics Anonymous and has remained sober for the past eight years. Another man, president of an important firm, chartered a plane for South America when drunk and woke up in Lima, Peru, penniless and with no memory whatsoever of his trip and no inkling of why he had done it. Since he was a self-made man with a deprived background, we might conjecture that this grandiose bit of acting out made him feel important.

Patients may act out their infantile needs not only by drinking, but by various acts even when not drinking—by aggressive behavior, demanding attention, refusing to work, maneuvering their family or friends into supporting them, causing confusion by infantile rage reactions and violent, angry outbursts, by truancy, threats of suicide, self-injury, throwing up a job, walking out on the family, etc.

The type of acting out among alcoholics also varies greatly, depending on the underlying personality types. A psychotic who is also alcoholic may show extremely bizarre behavior when intoxicated, whereas in sobriety he may be able to manage at least marginally. One paranoid schizophrenic when drunk would expose his genitals, chase people with knives, and showed a well-defined paranoid reaction—the food was poisoned, the living room was wired, the devil was out to get him, attendants were all monsters, etc., and he himself was God. Within hours after the alcohol had been eliminated, he reverted to his old self, rather schizoid and *slightly* paranoid but able to continue a responsible job he had held for many years. Another ambulatory schizophrenic girl would fly into rages when drunk and would mutilate herself, sticking pins in her arms and hacking off all her hair, acts which she deeply regretted after the drunken episode was over. In spite of two to three short episodes of this kind a year, she is able to work fairly regularly if she does not resort to drinking.

Though formerly I felt that alcohol might be used as a defense against psychosis (and perhaps it sometimes is), I have had many ambulatory schizoprenics and cyclothymic personalities who function fairly well outside of a hospital if they can remain sober. Alcohol totally disorganizes them and they then need a short- or long-term stay in a hospital.

Acting out among psychopathic alcoholics can be dangerously antisocial, with beatings of the wife and children, stealing, writing worthless checks, promiscuity, prostitution, perversions, rape, wild homosexual experiences, etc. Such behavior should be considered as characteristic of the psychopathic personality with absence of or severe deficits in the superego structure, and not as entirely due to the superimposed alcoholism. In my experience, even though it is possible to bring the drinking in these individuals to an end, the antisocial acting out continues as before. Though the psychopathic individual may have anxiety, it is usually merely a fear that he will be caught and not an inner conviction that his behavior is in any way wrong. This is in sharp contrast to the usual alcoholic who, after an episode of severe drinking, feels deep remorse and an overwhelming guilt and sense of worthlessness.

Alcoholics who have deep-seated neurotic problems, as well as their addiction, run the gamut of symptoms. Among them there are many who are phobic, hysterical, obsessive, depersonalized, compulsive, overconforming, schizoid, helplessly dependent on a partner, masochistic, sadistic, chronically depressed, etc. The list could be almost endless.

Many alcoholics, however, fall in the class of character disorders, a loose conglomerate of inadequate personality traits which range from the severely unhappy to the fairly well-controlled, though often conflicted, individuals.[43] They show Horney's "basic anxiety."[32] Projective tests show many disturbances, such as unbearable tension, fears of social situations, alienation from the self and others, and irreconcilable conflicts. There may be a lack of self-identification, a feeling of fragmentation, inability to judge others as friendly or unfriendly, impulsive acting out with regrets and guilt feelings, ambivalence, suggestibility on the one hand and stubbornness on the other. Most are extremely sensitive and vulnerable to criticism, which denotes a weak ego structure and an exceedingly poor and nebulous self-image. Many show confusion as to their sexual role, and some seem fixated at the pregenital level. The superego may be harsh, punitive, and archaic or it may show "lacunae," i.e. it may be effective in some areas and not in others. Instinctual drives may be inhibited, leading to restrained, cautious behavior, rigidity, a lack of spontaneity, and an inability to enjoy life. If the instinctual drives, on the other hand, are not under control of the ego, there can be gross acting out with a feeling that the world should gratify their every whim. Since this is impossible, the individual may become demanding, abusive, enraged, and threatening.

Different defenses are used in the various character disorders, the compulsive characters often using reaction formations, isolation, and withdrawal from life with rigid repression of the id impulses. Occasionally the underlying sadistic and anal components may break through. The oral characters, though narcissistic and vain, can be generous and giving, provided there is always a "source of supply." If not, there is depression, rage, exploitation, and revenge. The schizoid type is withdrawn, shy, and lives in fantasy in an autistic world. The paranoid type is suspicious, thinks others are out to harm him, and is generally jealous and envious.

While the individual is in the active stage of his alcoholism, there is a disturbance in the normal inhibiting function with little capacity to delay action, to tolerate aggression, anxiety, or frustration, to maintain lasting and loving object relationships, to learn from experience, and little ability to think abstractly. Life tends to be lived according to the pleasure principle, which creates difficulties in the environment. Owing to fixation or regression, the patient continues to act as he did in early childhood, and he has lost mastery over his impulses. He may revert to truly psychopathic behavior when he is drunk. When sober he often has excellent control over his aberrant impulses, can deny them, sublimate them, or change them through reaction formations. If his impulsivity can be checked, this may help him bind his anxiety and thus help him to desist in his acting out.

PSYCHOTHERAPY OF THE ALCOHOLIC

In treatment of the alcoholic, one must be aware of the many functions alcohol may have played in his life, not only in helping him to cope with his neurotic conflicts, but insofar as it has often become his chief source of pleasure, allowing him to feel friendly, manly, or feminine, relaxed, worthy, lovable, generous, witty, carefree, and original. We must, however, try to convince him that these feelings of well-being when drunk are not only illusory and temporary but are paid for with awful pain and misery in the long run after addiction occurs. Pointing out these negative factors alone is rarely ever effective, however, and one must put the emphasis on the fact that life can be better without alcohol than with it. One must point out and foster all the healthy elements of the personality and build up enough motivation in the patient so that he will be willing to undertake the long, hard battle toward permanent sobriety. He will need help in his struggle to overcome the ever-present pressures to drink, pressures from within himself as well as from his environment.[23]

An analytic type of therapy aimed primarily toward the production of insights into the "whys" of drinking can be spectacularly ineffective until and unless the drinking can first be stopped. Though this is a direct intervention aimed at symptom removal, it is a necessary first step before one can evaluate the underlying personality. As in most of the acting-out disorders— alcoholism, delinquency, homosexuality, etc.—the aim should be to help the patient control his antisocial behavior by helping him to find a more rewarding type of life, by enhancing his sense of worth, by helping him find substitute gratifications. That even deep analysis rarely helps the alcoholic unless he stops drinking early in therapy can be illustrated by one case of mine, a psychoanalyst himself, who had had seventeen years of analysis trying to determine *why* he drank. He grew steadily worse, lost his professional standing, his family, etc., because no analyst had ever emphasized to him the need to stop drinking first if progress was to be made. He finally went on Antabuse®, stopped drinking for the last seven years of his life and had only one "slip" when he stopped the Antabuse for just "one evening's holiday." The disastrous effects of this loss of control while taking part in an important psychoanalytic convention put him immediately back on Antabuse, which he took for the rest of his life. After this relapse he made the wise observation that "one martini threw all my hard-earned insights out the window." Later in teaching young analysts he stressed that one could not gain by the insights when overwhelmed by alcohol and that in an alcohol-dependent individual even one drink can start up this abnormal process. After sobriety, however, the insights can be enormously helpful.[48]

This direct intervention is not always possible at first, but with patience, tolerance, and the development of rapport, the patient can usually be motivated *in time* to give up his alcohol.

Through the years I have devised a technique which seems to work quite well. I set aside two hours for a new patient, and if possible, have the spouse also present in an adjoining room. If the patient objects to the spouse being there I, of course, do not insist. Since almost all patients are there against their will, and do not want to stop drinking, the first hour is spent trying to smooth down their ruffled feathers, and make friends with them. During this period I try to learn a little about their background, something about their work situation and their family problems, which are nearly always quite acute. We then begin to talk about their drinking. Since the word "alcoholic" is so pejorative, I go out of my way at first to speak of a "problem with alcohol," rather than using the term "alcoholic." We discuss nature with emphasis on the fact that if they are truly addicted, they do not have willpower to stop when they once have started to drink. It is pointed out that this is probably due to the mistaken idea that alcohol will cancel out their anxiety and tension. It does do this for about a two-hour period of sedation, but as the sedation wears off, their feeling of anxiety or nervousness increases, becoming more pronounced with each drink. This makes it possible to point out that they do not continue drinking because they have no willpower, but are using alcohol as a medication to, temporarily at least, overcome the increased tension.[28] When showing a diagram that covers this, patients frequently say, "That makes more sense than anything I have ever heard and describes me exactly." This abolishes a good share of their guilt about being alcoholic and helps the family to become more compassionate toward them. The next step then is to go into their pattern of drinking, with emphasis on the progressive nature of the disease. A chart devised by Glatt is a great help[29] (see Chart I). The patient goes over each symptom with me step by step to try to determine just how far into his addiction he is. Early signs, of course, are sneaking drinks, unwillingness to talk about his intake of alcohol, preoccupation with drinking, and the beginning of blackouts (which are periods of amnesia.) If they are further along in their problem, loss of control starts. The disturbances in the family members, alibis, rationalizations, denials, and persistent blaming of others for the plight they are in begin to become quite apparent. Also when drinking, many of them show a marked change of personality all the way from becoming merely verbally argumentative up to actual physical violence. Persistent remorse starts, with a feeling of guilt, a lack of self-confidence, and a feeling that they are "no good." Loss of jobs or demotions begin to occur as well as loss of friends and unreasoning resentments which may continue not only while they are drinking, but in their intervals of freedom from drinking. The endless trips to hospitals and AA rest homes begins about this time. Morning drinking starts in order to overcome the nervousness and guilt and to decrease the tremors, which are sometimes so severe that they cannot hold a cup or sign their names. Benders of a few days or a few weeks duration may begin to occur. There is, of course, progressive loss of interest in things which used to be important to them. There may be an ethical deterioration, indefinable fears, and perhaps finally a willingness to accept the fact that they do have a problem.[35] Sometimes this will not be accepted until there is the loss of a job, or threatened loss, or a wife leaving them. These crises make it impossible for them to continue their denials and rationalizations.

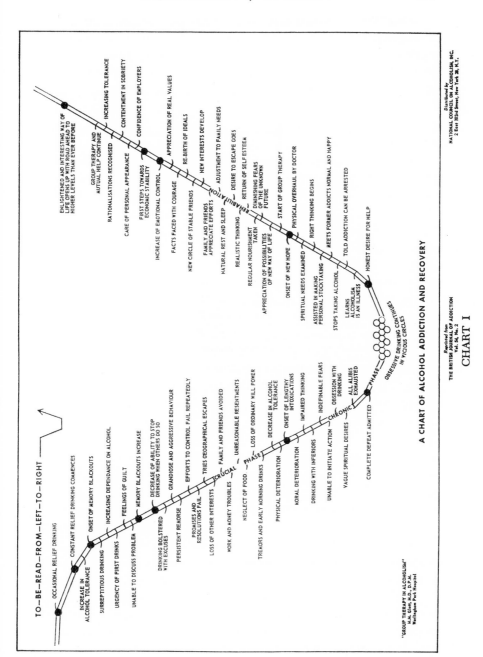

A CHART OF ALCOHOL ADDICTION AND RECOVERY

CHART I

"GROUP THERAPY IN ALCOHOLISM"
M.M. Glatt, M.D., D.P.M.
Warlingham Park Hospital

Reprinted from
THE BRITISH JOURNAL OF ADDICTION
Vol. 54. No. 2

Distributed by
NATIONAL COUNCIL ON ALCOHOLISM, INC.
2 East 103rd Street, New York 29, N.Y.

TO—BE—READ—FROM—LEFT—TO—RIGHT →

OCCASIONAL RELIEF DRINKING

CONSTANT RELIEF DRINKING COMMENCES

INCREASE IN ALCOHOL TOLERANCE

SURREPTITIOUS DRINKING

URGENCY OF FIRST DRINKS

UNABLE TO DISCUSS PROBLEM

ONSET OF MEMORY BLACKOUTS

INCREASING DEPENDENCE ON ALCOHOL

FEELINGS OF GUILT

MEMORY BLACKOUTS INCREASE

DECREASE OF ABILITY TO STOP DRINKING WHEN OTHERS DO SO

DRINKING BOLSTERED WITH EXCUSES

GRANDIOSE AND AGGRESSIVE BEHAVIOUR

PERSISTENT REMORSE

EFFORTS TO CONTROL FAIL REPEATEDLY

PROMISES AND RESOLUTIONS FAIL

TRIES GEOGRAPHICAL ESCAPES

LOSS OF OTHER INTERESTS

FAMILY AND FRIENDS AVOIDED

WORK AND MONEY TROUBLES

UNREASONABLE RESENTMENTS

NEGLECT OF FOOD

LOSS OF ORDINARY WILL POWER

TREMORS AND EARLY MORNING DRINKS

DECREASE IN ALCOHOL TOLERANCE

PHYSICAL DETERIORATION

ONSET OF LENGTHY INTOXICATIONS

MORAL DETERIORATION

IMPAIRED THINKING

DRINKING WITH INFERIORS

INDEFINABLE FEARS

UNABLE TO INITIATE ACTION

OBSESSION WITH DRINKING

VAGUE SPIRITUAL DESIRES

ALL ALIBIS EXHAUSTED

COMPLETE DEFEAT ADMITTED

CRUCIAL — PHASE

CHRONIC — PHASE

OBSESSIVE DRINKING CONTINUES IN VICIOUS CIRCLES

LEARNS ALCOHOLISM IS AN ILLNESS

STOPS TAKING ALCOHOL

TOLD ADDICTION CAN BE ARRESTED

HONEST DESIRE FOR HELP

MEETS FORMER ADDICTS NORMAL AND HAPPY

ASSISTED IN MAKING PERSONAL STOCKTAKING

RIGHT THINKING BEGINS

SPIRITUAL NEEDS EXAMINED

PHYSICAL OVERHAUL BY DOCTOR

ONSET OF NEW HOPE

START OF GROUP THERAPY

APPRECIATION OF POSSIBILITIES OF NEW WAY OF LIFE

DIMINISHING FEARS OF THE UNKNOWN FUTURE

REGULAR NOURISHMENT TAKEN

RETURN OF SELF ESTEEM

REALISTIC THINKING

DESIRE TO ESCAPE GOES

NATURAL REST AND SLEEP

ADJUSTMENT TO FAMILY NEEDS

FAMILY AND FRIENDS APPRECIATE EFFORTS

NEW INTERESTS DEVELOP

NEW CIRCLE OF STABLE FRIENDS

RE-BIRTH OF IDEALS

FACTS FACED WITH COURAGE

INCREASE OF EMOTIONAL CONTROL

APPRECIATION OF REAL VALUES

FIRST STEPS TOWARDS ECONOMIC STABILITY

CARE OF PERSONAL APPEARANCE

CONFIDENCE OF EMPLOYERS

RATIONALISATIONS RECOGNISED

CONTENTMENT IN SOBRIETY

GROUP THERAPY AND MUTUAL HELP CONTINUE

INCREASING TOLERANCE

ENLIGHTENED AND INTERESTING WAY OF LIFE OPENS UP WITH ROAD AHEAD TO HIGHER LEVELS THAN EVER BEFORE

REHABILITATION

The "Twenty Questions Test" of Seliger[46] is also a great help (see Chart II).

CHART II

THE TWENTY QUESTION TEST

Are You an Alcoholic?

To answer this question, ask yourself the following questions and answer them as honestly as you can.

	Yes	No

1. Do you lose time from work due to drinking?
2. Is drinking making your home life unhappy?
3. Do you drink because you are shy with other people?
4. Is drinking affecting your reputation?
5. Have you ever felt remorse after drinking?
6. Have you gotten into financial difficulties as a result of drinking?
7. Do you turn to lower companions and an inferior environment when drinking?
8. Does your drinking make you careless of your family's welfare?
9. Has your ambition decreased since drinking?
10. Do you crave a drink at a definite time daily?
11. Do you want a drink the next morning?
12. Does drinking cause you to have difficulty in sleeping?
13. Has your efficiency decreased since drinking?
14. Is drinking jeopardizing your job or business?
15. Do you drink to escape from worries or troubles?
16. Do you drink alone?
17. Have you ever had a complete loss of memory as a result of drinking?
18. Has your physician ever treated you for drinking?
19. Do you drink to build up your self-confidence?
20. Have you ever been to a hospital or institution on account of drinking?

If you have answered *Yes* to any *one* of the questions there is a definite warning that you may be an alcoholic.
If you have answered *Yes* to any *two*, the chances are that you are an alcoholic.
If you have answered *Yes* to *three or more,* you are definitely an alcoholic.

These questions were made up by Dr. Robert V. Seliger for use at John's Hopkins University Hospital, Baltimore, Maryland, 1945. Out of his original 35 questions only 20 appear on this chart.

The next step in the first interview is to discuss various methods of treatment in enough detail so that they understand them. The spouse is usually present at this time.

Of first importance is affiliation with AA, but 80 to 90 percent of my patients do not want to hear of it on their first visit. We do not push them, but since I have a direct telephone line to AA, and know many talented individuals at AA Intergroup, I can sometimes persuade patients to be introduced by telephone to

AA. Because of their friendly reception over the telephone, much of their resistance to AA can be overcome, and they may be willing to meet the individual they talk to for dinner or for a meeting the same day. There is no question but that the results of AA affiliation have proven to be more effective than any other form of treatment. It is estimated that there are four or five hundred thousand persons in the United States who have recovered through AA, which, I believe, gives the soundest and most lasting recovery. Many patients, however, may need a short (or sometimes long) period of psychotherapy to be willing to accept AA.[2]

If AA is refused, I then explain the nature of our group therapy meetings which are smaller than the AA meetings and which they are willing to attend once a week.[20] The first four of these meetings are mostly didactic with the patient and the spouse both attending (provided the patient allows the spouse to be there). The didactic sessions are led by a trained recovered alcoholic and last two hours. He covers all sorts of ground, not only the physiological effects of alcohol and the progressive symptoms, but also variations of cultural patterns. After these initial discussion groups are over (I try to be present at all of them, at least for the last hour of discussion), they are then urged to attend psychodrama sessions two or three times to see whether this technique would be of help to them. The majority of patients like it and profit greatly from it, provided they are assured that they do not have to participate in the first few sessions but can simply observe. Psychodrama sessions, each of which lasts two hours, can be attended for as long as they feel they are useful. This may be anywhere from one or two sessions up to a year or two of weekly sessions. A few come for years. I am fortunate in having an excellent psychodramatist, Miss Hannah Weiner.[50]

Since there are frequently other psychiatric conditions present, I try to see each patient once a week for at least a short period of time until I know they are on the road to recovery. This is not an analytic type of therapy but would be classified more as guidance. If it becomes evident that the patient needs a deeper form of therapy, this can be arranged for, usually with some other psychoanalyst, as I have not enough open hours to undertake it myself. A diagnosis must be made since there are often underlying problems. A few act actually schizophrenic as well as alcoholic, and many show an underlying depression for which appropriate therapy may be required.[27]

What I am describing here is, of course, the outpatient treatment, but there are a sizable number of alcoholics who need to be detoxified first in a hospital, and then may need to undergo rehabilitation in a living-in facility for anywhere from two to four weeks, and sometimes longer. I have found great resistance in many voluntary hospitals to take in alcoholics. However, wherever this has been done, alcoholics have been found to be no more trouble than nonalcoholics if the nurses and the resident staff know how to handle them.[4, 14] As a matter of fact, they are quite grateful for the care they get. The new tranquilizers have proved extremely beneficial here, but should almost always be discontinued after the withdrawal period is over.

I have found that after detoxification the period of inpatient rehabilitation, if needed, is best carried out in a setting where alcoholism itself is stressed as well as the underlying personality "hang ups." These facilities are usually run by recovered alcoholics, almost always AA members, and the emphasis on rehabilitation is geared largely toward the problem of alcoholism.[2] They are modest in cost. Of course, there are some patients who require long-term care in a private psychiatric hospital, but too many of these hospitals frequently ignore or do not recognize the alcoholism itself. Frequently psychiatrists make the mistake of telling the patient that alcoholism is always the result of an underlying personality disorder, that they will help with this disorder, and then the drinking will automatically become normal. This, of course, never occurs, possibly for chemical reasons, so that the patient may leave even some of our best psychiatric hospitals unequipped to deal with alcohol in the outside world. Unless the patient becomes convinced that, because of this underlying metabolic disturbance in the addictive process he never can drink safely again, he will most probably try to return to social drinking with inevitably disastrous effects. Should a way ever be found to correct this metabolic defect or to compensate for it, as is done with insulin and diet in diabetes, or methadone in heroin addiction, the situation may change and the alcoholic might again enjoy moderate social drinking. So far this goal has not been reached.

Antabuse (disulfiram) has proven of great help. Discovered in the late forties, it is now in use in hundreds of thousands of cases all over the world. I myself have given it to well over three thousand cases with no deleterious effects, provided the proper dose is used, i.e. .5 gm (one pill) once a day for five days, then .25 gm (a half pill) daily for an indefinite period. It can be started safely twelve hours after the last drink. However, as a safety measure, if the recent drinking has been very heavy, I may start off with a half pill b.i.d. on the first day. Antabuse should *never* be given without the patient's full consent, knowledge, and understanding of its incompatibility with alcohol. There are virtually no contraindications except a decompensated heart and psychosis. I have avoided using it early in pregnancy since adequate studies have not been made but a number of women have taken it safely after the first six months of pregnancy with no danger to the child. As a precaution, I have used half the usual dose in these persons.[5, 7, 18, 30]

In most cases Antabuse may be taken for many years. My longest case is a plastic surgeon who has been on it safely for twenty-one years and I have several who have taken it for fifteen or more years. Such prolonged use would probably not be needed were the individual willing to avail himself of the therapy Alcoholics Anonymous could give him. Most patients stay on Antabuse regularly for one to two years but keep it around and take it for five days before conventions, trips away from home, weddings, etc., as an added insurance that they will not drink. Its value lies in relieving the alcoholic of all the conflict over and preoccupation with drinking and since it takes four to five days to be eliminated from the body, it gives him time to think things over should he become upset about something which formerly would have led to a drinking bout.

The claims and hopes that sedatives and, more recently, tranquilizers would cut down on the need to drink have been disappointing. These medications are, of course, often lifesaving in the acute withdrawal stage, but their use should be discontinued as soon as possible because there are few which are not in themselves eventually addicting. Exception must be made in the ambulatory schizophrenics who are also addicted to alcohol. They may need to be kept on phenothiazines as well as Antabuse. If not too seriously ill, I have had some good results on these patients using a combination of thorazine, Antabuse, psychotherapy, and hopefully, AA.[22] Recovery, Inc. has also helped many of them.[37]

Another attempt to "cure" alcoholism by the use of LSD a few years ago has also proved disappointing.[21] Of the twenty cases I treated eight years ago, a large proportion did well, but it seemed evident then that it was the extra attention these patients received and not the LSD which broke down their resistance to accepting the fact that they did need help in overcoming their alcoholism and becoming willing to accept this help. A recent report, however, of a well-controlled study shows that some alcoholics receiving LSD do have fewer relapses than the controls.[42]

Although I was unable to produce a lasting aversion to alcohol by means of hypnosis, I found that the learning to relax which can occur with hypnosis was distinctly helpful to the tense, nervous and sleepless alcoholic. Some patients have used a mild self-hypnosis or relaxation for years after the hypnosis sessions were over to help them sleep. This technique, I believe, also helps these persons to overcome some of their depressed feelings and improves their self-image. It may also help in establishing a good feeling tone between the patient and the therapist.[44]

Some of the behaviorists (e.g. Wolpe,[51] Franks[26]) are claiming good results from their techniques with the alcoholic. These techniques have been used for twenty-five to thirty years at the Shadel Sanatorium in Seattle, along with other methods of treatment. Since I have done a little work in this field myself, I believe that the negative approach of producing an aversion is, by itself, not very effective. Wolpe's technique of reciprocal inhibitions can be effective in eradicating and desensitizing some of the most deep-seated and persistent phobias. Not only must the "hierarchy of fears" be carefully constructed, but I believe the patient definitely needs other psychotherapy. In other words, I feel that the patient must be convinced that not drinking will give him greater rewards than drinking, which does mean patient psychotherapy along with the conditioning. One recent excellent example of stressing the positive is a study being carried on in Colorado by Lehmkuhle.[36] First-offenders arrested for drunken driving may be given an opportunity to continue to drive their cars provided they will undertake weekly group therapy sessions for a two-year period of time. They also must take Antabuse daily. Wives are also treated in separate groups, and efforts are made to interest the patients in Alcoholics Anonymous. If the patient fails to appear even for one group therapy session, or omits his Antabuse for one day, he is immediately put in jail, pays a fine, and of course, his license is revoked. Though the number of cases is still quite small, the results seem remarkably good.

Though I have not had personal experience with the videotape technique, it is sometimes extremely effective. About sixteen years ago I was shown a film at a hospital in a suburb of Paris of a patient in the midst of severe delirium tremens. When shown back to the patient about three weeks after recovery, he had been so shocked by this bit of truth about his condition that he had been totally abstinent for the five years up to the time of my seeing the film. He said, "My wife told me I was like this, but I never believed her."[8]

Spiritual counseling is of great help to many individuals. Though few of my patients attend any church and may not need religion in the formal sense, it may be necessary to help them face the fact that we all do need some guiding ethical principles for our lives. Things like love, loyalty, tolerance for others, honesty, justice, humility, hope, and so on are as important to one's proper psychic functioning as any medications are to one's body. Some ministers and priests have become very gifted in helping the alcoholic. To be helpful to the patient, however, I believe clergymen must and usually do accept their spiritual counseling as just one part of the total program.[10]

There are about 250 self-help groups in the United States. Many of them, patterned after Alcoholics Anonymous, give additional help for certain specific psychological problems and often help to reintegrate an individual into a more satisfactory social life. Such organizations are Recovery, Inc., Parents Without Partners, Schizophrenics Anonymous, Fathers At Large, Synanon, Gamblers Anonymous, Weight Watchers, AFTLI (Association Feeling Truth and Living It) and many others.

Marathons or workshops lasting anywhere from twenty to forty hours of intensive group therapy can be extremely important, but so many of these groups have sprung up that there is a certain danger of their being used indiscriminately on patients who have not been properly screened and led by persons who have not been carefully trained and supervised. Marathons can, however, produce profound emotional insights and changes of the patient's concept of himself and others. Frequently this can also be produced by the psychodramatic technique. Since marathons do show great promise, they should be conducted but, hopefully, better supervised.

SUMMARY AND CONCLUSIONS

Since this paper is long and perhaps too discursive, I will not attempt to give a complete summary. Instead I will try to state what seem to me to be important concepts in understanding and treating the alcoholic. Since drinking is only one facet of a person's life, treatment of the total personality is indicated, which may take several years depending upon the underlying maturity of the individual who has become addicted to alcohol. In my own practice I have found that the multidisciplinary approach, using a number of modalities all at the same time, gives better results than one method used exclusively.[22]

1. Alcoholism is a disease of unknown etiology with eventually physiological, psychological, social and spiritual overtones operating often both in a cause and effect manner.[40]

2. Probably anyone who can tolerate alcohol at all can become addicted to it if he drinks excessively for a long enough period of time.

3. An immature and conflicting young person may gain a great deal from alcohol when he first starts to drink and may

therefore continue to use it in place of using other avenues of self-expression. Thus he remains fixated emotionally and continues in adult life to act in an immature and adolescent way—and the longer he continues alcoholic drinking, the more infantile his behavior becomes.

4. Other persons who have matured more and have often accomplished a great deal (doctors, lawyers, etc.) may also become addicted through excessive social drinking. Though their behavior when drunk—or between bouts—may also be infantile, this may represent a regression rather than a fixation. When these persons stop their alcohol intake, they can revert rather quickly to the former fairly good emotional adjustment of their pre-alcoholic lives.

5. Though the alcoholic may "act out" as any maladjusted person does, it is probably a mistake to consider the bizarre and often violent behavior of the alcoholic when drunk as typical acting out. Recent metabolic studies seem to show that some toxic substance produced by alcohol in the alcoholic and not in the moderate social drinkers is responsible for a very toxic psychotic state. The alkaloid isoquinoline formed has been found to occur also in the person hallucinating because of LSD, peyote, mescaline, and possibly many other drugs capable of producing a toxic psychosis.[11]

6. A purely psychoanalytic approach is rarely, if ever, effective in treating the alcoholic unless total sobriety can be brought about before an analytic approach is undertaken.

7. Treatment of the alcoholic must take into account the many and various needs of the alcoholic. He must be helped to attain a good state of health, which may require detoxification in a hospital[14] or Alcoholics Anonymous rest home,[2] good diet, a chance to gain back a state of emotional equilibrium, usually help with his ever-present family problems,[1, 3, 13, 15, 19] and perhaps help with his employment situation.[49]

8. Since alcoholism is not a unitary disease, treatment must be flexible and, when possible, tailored to the patient's individual needs. Since we do not know the cause, the most effective type of treatment seems to be a multidisciplinary type with the use of AA if possible, often Antabuse, group therapy for the patients

and spouses,[1, 13, 15] psychodrama, some individual psychotherapy, usually of a reality-oriented type for selected persons, etc. One should be open to new methods of treatment and always aware of the meagerness of our real knowledge of the disease of alcoholism.

9. Underlying all treatment of the alcoholic must be an acceptance of him as an ill individual and not merely a perverse person with no willpower. Though he must gradually give up his neurotic and often demanding egocentric attitude of life, in the beginning of treatment it is best to let him see that you are accepting, flexible, understanding and patient. Above all else one must give him hope of a life better without alcohol than with it. Stressing his good points is important. Humor plays a role also in group therapy and AA so that giving up alcohol does not seem so dreary.

10. Any doctor, psychiatrist, internist, psychologist, social worker, AA member or well-trained counselor can, if he will, learn to treat a large number of alcoholics successfully. This gives the helping person the rewards we all need.

REFERENCES

1. *Al-Anon Faces Alcoholism.* New York, Cornwall Press, 1965.
2. *Alcoholics Anonymous Comes of Age.* New York, Alcoholics Anonymous, 1957.
3. Bailey, M. B.: *Alcoholism and Family Casework.* New York, Community Council of Greater New York, 1968.
4. Berke, M.; Gordon, J. D.; Levy, R. I., and Perrow, C. B.: A study on the non-segregated hospitalization of alcoholic patients in a general hospital. *Hospital Monograph Series No. 7.* Chicago, American Hospital Association, 1959.
5. Billett, S. L.: The use of Antabuse: an approach that minimizes fear. *Med. Ann.,* 33:612, 1964.
6. Block, M. A.: *Alcoholism: Its Facets and Phases.* New York, John Day, 1965, p. 197.
7. Bourne, P. G.; Alford, J. A., and Bowcock, J. Z.: Treatment of skid row alcoholics with disulfiram. *Quart. J. Stud. Alcohol.,* 27:42, 1966.
8. Carriere, J.: Cinematographic psychoshock in delirium tremens. *Ann. Med. Psychol.,* 12(2):240-244, 1954.

9. Chafetz, M. E., and Demone, H. W., Jr.: *Alcoholism and Society.* New York, Oxford University Press, 1962.
10. Clinebell, H. J., Jr.: *Understanding and Counseling the Alcoholic.* New York, Abingdon Press, 1956.
11. Cohen, G., and Collins, M.: Alkaloids from catecholamines in adrenal tissue: possible role in alcoholism. *Science, 167*:1749-1751, March, 1970.
12. Delany, L. T.: The significance of acting out in the group treatment of the alcoholic. Presented at the annual conference of the American Group Psychotherapy Association, 1962.
13. *The Dilemma of the Alcoholic Marriage.* New York, Al-Anon Family Group Headquarters, 1967.
14. Fox, R.: The alcoholic in a general hospital. In L. Linn (Ed.): *Frontiers in General Hospital Psychiatry.* New York, International Universities Press, 1961.
15. Fox, R.: The alcoholic spouse. In V. W. Eisenstein (Ed.): *Neurotic Interaction in Marriage.* New York, Basic Books, 1956.
16. Fox, R.: *Alcoholism as a Form of Acting Out.* New York, Grune & Stratton, 1965.
17. Fox, R.: Alcoholism in industry. *J. Amer. Women's Assoc., 20*(12): 1109-1119, 1965.
18. Fox, R.: Disulfiram (Antabuse) as an adjunct in the treatment of alcoholism. In R. Fox (Ed.): *Alcoholism—Behavioral Research, Therapeutic Approaches.* New York, Springer, 1967.
19. Fox, R.: Effect of alcoholism on children. In *Proceedings of the Fifth International Congress on Psychotherapy.* New York, Karger, Basel, 1963, pp. 55-65.
20. Fox, R.: Group psychotherapy with alcoholics. *Int. J. Group Psychother., 12*, 1962.
21. Fox, R.: Is L.S.D. of value in treating alcoholics? A paper given at an International Conference on L.S.D. at South Oaks Hospital, Amityville, L.I., New York, May 8-10, 1965.
22. Fox, R.: A multidisciplinary approach to the treatment of alcoholism. *Amer. J. Psychiat., 123*:7, 1967.
23. Fox, R.: Psychiatric aspects of alcoholism. Talk given at the Fifth Emil A. Gutheil Memorial Conference of the Association for the Advancement of Psychotherapy. New York, October 25, 1964.
24. Fox, R.: Unpublished data, 1970.
25. Fox, R., and Lyon, P.: *Alcoholism, Its Scope, Cause, and Treatment.* New York, Random House, 1955.
26. Franks, C. M.: Alcohol, alcoholism and conditioning: a review of the literature and some theoretical implications. *J. Ment. Sci., 104*:14-33, 1958.

27. Freed, E. X.: Alcoholism and manic depressive disorders. *Quart. J. Stud. Alcohol*, 31(1):62-89, 1970.
28. Gitlow, S. E.: Treatment of the reversible acute complications of alcoholism. *Modern Treatment*, 3(3):472-490, 1966.
29. Glatt, M. M.: Group therapy in alcoholism. *Brit. J. Addict.*, 54:140, 1958.
30. Greenbaum, H.: Group psychotherapy with alcoholics in conjunction with Antabuse treatment. *Int. J. Group Psychother.*, 4:30, 1954.
31. Health Services Administration. Advisory Council on Alcoholism, Report of Committee on Relation of Alcohol to Other Drugs. Data from several Narcotic Rehabilitation Centers. New York, April 22, 1970.
32. Horney, K.: *The Neurotic Personality of Our Time*. New York, Norton, 1937.
33. Jackson, J.: The adjustment of the family to the crisis of alcoholism. *Quart. J. Stud. Alcohol*, 15:562-586, 1954.
34. Jellinek, E. M.: *The Disease Concept of Alcoholism*. New Haven, Hill House, 1960.
35. Jellinek, E. M.: The phases of alcohol addiction in males. From a lecture given to the World Health Organization, Geneva, Switzerland, October, 1951.
36. Lehmkuhle, J. M.: Personal communication, 1970.
37. Low, A.: *Mental Health Through Will Training*. Chicago, Recovery, Inc., 1950.
38. Maisel, A. Q.: Alcohol and your brain. *Reader's Digest*, June, 1970, pp. 65-69.
39. Mann, M.: *New Primer on Alcoholism*. New York, Holt, Rinehart, and Winston, 1958.
40. Milt, H.: *Basic Handbook on Alcoholism*. Maplewood, New Jersey, Scientific Aid Publications, 1969, pp. 40-43.
41. Newell, N.: Alcoholism and the father image. *Quart. J. Stud. Alcohol*, 11:92-96, 1950.
42. Pahnke, W. N.; Kurland, A. A.; Unger, S.; Savage, C., and Grof, S.: The experimental use of psychedelic (L.S.D.) and psychotherapy. *J.A.M.A.*, 212(11):1856-1863, 1970.
43. Portnoy, I.: Psychology of alcoholism. From a lecture given to The Association for the Advancement of Psychoanalysis, New York City, 1947.
44. Reardon, W. T.: Modern Medical Hypnosis. Wilmington, Delaware, Reardon, 1962.
45. Report of Committee on Relation of Alcohol to Other Drugs of the Advisory Council on Alcoholism to the Health Services Administration. New York City, 1970.

46. Seliger, R. V.: *Alcoholics are Sick People*. Baltimore, Alcoholism Publications, 1945, pp. 9-12.

47. Silverberg, W. V.: Acting out versus insight, a problem in psychoanalytic technique. *Psychoanal. Quart.*, 24:527-544, 1955.

48. Tiebout, H. M.: The act of surrender in the therapeutic process. Paper given at the New York Psychiatric Society, October 3, 1945.

49. Trice, H.: Alcoholism in Industry. New York, The Christopher D. Smithers Foundation, 1963.

50. Weiner, H. B.: Treating the alcoholic with psychodrama. *Group Psychother.*, 18:27-49, 1965.

51. Wolpe, J.: *Psychotherapy by Reciprocal Inhibition*. California, Stanford University, 1958.

DRUG ADDICTION, STEMMING from character problems, is currently the major pathway for many of our youths to act out conflicts both with society and within themselves. Dr. George Stricker, a Professor of Psychology at the Institute of Advanced Psychological Studies, has extensive experience with young drug addicts utilizing group process methods. He describes the characteristic "rap sessions" with the nonhabitual, nonheroin drug user. Although his approach emphasizes prevention rather than cure, the techniques seem also obviously quite therapeutic. He includes an extensive description of leader selection as well as the dual focus of the training experience. The training includes both group process participation and an awareness of leadership roles and techniques. The leader training program is further supplemented by didactic material detailing relevant data on drug usage.

Prior to describing his group techniques, Dr. Stricker provides a thorough psychodynamic rationale for drug use by the teenagers and these formulations serve as an outline for the development of a treatment plan. He postulates that with a group leader involvement characterized by honesty and integrity, the group members are enabled to redirect their energies into more constructive activities rather than drugs. He ends the paper by outlining two additional advantages of his method for leadership training: first, his paraprofessionals would be utilizing their skills in the future, and secondly, their personal growth and development resulting from the training program is a factor that would facilitate commitment to their work.

In this clear and concise paper, Dr. Stricker offers us a group process method found to be quite effective in working with youthful soft drug users. The extensiveness of the symptom of drug use among our youth requires some concerted action by mental health professionals. Dr. Stricker's paper, with a promise of possible approaches to a solution to this crisis, is a crucial and important contribution at this time.

D.S.M.

G.D.G.

Chapter 15

Training Nonprofessionals to Work with Soft Drug Users

GEORGE STRICKER

THIS PROJECT WAS designed to focus on a particular target group, the adolescent soft drug users in Nassau County. In the title of this paper and in the identification of these youngsters as soft drug users there is a dichotomy implied between soft and hard drugs. That dichotomy is a foolish one and one which could not be defended. Anyone who has seen a toxic reaction to amphetamine usage, who has seen an addictive reaction to barbiturate usage, who has seen a fatal response to barbiturate usage, would not be inclined to label those drugs as soft drugs. What we mean to convey by that title is that heroin was rarely the preferred drug of the adolescents who were served by the project. While I would not like to distinguish between soft and hard drugs, I think we can distinguish between hard-core and soft usage of drugs. It is not the drug, then, but the method of usage that we focused on. Soft usage can be defined as occasional, experimental nonsalient usage of drugs. The important point about it is that the user's life does not revolve around drug usage. There are many things that he does, one of which is take drugs. With hard-core drug usage, on the contrary, we have an individual whose life revolves about the acquisition and the taking of drugs.

Our target group for the project was predominantly soft users of drugs other than heroin. It is possible to look upon our

The work described in this paper was sponsored by the Nassau County Drug Abuse and Addiction Commission. I would like to thank a number of colleagues, particularly Abraham Cohen, Gerald Edwards, and Victoria Sears, for their help and encouragement.

251

groups as rap groups rather than as treatment groups, with our focus on prevention rather than on treatment. These distinctions probably are much more a matter of degree than absolute divisions. It is very difficult to tell when the intensity of a rap group is such that we really ought to call it treatment, or when the focus is on the solution of current problems rather than the anticipation of future problems. Our intent was to conduct prevention-oriented rap groups, but many of the sessions would not be recognizable as such.

The major decision that we had to make was in our choice of the type of leader that we would select. This decision was influenced by the experience of community psychologists with paraprofessionals.[2] It indicated to us the ability of people who do not have conventional training, and their potential usefulness in a project of this sort. We are dealing with drug users, and in the field of drug use we looked to the experience of the Synanon and Daytop type of community.[3] These communities suggested to us that the paraprofessionals we looked for might be most useful if they had had similar experiential and sub-cultural backgrounds to the target groups.

With Synanon and Daytop, and with Topic House, which is our own residential, therapeutic community in Nassau County, the approach has been to take ex-addicts and to use them as drug group leaders. Part of the Nassau County Drug Commission's program originally included sending Topic House residents into the community to address various high school groups. The experience was not altogether an effective one, or one that was received favorably. There was an enormous gap separating the Topic House resident, who was an ex-heroin addict, most likely from a lower middle-class family, from the experience and background of the adolescents in upper middle-class communities like Great Neck, Locust Valley, and the Five Towns, where our groups have tended to be located. What happened was that the high school students would look at the ex-addicts and say, "Wow, groovy, great story, but it has nothing to do with me." In terms of any kind of personal identification and integration of the message, the ex-addicts were being turned off. Therefore, we did not feel that we could look to this traditional group as a source for our leaders. We wanted indigenous leaders and, for our particular target group, the indigenous subculture is the middle-class adolescent drug scene. Thus, it was to the middle-class drug scene that we looked for our leaders.

Among the criteria that we adopted in choosing leaders was, first of all, that they be young. We wanted them to be close enough in age to the people they were going to relate to that they would not be disqualified before they opened their mouths. Secondly, we wanted them to have drug experience, so that this was something they could also share with the people that were going to be involved with them. Finally, while we wanted them to have drug experience, we made it a specific rite of passage that drug usage could not continue while these people were connected with the project. Each of the leaders, at the beginning of the project, had to indicate his resolve to discontinue his own personal use of drugs. This was not presented to them as a moral issue or as a treatment approach. It was presented to them in a very pragmatic way: If you are going into the community, if you are representing the Drug Commission, if you are dealing with people who are troubled with drugs, you are going to put yourself in a very difficult position if you have to respond to questions about your own drug use by saying, "Well, it's OK for me, but you really ought to look into that and stop it yourself." The group leaders agreed for these reasons that they would relinquish personal use, although, in both of the training groups that we have had, this was a topic of discussion at the beginning of the groups, and it took a number of sessions before the issue was resolved to the satisfaction of the group members.

In addition to age and prior drug experience, we were looking for a number of personal characteristics. Since applicants had called and volunteered to participate, we had *prima facie* evidence of their motivation. We were also looking for sensitive human beings and people with the personality skills to be interpersonally helpful. Some of these criteria were much easier to identify than others. It was much easier for me to determine who was young than who had the personality skills to be interpersonally helpful.

The procedure of selection was to have each of the people

who had heard about the groups, and the grapevine does wonders in recruiting people of this sort, come in for an individual interview. During the interview I inquired about such things as the reasons behind their motivation, what their drug experience had been, what their experience in groups had been, and what they themselves saw as being personally beneficial about participation. On the basis of the interview and vague clinical hunches I chose the people who were going to participate in the project.

The first group began in December, 1968. We started with twelve people in the group, and currently ten of them remain. The two who dropped out did so, as best as I could tell, because they wanted to continue with their own drug use, and they found that the promise they had made upon entry was going to be too personally difficult for them, so they made the choice to give up participation. The other ten have remained and each of them has had about a year's experience functioning in the community. The second group began in January, 1970. It began with ten leaders and is now reduced to eight. One of the drop-outs occurred before the first group session and was due to the candidate having found alternate employment. The second person who dropped out did so after the first session because he found the stress of group participation too difficult, rather than for a drug-related issue. These eight people should be going out into the field in the next two or three weeks, and at that point we will have eighteen functioning group leaders in Nassau County. Although some members of the first training group have begun to work individually, initially they go out in pairs, largely for the mutual support they can provide each other through that method of functioning.

About half of the eighteen are Adelphi graduate students in clinical psychology. The other half have enormously variable backgrounds. They all have a minimum of two years of college education, although this is a civil service requirement rather than a criterion which necessarily is meaningfully related to job functioning. Some have advanced degrees in fields other than psychology. All of them, whether or not they are graduate students, have in common their youth, drug experience, sensitivity, and personality skills.

The philosophy of the training, which is one of the pivotal aspects of the program, is that the training should be experiential rather than didactic. Dr. Abraham Cohen, who co-led the first training group with me and is now leading the original group while I am leading the second separately, originally wrote a statement about what he visualized the training should be, and I would like to present a portion of that:

> The experience will consist of participation within a viable laboratory model of an encounter group. All those training for group leader roles will themselves be active group members, experiencing and sharing all of the vicissitudes typical of a confrontation self-help group. Through this kind of first-hand participation, potential leaders will be able to experience and cope with many of their own interpersonal anxieties. Such interaction should provide its members with personally meaningful knowledge of group dynamics as well as practical experience pertinent to the organization and operation of such groups. Social interaction between peers should be emphasized rather than the intrapsychic exploration between the specialist and his patient. Although the term leader has been used, the role of leadership should be delegated and shared within and amongst the group membership. Participant-leaders, because of their special knowledge of group process, tend to lead through example. Leadership is best shared by all group members through the emulation and incorporation of an attractive model.

That was from the original proposal that Dr. Cohen and I had agreed upon. It describes the way we approached the groups, and I think it's the way that has been carried through with some adherence to the letter of the proposal, and with some success.

Now let me quote from a second paper. This is something that has been written by Allen Schwartz, who is one of the Adelphi graduate students who was trained in the first group and who has been participating in the community. As a representative of the first group he wrote a rather extended statement about the values and activities of that initial group which I, with Allen's permission, will quote liberally throughout this presentation. Let me present what Allen has written about his experience as a member of such a training group:

> Training activities are undertaken in the leader group which meets once weekly for three hours. The training is experiential in

nature; that is, we are learning to lead groups and perform our service to the community by observing and then discussing the way in which one group is led. We believe this to be the most meaningful kind of training which we could receive in a group setting; and we all feel it continues to be tremendously successful in helping us develop both the clinical skills in group leadership, and the personal growth and maturity required of a group leader. We are learning to relate to the members of the groups which we lead in an honest and helping manner as a result of our membership experience in the leader group. We believe, for these reasons, the training is working and working well. It is enabling us to perform effectively in providing a service for the community which we all feel is vital.

So much for personal testimony. In short, what both of these statements suggest is that the twin foci of the training experience is the provision of the experience of group process for the members and also the modeling of an effective leader and effective leadership techniques. This experiential aspect of the training has now been supplemented by a didactic program which is presented to the group members by the Drug Commission. This portion of the training is currently being expanded for future groups. Beside the skills of group leadership that the experiential group provides for the members, we also want to give them a certain amount of information about the drug area which they are likely to be called upon to give by both members of their groups and people in the community where they are functioning. There are didactic lectures about the effects of drugs, the history of drugs, the laws as they pertain to drugs, the programs of the Commission, and the presence of various kinds of treatment resources in the community.

The information about drugs and about the Commission's programs are offered both to inform the group members and also to provide them with some identification with the Commission. Probably the single greatest problem that we have run into with the groups is that they tend to become very insular, and the group members have enormous loyalty to each other, enormous identification with Dr. Cohen and myself, but very little recognition of their relationship to the Commission. That can lead to a number of practical difficulties when they are working in the community, and the use of Commission members to provide these didactic programs we hope will be useful in overcoming some of this feeling of separation that has existed in the past.

All of our work is guided by a central treatment philosophy, and for that I will again quote from the statement that Allen Schwartz wrote. This is the philosophy as it is perceived by one of the more articulate of the group members, and is one which, in large part, most of the other members would probably endorse:

> We fundamentally value verbal communication in a group setting as a process through which adolescent problems in living may be explored and helped. We believe that the source of most human problems derives from the failure of or disturbance in the communication between the people we see and significant people in their lives; their parents, siblings, peers, and teachers. We feel that by listening to these people discuss difficulties in relating to their parents, and by guiding them to relate better to each other, both within and outside of the group setting, we are providing an experience through which these people can develop a more successful life style. We believe drugs to be an important issue, but it is only one of many important issues. It has been our experience that the use of drugs is inextricably linked with other behavior patterns and life styles, so that often the focus of deep involvement necessarily moves far afield from the drug issue; in addition, an early focus on drugs may turn group members off to the experience we are offering. We see ourselves as treating people in their entirety; to some degree following their leads and exploring areas which they find profitable. We do not, for we believe we cannot, treat a symptom or a circumscribed area of behavior in a group setting. It is not feasible to do so for we believe it would not be successful.

Drug abuse, then, is seen as a symptom of interpersonal difficulties and breakdowns in communication. While we are interested in symptom removal, we would not like to settle for it. Indeed, we have some questions as to whether symptom removal could be achieved without some fundamental alteration in the values and communication patterns of the young people. The sociological impact of the peer group and the allure of the drug scene cannot be overlooked. Rather, through the judicious management of group process we would hope to use the peer group in a constructive way and harness this pressure toward a more positive and growth-producing direction. It is hardly novel to remark upon the enormous influence that a peer group has on an adolescent and how attractive and how influential the drug scene can be. What we hope to do is to create our own scene in the group and provide a group process which would give the group members a meaningful, viable alternative to participation in the drug scene.

Finally, we have the question, What it is that the young people are looking for? What is it that drugs substitute for? What is it, the absence of which, leads to supplementation by drug abuse? One simplistic formulation is that what youth wants is honesty and integrity. We have noted from a number of past experiences that where someone or something can provide a meaningful alternative, drug use can be reduced. We have heard that drug use was reduced markedly in the Village during the time of the McCarthy campaign and in Berkeley during the Free Speech Movement. When there is something that can involve youth meaningfully, they are willing to put their energy into it and to pursue that goal in a manner that is marked by honesty and integrity. This pursuit becomes more important to them than the drug scene or drug usage. We would like to provide them with such an alternative. If our groups can provide them with this experience, if the leader can model these values, then the group and the way of life it represents can be a meaningful and attractive alternative to drug abuse. Parenthetically, the involvement of many young people in activities surrounding the war, such as during the recent Cambodian crisis, can provide them with exactly such meaningful alternatives. The adult community, which can be so up in arms about drugs, can either encourage their participation in such an important and meaningful pursuit or they can turn them off and send them back to drug abuse.

Now I would like to address a question about the techniques which have been used in the groups as they have functioned in the community. These are not techniques in the original training groups but in the groups that are being led by the young people. The techniques are many and they are varied. The leaders were encouraged to work in their own way, in the way which they find most comfortable and most productive; and, as a result, they have spread out in a number of alternate paths.

Let me again quote a summary of some of these directions from Allen Schwartz' paper:

> Service activities consist of leading groups of adolescents, junior high school, high school, and college students, which employ various techniques and approaches to group interaction. There is some truth, no doubt, in the belief that all the groups we lead are different, inasmuch as each leader pair tends to emphasize different issues and employ different techniques. However, some of the more common activities engaged in by most groups may be outlined as follows:
>
> 1. Focusing on and defining significant issues in the current lives of the group members. Helping them first to be aware of and then to try out alternate ways of behaving with each other and with persons beyond the group.
>
> 2. Building relationships which are both meaningful and satisfying. Directing group members to "find out who they are."
>
> 3. Offering young people a place where they can receive support, friendship, and help as they see to define it.
>
> 4. Providing a place for individuals who are experiencing emotional upheaval and pain. In such instances the group leaders may seek to reach out to the individual and help him to label the problem.
>
> 5. Providing an experience in which group members may learn the meaning of group pressure and group power. Directing them to understand the consequences of group power and, hence, the responsibilities associated with its application.
>
> 6. For college level groups, offering a forum for the discussion of transition issues relating to drugs, work, money, adulthood, sex. Such groups reach people who are not reached by university clinics and psychological services.
>
> 7. Working toward an integrated community approach to problems in living encountered by adolescents. This includes providing a decentralized unit from which psychiatric and psychological referrals may come, participating in parent and school panels concerned with issues relevant to group activities, working with schools in developing in-school programs, etc.

I doubt if a technique-oriented focus is relevant in understanding our groups. Rather, to the extent that each group mirrored honesty and integrity and was able to inspire more open communication, regardless of techniques, they should have been successful.

As far as evaluation of the entire project is concerned, I'm embarrassed. We have nothing in the way of substantial evidence to offer. The kind of evaluation that I will offer you I would never accept from anybody else, and I hope you'll be kinder to me.

The groups seem to be well received by the adolescents. The members are coming in the evening, on their own time and with no requirements. Perhaps they began to come out of curiosity, but they come week after week after week. The groups range in size from eight or ten in one community to thirty or forty in another community; and the majority of members will come over and over week after week. With no visible reward other than what they get in the group, I can't help but believe that the group must be offering them something. The groups are also well received by the communities, who have reflected their appraisal by asking the Drug Commission for so many additional group leaders that we are completely at a loss as to how to meet those requests. Finally, the clinical impression of the group leaders themselves is a very favorable one. They feel that they are reaching the adolescents and that the adolescents are responding to them in the ways that they had hoped for. We are still left with the question of just how successful this program has been, and I hope that we can do a more thorough and more well-founded type of evaluation in the future.

There are two other comments that I would like to make about the group program in reference both to the leaders themselves and to general issues which we have seen in the training of paraprofessionals. One such issue is the necessity for providing paraprofessionals with a career ladder. It has been the experience in a number of different communities using paraprofessionals that they get involved in meaningful work, make a real contribution, are given a feeling for their abilities, and then are stopped at that point. There is no place that they can go from the particular task that they are doing. With half of our group leaders, that is not a real problem. They are graduate students who will, within two or three years, earn PhD's in Clinical Psychology. They will go into the community and function as full-fledged professionals, so that for them this is not paraprofessional training, but it is more nearly an additional kind of practicum experience. For the people who are not graduate students, and who are more nearly paraprofessionals in the way that the term has been used, the problem has arisen as to where they go from here. After they spend their two or three hours an evening in a community, what further use can they make of the training that we provide for them. I am very pleased that of this group, about three quarters of them either already have been or shortly will be employed by the County Drug Commission. They are having jobs provided for them which will make full use of the kinds of skills that we are training and developing in our groups. There really is a place that they can go from here, and they can see a career ladder for themselves. There is use that they can make of the training outside of the specific groups that they lead.

Secondly, there is the operation of what Frank Riessman has called "the helper principle."[1] He has noticed in his work with paraprofessionals that very frequently at least as much benefit accrues to the people offering the help as to those receiving it. Our eighteen group leaders were people, a substantial number of whom, at the beginning of the program, were wrestling with real drug problems. At the present time I would guess that this is an issue that is in the past for all of them. The issues surrounding their own drug usage have been resolved in a productive and mature manner. There also has been, again through clinical observation, a substantial amount of personal growth in many of these people. I would attribute this personal growth partially to their experience in the training group, which has a great deal of therapeutic impact, but at least equally to the assumption of responsibility for other groups. They are working in the community in a responsible manner and having to deal with a number of countertransference issues and explore their own feeling as helpers, and in doing so have benefitted themselves as human beings. Thus they not only have been able to deliver a meaningful clinical service, thereby helping a large number of troubled and puzzled adolescents, but by doing so, they have succeeded in helping themselves.

REFERENCES

1. Riessman, F.: The "helper" therapy principle. *Social Work, 10*:27-32, 1965.
2. Riessman, F.: Strategies and suggestions for training nonprofessionals. *Community Ment. Health J., 3*:103-110, 1967.
3. Stricker, G., and Weiss, F.: *Kicking It.* New York, Pyramid, 1971.

$\mathbf{M}$RS. MARIA V. BERGMANN, a practicing analyst, demonstrates the same high standards in translating theory into a practical application as she had in an earlier Adelphi conference. Mrs. Bergmann is an ego psychologist and, in part, a follower of the teachings of Margaret Mahler whose framework she uses to begin her paper. The predisposition to act out is postulated as occurring in character formations where oral fixations predominate. Using this thesis and integrating it into her ego psychological developmental approach, Mrs. Bergmann gives us an excellent frame of reference for conceptualizing the three illustrative case histories that enliven her theoretical formulations.

Mrs. Bergmann has thus furthered our understanding of both the etiology and dynamics of acting out in this fascinating clinical paper which brilliantly integrates ego psychological theory with case material covering techniques for handling patients at a particular development level.

D.S.M.
G.D.G.

Chapter 16

On the Relationship Between Words and Actions: Examples of Technique from Psychoanalytic Practice

MARIA V. BERGMANN

IN THIS PRESENTATION I plan to deal with situations from a patient's infantile past where acting out or taking action is the only possible form of communication of an inner need or representation of a past event. Recent psychoanalytic literature has stressed that a predisposition toward acting out can be expected in character formations where oral fixations predominate, where narcissistic needs have remained ungratified during the early stages of life, and where early traumata have predominated.[8, 9, 15] Several authors stress that early separation traumata are likely to play a predominant role. As a result of deficient reality testing capacity on the part of the young child who has been left, a restitutional, anxiety-reducing fantasy, often with magical content will be reenacted repeatedly, presumably serving the unconscious intent of mastering the trauma in a nonverbal manner.

The psychological characteristics of the relationship between words and acts have their origin in the second year of life. At that time, both speech and motor activity develop with a great maturational spurt. The development of the child's ego functions at this stage are best observed through speech and actions. These carry the infant from symbiosis toward separation.[12] It is through these functions that memory formation, perception, and the synthetic functions of the ego find expression. As the infant grows into a toddler he moves on his own behalf and expresses his needs, wishes, and opposition[16] in words, as well as actions. In a rudimentary form a distinction can already be made at this period between communication and discharge; whether words are in the service of one function or the other. When speech is libidinally cathected as a communication between mother and child it becomes the carrier of a new form of love relationship between them, distinct from the symbiotic one. Verbal communication contributes toward the establishment of individuation, the formation of the body image, and the sense of identity. Action and speech move together to discover the world, strengthening the growing powers of the synthetic functions of the ego and the development of the secondary process.

The basis for a gradual separation between thought and action has been formed. Thought will become trial action expressing words and followed by action when necessary. As Freud has taught us, thinking is experimental action. The use of language delays discharge of affect.[2] The capacity to use speech promotes reality testing and the integrative process of the ego.[11] The extent to which wishes and phantasies can be verbalized and communicated successfully to the mother, action can be delayed and "confident expectation"[3] gradually developed. Under ideal conditions, discharge and communication will have to become separate functions of psychic life.

In pathological development this separation is achieved only partially or is regressively undone under the impact of anxiety or themes of stress as a result of a pathological object relationship between infant and mother. Under such conditions, action itself becomes a form of wordless communication; sometimes only if hostility has been discharged first, is ordinary intelligible communication possible. Verbalization may be used to ward off instinctual pressures rather than be used as an expression of thoughts or feelings.

During the separation-individuation phase, thought and speech are still secondary to action. Motor activity is the most important means by which the child separates from his mother.[14] However, a disproportionate need for motor activity at the expense of verbalization after the second year of life, or after speech has become firmly established, is characteristic of a personality structure developing toward a tendency of acting out.[10] If the child has been exposed to severe pathological conditions in his primary object relationship his psychic representations of his mother and of himself will be equally unstable. Internalization of the good self and good object will be easily disrupted by external pressures and inner tensions, both promoting rapid discharge. If object and self-constancy lack stability, the child will have only a moderate capacity to wait and will discharge his instinctual pressures through actions. This is a sign that the mother has not been able to communicate with the child by understanding his preverbal cues at first and later his verbal expression. The child cannot rely on words alone to reach his mother. Thus, he cannot be sure that when he expresses his needs in words help will be forthcoming. If differentiation between self and object has been incomplete due to an insufficiently good symbiotic or postsymbiotic relationship between mother and child, action or oppositional action, will be used by the child as a defense against the loss of identity.[1] Opposition will serve the preservation of a separate boundary between himself and his mother: acting for himself will mean acting against mother.

Freud's original formulation[7] regarding the motivations for acting out related to problems of repressed memories only: The patient who cannot remember in analysis reproduces his memories not in words, but in actions. Due to the repetition compulsion, which is an ever-present characteristic of psychic life, he repeats his memories in action over and over again without knowing that he does so. The transference relationship becomes a vital arena for such repetitions, particularly under the pressure of intense feelings of love or hate. Thus, transference occupies an intermediary position between recall and acting. In view of the fact that each transference relationship carries in it the original themes of primary object love, as well as later relationships, the original modes of the relationship between speech and action will become apparent during regressive phases of analytic work. It may even be possible to pinpoint some of the developmental way-stations when the child gave up trying to be heard and understood, became resigned, experienced being ignored beyond hope, and found adaptive measures other than speech to communicate with his environment.

Acting out within the transference has traditionally been understood as a way of remembering that has to be translated into words and proper memories by the analytic process. In recent years, many psychoanalytic authors have stressed the transference neurosis as a therapeutically induced relationship in which early feeling states are relived, with or without access to original memories. In a symposium in 1968 Anna Freud[6] elaborated on Freud's original definition of acting out. She stated that the preverbal period in human development corresponds developmentally to the period preceding ego organization and the consolidation of secondary process thinking. Therefore, memories from this period fall under the category of primary repression and are not recoverable, as the memory function as such, has not as yet been established. Such events, therefore, *have to be relived, as they cannot be remembered.*

It follows that traumata from the preverbal, or "semi-verbal" period that leave a lasting impact on the development of the psychic structure and on character formation will become carriers of action patterns established for the purpose of discharging psychic stress. They will form the nucleus of nonrecoverable memories and "nonrememberable" events resulting in developmental defects and discrepancies of various sorts: retardation of speech development, inhibition of locomotion, or noncommunicative, nonobject-directed behavior. We know from clinical practice that desertion of infants, premature separation, or lack of communication with them, stemming from the pathology of the mother, will leave them repeatedly in states of physical and psychic distress and will lead to a disproportionately large quantity of aggression within the psychic system.[5, 9] This excessive aggression will have to be discharged by all available means in order to preserve the inner cohesion of the psychic structure of the child and to preserve the object. True, the antecedents of these disturbances cannot be recaptured, but this developmental frame of reference is a very useful therapeutic tool in reconstructing early stress situations with patients when repeated in the transference. By making disturbances in the primary relationship with the mother conscious, patients become able to relieve excessive amounts of stress, anxiety and guilt by means other than acting out. In other words, the themes of early pathological object relationships leading to severe traumatization of the child can be put into words for the first time in a therapeutic relationship. This is not to suggest that verbalization is a cure, nor that irreversible pathology can be mastered by such means. But verbalization of distressing and anxiety-laden feeling states previously uncontrollable become organized when understood and put into words, thus becoming potentially accessible to ego control: Verbalization enlarges the emotional and experiential field that is accessible. The delay of action and thereby of discharge of instinctual gratification is a step toward autonomy of the ego.

A professional man in his early thirties came to analysis because of incapacity to work. His intellectual talents had made it possible for him to pass highest academic degrees without serious study. At a certain point, he missed out on a crucial opportunity in his career because he could not work and sought analysis. He was unable to sit still at his desk, to listen without becoming very sleepy and inattentive. In analysis he would withdraw into a sleeplike stupor, or when awake, behave like a small, hyperkinetic child: He would play with small objects he carried on his person. Verbalization was superficial, and in the service of discharge, and therefore closer to action than thought. He called such talk "radio static," designed to implement his flight from severe states of anxiety. His object relationships were tenuous and nonsustaining. He could function best when making a speech in an impersonal situation, but could not write his speeches, except in "bite-sized" statements of a page or two, associated to his mother's force-feeding where each bite was named after a relative-beneficiary.

Certain crucial facts about his first two years of life could be ascertained from his mother and his pediatrician whom the patient went to visit during his analysis. Although the patient was breast-fed for a short period, he was kept in an antiseptic environment. He was the first child of a very anxious unstable mother. He was given to throat infections and colds, was sickly and weak, and at the insistence of an obsessive pediatrician, handled as little as possible to avoid contagion. His toys were frequently washed. He was rarely held, rocked or fondled, and physical intimacy between mother and child left the mother with a feeling that she was putting him in danger by disobeying the physician.

When a younger brother was born, when the patient was almost three years old, the mother disobeyed the doctor and raised him "her way," erratically, but much more closely and lovingly. By this time the patient was an envious and enraged observer, who tried to hurt the new baby at every turn.

The patient was toilet trained at six months and force-fed. He was raised with hypochrondriacal fears related to his well-being. He was small in build and height, and exceptionally intelligent, causing him to be skipped repeatedly, so that his classmates were always much older. From them he felt a keen sense of exclusion, athletic giants, who related to him with a mixture of admiration and contempt.

Early analytic attempts to question the patient's hyperkinetic movements and discharge-type speech activities in the analysis were met with sardonic rhetoric, typecasting me as German, antiseptic in orientation, and inhuman. It was not difficult for the patient to relate this to the pediatrician, but more difficult to his mother, who had remained a very important figure in his life until he left home. It became apparent that the touching of objects that needed to accompany his speech helped him to ward off massive amounts of hostility and frustration which covered a deep and lonely yearning for communication through being touched. When he felt alone and without the opportunity to look or to touch, he became hostile and disorganized. His speech became withdrawn and sleepy or impersonal rhetoric. An analytic observation that "touched him" would temporarily relieve him, but our work was "bite-sized," and interspersed by long periods of flight. As a result of the physical closeness denied both mother and child, they developed very early verbal communication. The patient developed verbal precocity before the second year of life and was able to read at two and one-half years. Looking and speaking became substitutes for touching. An intense hostile, intrusive curiosity marked his adult relationships and transference relationship at times. The narcissistic trauma of seeing his brother handled and fondled by his mother at a time when he still craved such closeness had prompted him to develop various forms of "hostile touching" in order to provoke a response from people. From an early age these touches frequently were snide or sarcastic remarks. His narcissistic supplies had to come primarily from outsmarting others, using his intellect to demonstrate his superiority. He had needed to build his sense of well-being on a myth of intellectual invulnerability—the only area where he could compete successfully. Work, by contrast, was associated with mother's touch. She "worked" on him to feed him, but in a manner that withheld gratification—being forced and disciplined in an erratic unpredictable manner. We can see that precocious verbalization was a substitute for touching. In its discharge function, it became action-oriented, served the purpose of releasing hostility and tension, and of reestablishing a narcissistic myth about his intellectual invulnerability whenever his feelings of infantile omnipotence were threatened. In its communicative function speech was designed as a substitutive reaching out for the human touch. The patient's internal representations about himself and his mother were unstable—related to the fleeting quality of her touch with all its unpredictability, and to the manner in which she had forced him to survive on the physician's terms as an infant. Added to this was the traumatic impact of his mother's rages. Although he had attained object constancy, it was tenuous in quality, interrupted by anxiety states that were traceable to fears of sudden traumatic desertion. The superficial affect that prevailed in the early phases of analytic work was manifested by superficial verbal communications and random fidgety body motions. These condensed the positive, but emotionally limited function of verbalization in his early relationship to his mother, and his fear of the trauma of being suddenly robbed of her if he openly exhibited the depth of his rage and frustration.

The initial focus of the patient's treatment led to an examination of his overt behavior with its mixed messages of communication and discharge. At times his hyperkinetic motions assumed the character of a sign language, comparable to the physical stress signals of very small children, whose behavior Mahler[13] has described as manifesting "organismic distress." Very gradually, the patient learned to differentiate discharge behavior from communication. It became clear that much of his frantic fidgetiness was a replication of his mother's anxiety states—his imitative version of them. The patient identified with her shiftless, flighty behavior, as though he had to chase after her, in order not to lose her. There was also a reliving of mother's tantrums during which she would run out of the house, followed by the father. She would threaten not to return. The hyperactive state, therefore, represented the period *before* the threatened traumatic loss of the mother, as well as the undoing of this threat.

It was only after this nonverbal communication from his past had become intelligible to the patient that we were able to turn our attention more closely to the character of his object relationships. He characterized them as "touch and run," as he did the physical ministrations by his mother. Through a careful scrutiny of his behavior, the patient became aware that "touch and run" induced hostile responses from others, as they once had in him.

As the patient gradually separated hostile discharge from genuine communication, and as he became increasingly able to remember the feeling states induced by his early traumata, his behavior became much calmer and his anxiety states more controlled. He developed a certain capacity to verbalize his anxieties and to control his hostile outbursts. His behavior became less flighty. Simultaneously, he developed an anticipatory function related toward his verbal behavior and its effect upon others. He gradually relinquished the phantasy that he could reach his mother when she was in her tantrum states by seeking to fuse with her.

It was after the patient was capable to discharge hostility verbally and to distinguish it from other forms of communication that his analysis gained in continuity. Only then did he begin to produce phantasies, analyze dreams—in short, behave more like other analytic patients. In states of distress he would ask to sit up, so he could "touch me" with his eyes, thereby regaining control over his anxieties sufficiently to continue analytic work. As his anxiety states lessened, his hostile feelings became more organized and he developed transitory obsessional phantasies. Once, when it took an extra minute to open the door for him when he came for his hour, he phantasied I had died, and he wondered whether to wait until they took the body out on a stretcher. He was glad he had not paid his bill, as my estate may overlook to collect it. The phantasy demonstrates that the patient was learning how to wait. In the past he has used a stopwatch (action) to time his waiting. Now, hostility which covered the threatened object loss could be verbalized. In his anger that he would not get fed, the situation turned into a force-feeding of me (the fee) and a withholding (to feed himself). He was angry about being deserted but did not become disorganized. Object constancy had reached a more stable level and his internalizations permitted a more focussed expression of his needs. The step from action to verbalized phantasy was his first analytic triumph.

This example demonstrates that by the fortunate coincidence of having been able to ascertain a sufficient amount of data from his first two years available during the very early stages of treatment, the patient's nonverbal stress behavior became sufficiently intelligible to permit it to be relinquished rather rapidly and to open the vistas for genuine recall.

The following example is taken from an analysis I supervised. A young woman artist in her thirties would usher in each new analytic topic by first submitting an artistic product to her analyst which contained the psychological theme toward which she was moving in an artistic form. For instance, when yearning for closeness toward her father, the patient would paint a number of portraits of older men, including that of the analyst. She would bring them to the hour, sometimes associate to them later, but at first submit them to be viewed without verbal communication. When it became evident that she would soon discuss the conflicts of her phallic period, she began making mobiles; when some bisexual phantasies related to her body image were her uppermost concern, she began making flowers; when she was about to embark on the problem of her frigidity, she engaged in making jewelry.

At the outset of the analysis it was suggested that these nonverbal, concrete offerings that so frequently accompanied the patient to her sessions would be treated with a neutral friendliness, with impartiality, and not be subjected to analytic scrutiny unless the patient herself initiated this. The patient would be left free to associate to her artistic productions, or not, and the fact of being accompanied by them would not be raised as a subject for analysis at this time. The idea of this technique was an adaptation of a principle taken from child analysis, where the paramount importance of leaving current autonomous functions and sublimations intact, in favor of analyzing past developmental conflicts is described as being of crucial importance for permitting the continuing development of children under analysis. This therapeutic technique was adopted to keep the patient's artistic sublimations intact while proceeding with the analysis. That this method was correct was borne out by the fact that the patient indeed began to talk, or at least to dream about, and then talk about the conflict themes she had at first presented visually to her therapist.

The patient's mother had never encouraged verbalization of her children's needs and for many reasons even discouraged their expression in relation to pivotal life experiences during childhood. The patient developed an obsessive character structure with many adaptive characterological devices for isolating feelings. The mother possessed a "lady doll," who was fancifully dressed in grown-up clothing, was dressed, patted, and handled lovingly by the mother. That doll could be looked at by the children, but not touched. There was a striking parallel between the mother's use of her doll that bore some features of a transitional object and of a seemingly idealized version of the mother's body image, and the patient's use of her art work—which could be looked at, but not touched by analysis—at least not on the first viewing.

There were additional reasons why the patient's artistic productions were reminiscent of a transitional object: They belonged to the patient alone; they were viewed in an initial, tentative state of creativeness before they assumed full-fledged independence of a true sublimatory nature. They started as a "me-not-me" possession, but after the patient had expressed some of her feelings related to them, she went back to work and turned out independent completed products. Verbalization created a more independent status for her work.

As a child, the patient's father had subjected her to repeated and traumatically painful episodes of administering enemas with ritualistic regularity. The mother assisted in these ministrations and the child was expected to tolerate them without making a sound. Of the many meanings of this wordless, traumatic and painful procedure, the following relates to our discussion. The patient needed to test her analyst repeatedly and before each new analytic theme could be verbalized, whether she would be permitted by him to retain autonomous control over her productions. By substituting a visual symbolic representation for an inner psychic preoccupation initially, she assured her autonomy and the subsequent analysis was consequently less frightening. The original enema trauma of childhood had been too traumatic to permit a trusting attitude without action when it came to her inner products. By showing first what she planned to produce and being assured by the analyst's attitude that she would not be robbed, or forced to share beyond her inner capacities, she became able to share verbally, and simultaneously, enormously enhance her artistic capacities.

This mode of handling the enema trauma in the analytic situation permitted the patient an initial experience of restitution and opened the way for the analysis of the trauma per se.

I hope to have demonstrated with these examples that certain actions by the patient or the analyst within the analytic situation may facilitate rather than inhibit recall. In certain situations where the infantile ego had been too weak to cope with a traumatic situation by at least being permitted to verbalize it and be given relief, the analytic rules "to put it into words" needs to be facilitated by an active move—or the permission of an active move on the part of the patient—before analysis proper can lead to the memory and mastery of the trauma. In this connection, it is important to realize that reconstructions given too early, or a premature interpretation of the action, may turn an attempt at a new mastery into a repetition of a failure. It seems important, though often impossible, to differentiate between unrecalled and nonrecallable memories[9] which have become part of the infantile, narcissistic and often impulse-ridden character structure. Bibring[4] made us aware that at a point in analysis where repression has been lifted, but a memory not yet produced in an analysis in verbal form, acting out will often ensue. This may take the form of a sudden need for action, a need for reality testing, or of a sudden feeling that adult ego functions cannot be trusted.

The following is an example where a sudden reliving of a disorganized infantile anxiety state interfered with direct access to a memory until a certain action was encouraged in the hour.

A patient began her session with an agitated and apparently pointless preoccupation. She wondered whether the shade on my desk lamp was crooked. She became increasingly preoccupied with this, could think of nothing else, and was markedly agitated. I noted that her view of the lampshade from her position on the couch was on a parallel picture plane and therefore should permit a viewing without perceptual distortion. However, the patient was unable to master the situation in its displaced form and I suggested that she sit up and look. She did so and with a sign of relief remarked that it was very crooked indeed! Her agitation had subsided. She then remarked that her perceptions seemed to her completely untrustworthy, and she produced a new memory from the age of two and one-half years where the reality of her perception played a central role. At that time, her mother was very self-preoccupied and sad, mourning the loss of a sibling, somewhat older than the patient, who had died. When her mother wanted to be alone she sent the patient to "go and play by the mirror," a large bedroom mirror which was designed to hold the patient's attention by viewing herself. The patient's mirror image became her companion and her twin, but sometimes she became very uncertain who this was, or whom she saw—presumably after she became lonely for her mother and it became increasingly difficult to maintain cathexis of herself in her separated state. She mentioned with great feeling that the child in the mirror never answered her.* In the feeling state that initiated the recall of the memory perception substituted for speech and a distorted object for a real one, as it once had in the actual situation. This was the reason for the reliving at the onset of the hour. The patient had to reaffirm her adult perceptions before she could verbalize her memory. My encouragement of the patient to test reality permitted her to reach her memory.

Each of the three patients here discussed were unable to reach their mothers emotionally and obtain relief during the original distressing situation or trauma reproduced nonverbally in the analytic situation. Each had given up on reaching the mother after repeated failures. In each case a very permissive, or active, encouraging attitude related to problems of mastery via the patient's ego functions, rather than free association facilitated recall and strengthened the therapeutic alliance. Following a newly acquired sense of mastery in which the adult ego could supersede the infantile one, the patients were able to return to verbal communication within the analysis, or acquire new verbal control over an infantile disorganizing feeling state for the first time.

REFERENCES

1. Angel, K.: Loss of identity and acting out. *J. Amer. Psychoanal. Assoc.*, *13*, 1965.
2. Balkanyi, C.: On verbalization. *Int. J. Psychoanal.*, *45*, 1964.
3. Benedek, T.: Parenthood as a developmental phase. *J. Amer. Psychoanal. Assoc.*, 6:389-417, 1958.
4. Bibring, E.: Therapeutic results of psychoanalysis. *Int. J. Psychoanal.*, *18*, 1937.
5. Elkisch, P., and Mahler, M.: On infantile precursors of the "influencing machine." *Psychoanal. Stud. Child*, 19:219-235, 1959.
6. Freud, A.: Acting out. Contribution to the Symposium on Acting Out. *Int. J. Psychoanal.*, 49:165-170, 1968.
7. Freud, S.: Remembering, repeating and working-through. In *Standard Edition*. London, Hogarth Press, 1958, Vol. XII, pp. 145-156.
8. Greenacre, P.: General problems of acting out. *Psychoanal. Quart.*, 19:455-467, 1950.

---

* Developmentally, this was the period of rapprochement,[13] but the patient did not feel free to run back to her mother.

9. Greenacre, P.: Problems of acting out in the transference relationship. In E. Rexford (Ed.): *A Developmental Approach to Problems of Acting Out.* New York, International Universities Press, 1966.

10. Greenacre, P.: Contribution to the symposium on acting out. *Int. J. Psychoanal., 49*:211, 1968.

11. Katan, A.: Some thoughts about the role of verbalization in early childhood. *Psychoanal. Stud. Child, 16,* 1961.

12. Mahler, M. S.: Thoughts about development and individuation. *Psychoanal. Stud. Child, 18*:307-324, 1963.

13. Mahler, M. S.: Notes on the development of basic moods: the depressive affect. In R. M. Loewenstein et al.: *Psychoanalysis—A General Psychology.* New York, International Universities Press, 1966, pp. 152-158.

14. Moore, B.: Contribution to the symposium on acting out. *Int. J. Psychoanal., 49*:182-184, 1968.

15. Rexford, E.: A developmental concept of acting out. In E. Rexford (Ed.): *A Developmental Approach to Problems of Acting Out.* New York, International Universities Press, 1966.

16. Spitz, R. A.: *No and Yes: On the Genesis of Human Communication.* New York, International Universities Press, 1957.

$\mathbf{D}$ R. LEON HAMMER, a graduate of the William Alanson White Institute where he was trained in psychoanalysis, very courageously in this paper criticizes both analysis and analysts and develops a new systematized approach to treatment that is minimally nonanalytic and, at time, violently antianalytic.

Dr. Hammer elaborates his "action-oriented" approach to psychotherapy and the reasons he evolved it. He begins with a critique of classical psychoanalysis which, Dr. Hammer believes, has failed miserably in providing the best environment for a patient's growth. This failure is attributed to the unequal relationship imposed by the psychoanalyst upon himself and his patient. For a patient truly to benefit psychotherapeutically, the therapist must be active, must be an initiator rather than merely a frustrator. Hammer includes an outline of specific traits which a therapist must possess to insure maximum growth for his patients and he supports his comments with illustrative examples.

The importance of being a total person, of taking risks and willingly admitting failure, of allowing genuine emotional interaction with the patient, perhaps, even including nonsexual and nonexploitative physical contact, was discussed and illustrated by case examples. Above all, the importance of flexibility on the therapist's part is emphasized by Dr. Hammer in his model of meaningful and helpful therapy.

In this paper, which is both innovative and highly critical of analysis, Dr. Hammer has advocated a real "core to core" emotional contact between patient and therapist as the minimal requirement for an effective therapy. A constructive utilization of action or even acting out is advocated. There are marked differences of opinion among professionals about the role of physical contact in psychotherapeutic practice. The majority of therapists, especially psychoanalysts, are opposed to this practice. The use of sexual contact, in particular with patients, is even more

279

strongly repudiated. (Dr. Hammer neither advocates nor participates in patient-therapist sexual contact.) Although we might disagree with some of Dr. Hammer's concepts, we believe that a university setting should be a place where new thinking can be aired and criticized. We are glad to exercise this role in presenting Dr. Hammer's challenging and provocative paper.

D.S.M.
G.D.G.

Chapter 17

Activity – An Immutable and Indispensable Element of the Therapist's Participation in Human Growth

LEON I. HAMMER

T HE SUBJECT OF this paper, like the goal of therapy, is healing, growth and change. Psychoanalysis and related disciplines fail to satisfy this goal. Without exception, they also fail to address themselves to the phenomena of growth, the conditions which are necessary for change in human personality. We are asked to "trust the process" as if the need to change was the means of change. The need, the driving force, and the means for harnessing this force, are not the same. In this paper we will explore this process, trusting that understanding can lead us to a more effective therapy, offering an alternative to current theory and practice.

The driving force "to become" demands a continuum of activity between a developing human being and a series of "significant others" (H. S. Sullivan). At any one time this activity is defined by the needs inherent to a stage of development. Maslow's[9] hierarchy of needs, or my own outline, are guides to the specific events of living around which contact and interaction optimally occur during these stages. The qualitative aspects of the contact are of enormous importance to the outcome of this development and are therefore central issues in this paper.

The process of change which takes place in adults is analogous to the process of growth which takes place in children. This change will take place only when all of the conditions for a child's real growth are possible in the therapeutic situation. This is nature's model from which man cannot depart without destroy-

281

ing himself and his environment. The core of such therapy is activity. There must be action, movement, behavior of a co-ordinated dynamic intense, spontaneous, emotional and contemplative nature. There must be an engagement between two people. First there is one totally responsible human being. He is called the therapist. And there is another human being involved. He who has bogged down in the stream of his unfolding.

This desire to create understanding of the theme of the *indispensability of action for growth* is one of the reasons for this paper. This growing appreciation for active intervention in people's lives is indicated by the appearance in the past decade of group and individual techniques such as Gestalt therapy, bio-energetics, encounter, sensitivity, and the entire "laboratory" increment as well as the increased role of psychodrama and behavioral assertive techniques.

To be effective, action takes place in the context of a developmental model of therapy. An explanation of the basic principles of this model is the second reason for this paper. There is no room for fantasy when we discuss change. We must study and obey the immutable laws for growth which are specific to our species, phases of interaction between the unfolding needs of a person and his environment. In therapy we actively reawaken needs long since unmet and we actively meet these needs. We create a new experience. This is our model.

In psychoanalytic literature, growth is associated with a vague concept of awareness called "insight" and "working-through." Therapy involves the dedication of patient and analyst alike to a unidirectional flow of ideas and feelings from the inside of the patient to both the conscious patient and the attentive therapist. (Glover[5]; Fromm,[4] "psychoanalysis is making the unconscious conscious"; Greenson[6]). The critical medium for this uncovering is the sensory isolation of the patient. It is written that when the voices of the outer world are stilled, inner voices never before heard will come forth into awareness. Once exorcised, these inner voices and the feelings they engender will join the stream of consciousness and be fused by the relentless skills of the analyst into an emotional understanding called insight. Insight then, in endless toil, bursts forth over and over again into revelation; and, by some still more mysterious and wonderful miracle, the patient is free.

The process of growth I have just abstracted is a fantasy. It has been embroidered and embellished by a stream of gifted artisans, each preferring one or more aspects of the original Austrian version to call his own.

The failure of psychoanalysis to be an agent of growth has several roots. One is its unswerving devotion to a setting of isolation and frustration. Another is its incredible blindness to the ineluctable conditions of human growth and survival. It fails to provide a model for growth based on natural laws. It has failed to use the increasing body of knowledge of childhood and of human development. In this context it fails to provide for a therapist who is willing to be an energetic active surrogate parent, an initiator of a living "experience-between" especially in the areas of need where development failed.

For the sake of discussion we must separate what is in reality a continuum. There is first the long, difficult, and painful body of "experience-between" which *leads* to trust. Then there is the other—the body of "experience-between" which is *rooted* in trust. In this latter context the therapist and the dissociated selves of the patient are engaged in a living interaction. It is a new experience which supersedes old experience, which relabels the psyche and through which the patient's hidden selves are realized.

I hope that the unfolding ideas in the paper will illuminate the concept of "experience-between." It cannot be summarized adequately in brief although words like "authenticity" and expressions such as "core to core"[4] and "gut to gut" are useful.

"Experience-between" is the direct and powerful intervention of one person in the life and psyche of another. It must be sufficient to engage the most selectively inattended, repressed or dissociated selves at any level of development. The intention, of course, can never match the total need, but the intention must be as total and complete and unafraid of failure as is humanly possible. For Bettleheim,[1] "one cannot help another in his ascent from hell unless one has first joined him there. This will always mean a descent to one's own hell, however far behind one has left it."

Most therapies which bring the patient and the therapist together only through the medium of the analyst's technical skill do indeed succeed in creating a variety of colorful fantasies, but real freedom and real growth eludes them. Any force which attempts to split those two inseparable aspects of human experience, the inner and the outer, the intrapsychic and the interpersonal, the patient and the therapist, rends itself the unwitting agent of alienation. Human life is, from its beginning to its end, a matrix weaved between inner and outer, a mesh of experience, the separation of which is sickness and death. By insisting on the separation of inner from outer, of patient from therapist, psychoanalysis becomes a catabolic agent which defeats nature.

We are witness to a situation in psychoanalysis in which one person is forced into relative exile in the presence of another for the purpose of growth. The contact is clearly defined and highly formalized. The patient, the excommunicated soul, is instructed to set out almost alone to find himself.

Instead, the analyst finds the patient moving always towards him. The analyst is trained to tell the patient that by turning toward the therapist he is turning away from himself. The patient persists. He gravitates again and again toward the therapist. But, the therapist persists and the patient is rejected with unremitting and unrelenting conviction. This is so basic to the art that we no longer even ask ourselves if the patient is indeed turning away from himself when he turns to the therapist. We no longer consider the matter open to serious question. In fact, though, it is.

It is the thesis of this paper that the move by the patient on the couch toward the doctor is far more natural and normal than the effort of the analyst to isolate the patient.

The human animal is inherently gregarious. He is a bonding creature. True separateness for this species means only one thing—probable death. By nature man is dependent on the world around him and particularly on other men for his sense and knowledge of self. This dependency is commonly so profoundly failed and so much is left unfulfilled in any single man that, given the opportunity we turn again and again to other of our kind to seek growth experience. Yet, this move by the patient toward the therapist rather than towards himself has been endlessly condemned as a subversion of the process called analysis.

The analyst notices only one aspect of this complicated but natural movement of his patient towards him. He loses sight of the fundamental principle of life which motivates the direction; he sees only what he has been trained to look for. He is permitted to observe only the way in which he is approached and not the larger picture, the *necessity* for the approach.

The patient innately longs for a corrective experience with this new person in his life (Fliess's Corrective Model of Reality) but in turning to the analyst he does something wrong. Life's earlier experiences have rendered this creature unable to make suitable or rewarding human contact. He complains; he is negative; he is too nice; he is irrelevant or autistic; he is hostile or obsessive; he is superficial or silent; he is demanding or self-effacing. In any case, he is a total bungler at direct productive contact, which is, incidentally, the reason he is seeking relief in the first place.

The analyst completely misreads the situation since the technique of turning to him is so poor and maladaptive. He frequently brands the entire maneuver as "pathological." With that curse on him the patient is lost for the second, and possibly the last time, in his life. He may never realize himself through a new growth experience but he will make the most of a bad situation. He will identify with the analyst and strive to feel equally superior to those who may try to depend on him. If he is obsessive to begin with he will be reinforced by the obsessive nature of his rejection and if he is "resistant" he will learn from the analyst new forms of "character assassination."

The analyst's goal of an "uncovering experience" for the patient is quickly undone by the analyst who enters into a long struggle with a person he labels resistant. The patient's resistance is his natural, though impotent, repudiation of what he knows is once again wrong in his life. The patient is easy prey, a perfect victim. Feeling defective to begin with, he can only assume that he himself is wrong and once again he is required to label that part of himself sick which is basically healthy. The wheel has turned full circle and nothing new will happen.

In childhood, during the normal evolution of human need, character develops not from the simple unfolding of needs and life skills, but from the interaction of those needs and skills with another human being. This second person is assigned by fate and may satisfy or deny those skills and needs entirely or in some part. (In real life we cannot "trust the process," and the process often fails.) The inner life of one man depends forever on the outer life of another. Men are thereby forever defined by the nature of this *dependency* both for initial growth and for an ultimate attempt to change.

The patient, by turning to the analyst rather than himself, is doing what comes naturally. In order to change or grow he knows, his chromosomes know, that he depends upon the heat, light, and energy of a searing and powerful direct involvement with another member of his species. The experience of being himself, he knows, can only change when his dissociated basic needs are lived out with another human being who will react to them differently from those who bore the original responsibility for labeling his psyche.

The analyst denies and attacks human nature when he derogates the patient's dependency on him for a new experience and refuses to be an equal partner in an active living engagement. The patient comes limping into therapy seeking contact, a contact upon which depends his life or his desire to live. However awkward, distasteful, burdensome, or defective, I regard his maneuver towards me for contact as sacred. Underlying all human endeavor and development is the necessity for an interaction which senses, validates, and grapples with real human need. Nothing that I have described before as necessary to change can take place without an intense emotional contact. Contact is the basic rule.

I begin with the patient's tenuous and often self-defeating gestures; whereas most of the gesture may seem to wave me away, as it does most other people. I make some safe return sign saying that I see its more basic intent.

I do not approach the contact as a negative force though I may make some comment on its limitations. I recognize my responsibility to take the initiative to provide alternative and more productive forms of contact, forms which the patient is afraid to make first. I make them as tentative as necessary to make the patient feel safe. Yet he is encouraged to see the importance of risking new contact in his search for real security. I respect his form of contact and I demonstrate other possibilities.

For example, a young lady came to see me and talked about her past life in a monotonous monologue for over an hour. When she was finished I asked her in a friendly way why she chose to bore me for an hour when we both knew she was on the verge of suicide, conveying to her my acute awareness of her underlying despair and desperation. For years she had "rapped" in this manner to analysts whose exasperation eventually led them to futilely exhort her to "buck up." Coming from a finishing school background she was "bucking up" in public while quietly slipping into madness and despair. No one seemed to recognize her desperation because everyone was concentrating on analyzing the details of the boring "rap" instead of recognizing the "rap" as a camouflaged way of saying "if you feel the deadliness of this you will know how close to death I am." In this instance, of course, there was no time to be tentative—just enough time to ask, "What does this contact really tell me?" She could not do this for herself.

The model of the analyst I am conveying is an active, sensitive initiator who accepts his responsibility for the patient's real dependency on him to create a living interaction centered around the patient's dissociated and repressed needs. A patient cannot act on a need which he knows nothing about and he does not learn about it by lying on his back in relative isolation examining fantasy after fantasy. The evolution of human development is a saga of interaction. Without interaction (action between) there is no evolution and there is no development. Nature has provided us, including analysts, with all the equipment for this kind of action. Nature has given us the power to observe her and record her precepts of growth, her laws of action-between. In brief summary these centered around the following:

1. Physical care.
2. Physical contact.
3. Communication: verbal and nonverbal.
4. Respect.
5. Structure.
6. Socialization.
7. A model of confidence to provide all the above within responsible human and professional limits.

Almost nothing of what has been learned about "nature's way"—of the natural development of the human being—has been officially incorporated into the main body of psychoanalytic practice or into its theory of therapy. This model for action is even more indispensable to the "neurotic" than to the "psychotic" patient.

The neurotic benefits less from conventional therapies than the psychotic for two interdependent reasons. First, these therapies preoccupy themselves with the patient's resistance. For the neurotic who is well prepared for defensive pseudo-mutual behavior this model provides the ideal diversion. The therapist's preoccupation with resistance is the neurotic's best defense. The psychotic's obvious defenses of denial and dissociation offer little challenge to a therapy which is so heavily designed to deal with resistance. Important issues are almost immediately available to the therapeutic situation. This frequently is frightening to the therapist who is trained to deal with pseudo-problems. He may be at a loss with the direct confrontation of a real need laid bare in its naked raw state. For the psychotic the dissociated material, that which is rooted in terror, is easily tapped as grist for the mill. Conventional therapies are not prepared for the dissociated. They are more comfortable with the less disturbing *repressed* material. They welcome all feelings on the level of castration. They reject with appropriate horror feelings associated with annihilation, murder and death, those dissociated insane feelings which seem so profoundly and elusively hidden in the well-defended neurotic. Unless one is dealing at this level, authentic growth and development does not take place in therapy. For these reasons the possibilities for this kind of growth for the psychotic are greater than for the neurotic. He is equally lost with the psychotic in the basic areas of unfinished business but he is better able to hide his defect. Psychoanalysis enhances this skill. Tragically the core of every neurosis is a buried and almost always untouched psychosis.

The patient, neurotic or psychotic, cannot take the initiative in making constructive contact. To achieve belated growth which was originally left behind because it was outside of, or damaged by, human involvement, the patient now needs his therapist. The therapist is responsible for this initiative; he is responsible for creating the opportunity for this new experience in the following ways:

1. He is presumed to be a lifetime student of basic human nature and development. In particular, he knows that life depends on *contact* and that it was a failure in *contact* that has led to the patient's inadequate experience in living.

2. Contact with the therapist is the basic guideline in therapy because there is a direct corollary between what a person avoids in his relationship with the outside and what he avoids on the inside. Since we can know others only to the extent that they will show themselves or allow themselves to be observed, we must make contact between patient and doctor the basic rule if there are to be any basic rules. The patient cannot know himself alone; he will begin to know new things about himself through his experience of himself with another—the therapist.

3. The therapist knows that the patient has survived, however poorly, with some method of his own to maintain contact. The therapist knows that this contact is designed to keep him at a safe distance. He deeply respects this contact as lifesaving to the patient. Therefore, he does not attack it, either through analysis, suggestion, or in any other fashion. Where pretense is concerned, the therapist will not attack. He will look for the positive side of the pretense. All defense is based on some substance (talent) which could become tools for expression instead of means to inflation. In this way the therapist shows he *cares*.

4. The therapist accepts the patient's real dependence on him

to lead the way out of isolation. He takes the responsibility of carrying out the development of real contact and he is willing without a struggle (and depending on his own mental and physical condition on any particular day) to take the initiative in making this contact. This initiative will take place primarily in the areas of relating which are either out of the patient's experience or deeply associated with bad experience. The therapist will take the initiative in making this contact. This initiative will take place primarily in the areas of relating which are either out of the patient's experience or deeply associated with bad experience. The therapist will take the initiative to understand these areas, to inform the patient and then to live with the patient in these areas rather than interpret them from a distance.

He will make the contacts which the patient cannot make in order to move away from the patient's base-line restitutive maladaptive contacts. In those situations where satisfaction of needs seems so remote and unreal, the therapist will provide the impetus and the hope on as realistic a basis as is possible. The therapist will do, therefore, whatever he can to responsibly provide the following:

A. Authentic direct emotional contact:
   1. Tenderness and affection
   2. Hostility, anger, and punishment
   3. Caring
   4. Empathy
   5. Ability to absorb hostility and react affirmatively without crushing the other
   6. Sympathy
B. Responsibility:
   1. Physical care
   2. Initiative
   3. Commitment
   4. Courage
   5. Firmness
   6. Availability
   7. A positive outlook on life
   8. Dependency (acceptance of people's real needs without derogation)
   9. Control
   10. Judgment

C. Authentic direct verbal contact:
1. Happiness and joy
2. Hostility
3. Education and learning (information)

D. Involvement:
1. Intention
2. Initiative
3. Flexibility
4. Support—through difficult times
5. Loyalty
6. Reaction
7. Friendship
8. Orientation to sensation to:
   a. Listen
   b. Watch
   c. Touch
   d. Smell

E. Respect:
1. To be a good *winner* and a good *loser*
2. For the value of restitutive maneuvers for:
   a. Safety
   b. Contact
   c. A view of hidden or abused talents
3. For different temperaments
4. Honesty

He may make one more or one hundred moves. Depending on his patient's real deficits he may have to talk, touch, see, scream, fight, hold, care; and show hurt, love, anger, trust, rage, reserve, aggression, tenderness, defeat, affection and despair, alter his schedule or work for nothing.

Most particularly, the doctor must be the first to care. Caring (and knowing) are the most catastrophic threats to the autonomy of a vulnerable person. To care for onself especially (popularly called motivation) may be the final surrender of one's greatest protection—to not exist. If you do not exist you cannot be hurt. We, the therapists, must exist; must provide the caring and the motivation when for these reasons the patient is unable to openly provide them.

No human animal is capable of caring for himself more than he is initially cared about. For our existence to be joyful someone somewhere has to experience us as joyful and show it. Young people say over and over about their parents "I want to just look into their eyes and see that I made them happy." To feel worth saving ourselves someone somewhere has to accept the responsibility for us, a basic human commitment to transcend our loneliness by "seeing things through" together. Especially in crises the therapist must stand firmly with the patient through the terror and disorganization which can accompany growth in the most hidden areas of personality.

We ask the impossible by asking our vulnerable patients to initiate the uncovering process. Revelation starts with us. We make this first move towards intimacy. We are the corrective mode of reality. We open up; if the patient attacks we show our hurt but we do not inflict hurt upon ourselves. We have our shortcomings but they cannot be used against us. Our faults do not deprive us of our autonomy.

No amount of suggestion, persuasion, interpretation, analysis, insight, or working-through will replace new experience. This gut-to-gut experience will not take place without the therapist's active initiative when the patient is unable to act.

5. Any distortion by the patient of the intentions of this contact will be dealt with as an interference to the ultimate satisfaction of the patient's basic needs. The therapist will not analyze transference in the conventional sense as a way of clarifying the past or even the present except in terms of contact and except as it may fulfill the need of all humans to have a past. He will not avoid attacks on, or affirmation of, his self-respect. Transference will be an opportunity for new experience.

Transference is traditionally that aspect of resistance which expresses itself in the patient's feelings about and behavior towards the therapist. The myriad meanings of transference in the literature of psychoanalysis constitute one of the most confusing episodes in the history of ideas. In light of my view of growth and change I would say that *transference and countertransference is that which interferes with direct constructive contact between the patient and the doctor, the former stemming from the patient and the latter from the analyst.*

My attitude toward transference and activity is determined largely by my concept of growth and change. I cannot conceive of, and have never observed, anyone changing fundamentally by simply unfolding to himself or to another person a series of fantasies about that other person even when they are clearly defined over a period of time as repetitive and enduring traits of his fantasy life or even when they are accompanied by a strong flow of feeling. People do change through new experience. Transference becomes, for me, therefore, an opportunity to have experience. It is important that the experience with me be real, that the patient's reactions are to a real person and to my real behavior. Fantasy and distortion can only be clearly seen by the patient in the context of reality. I am concerned that the patient sees how his distortion interferes with his achievement of real satisfaction with me over the broadest spectrum of human contact.

All of psychoanalysis and most of psychotherapies confuse reserve with neutrality. There is nothing neutral about reserve. Ironically, reserve is a most powerful activity.

Analysts and their patients are experts primarily on man's reaction to frustration, isolation and coldness. Seventy years of speculation about man, based on analysis, is simply a study of one tiny fraction of total humanity. Indeed psychoanalysis has always been active. It has, however, allowed itself only one activity, and its practitioners and patients have become dangerous to society because they define the true man only as he reacts in fantasy to frustration and they are taken seriously. What a picture of man! Whether or not man can be saved, what has psychoanalysis contributed to his salvation? What indeed has analysis done to treat man's real problems—his terror of his own dependency and ontological vulnerability and his violent and insane acting out for the power which would deny this vulnerability? Look at the world around you and ask what measure of softness or real strength this work has contributed to it. *We must not forget that by saying and doing nothing to another human being we are doing a great deal.*

I know that absolute neutrality is both impossible and undesirable. I refuse to contribute to man's madness by confining my activity as a therapist to the role of frustrator even though it might make my practice and life much easier. I will be as total a person as possible with my patients so that my patients may be total people. Frustration is, of course, a part of every man's life and is an experience sooner or later which patient and doctor must live through. When, however, we make the fraction the whole we join the common madness.

The endless fantasies stimulated by hours of relative isolation in a chair or couch are artificially stimulated and significant of almost nothing except the terror of isolation. Periods of time to oneself, the moment alone, the exhilaration of a separate self in meditation or in some kind of internal intellectual or emotional dialogue or contact is necessary to life. However, to quote John Heider,[7] who quotes a Zen priest, "One should allow thoughts (fantasies) into one's mind as one invites a person into one's kitchen, but do not ask them to stay for tea." Analysis is generally an endless tea party of fantasy, the natural reaction to a struggle for power between a frustrator (analyst) and the frustrated (analysand).

Meaningful fantasy and distortion come quickly and powerfully at the appropriate moment only in the heat of a broadly based relationship. This is the *natural* way for it to happen. Those powerful feelings such as love and intimacy with which the patient cannot cope and for which he needs our help are not evoked in isolation. The writings of Laing[8] and Bettleheim[1] and the life story of hundreds of people I have known equate isolation with emptiness. The "splendid isolation" of the schizoid is a living death.

Change occurs through new experience with one's hidden self, not through the revolving door of the established circuits of one's inner mind. Since an outer experience was indispensable to the original inner experience, a new outer experience is necessary to bring about a *new* inner experience. There is a dynamic field of action in which the natural quality of the exchange between analyst and patient creates a new experience before, during and after uncovering. Isolation of therapist from the patient or from his uncovered feelings perpetuates the deadness of the patient's life.

In the context of therapy the therapist is by definition the necessary active partner. Given this concept of change, the therapist has no choice but to be actively and powerfully involved. He cannot relegate this involvement to an activity outside of therapy.

For example, a female patient had an accident as she left my house—about six miles away. She called immediately and asked my wife to come. Later she stayed at our home because she had no way of being cared for properly. In the evening she began to feel "paranoid"—that she wasn't doing enough to earn her keep, that we resented her presence, that her bandages offended us and so on. These were almost overpowering and were exactly what she had been talking about for some time.

I told her to respect her senses. I am a person who likes my privacy and she probably sensed my reserve. Also, my wife, who was quite worn by this time and somewhat overtalkative, was annoying me and I was sure she sensed that. This was the valid part of her paranoia.

The invalid part was her feeling that we were not accepting her as she was, that we expected a major performance on her part in order for her to be accepted. On a somewhat deeper level she was afraid that she would be asked to relate to us in a way in which she felt inadequate. She believed that we would resent her for being unable to care as much for us as we could for her.

This was a critical issue in her life up to that time. This girl's distortions and valid feelings were evoked, clarified and realized in a natural life situation with her therapist. People who need help are avoiding these real situations in their own life to avoid the unhappy associations they make with everyday contacts. Their deeper feelings will not come to light in a relative vacuum. They are frequently experts at creating and maintaining vacuums such as we provide in conventional therapy. We must fill their void in order to get to their real feelings and to provide an opportunity for change. Activity limited to silence evokes only a tiny fraction of these deeper feelings. Activity directed to reality and to people's real needs evokes a broad range of inner feelings which in itself is a new experience. Once evoked, the therapist may engage the patient and his dissociated feelings in an original growth-producing encounter.

The evoking of the significant distortions in a patient's life is minimized by the almost totally unnatural environment of an analyst's office and of the traditional analytic situation. The narrowness of this condition has led over the past twenty years to group therapy and the Laboratory Movement (NTL, Synanon and Esalon) to broaden the range of interaction. This broadened range has created more realistic situations between people to which they could respond in their characteristic fashion providing more meaningful grist for the therapeutic mill. People transfer real feelings, distorted and otherwise, in real situations. It is our obligation to provide that reality. We must become active, reactive, interactive on a widened scale with people and accept the added emotional burden of being responsibly aware of ourselves.

The conventional use of transference is actually the principal issue of countertransference and it interferes with growth in other ways:

1. It creates a strong emphasis on the negative. Time and energy are spent primarily on attacking resistance aspects of transference or analyzing the character trait aspects or simply waiting for transference to appear.

Whereas people come to us because they experience life negatively, it is clear to me that the best way to help them is to not regard their negative qualities as strong points to overcome or analyze ad nauseum.

It is clear from my own experience that the lengthy emphasis on the negative in people (a) derogates them beyond belief, (b) reinforces their terror of the positive, (c) teaches them nothing of how one normally handles the "negative" in life, and (d) focuses on the wrong issue—their pseudo-self rather than on the real issue—their dissociated needs.

Glover[5] mentions this as a major problem of psychoanalytic practice as well as in the supervision of new therapists. He states, "In short, the general impression given is that the patient is *personally* resisting, instead of becoming the tool of his unconscious mechanisms and conflicts"; "these ego-resistances . . . are apt to create an impression of *perversity.*"

Reich argued that one must attack defenses before reaching the inner person. I disagree. However, by working with the body,

Reich is not making such an attack an endless dialogue on what is wrong with the patient. There is an enormous temptation facing the therapist to become endlessly involved with the negative feelings aroused by his own reserve because this involvement with pseudo-feelings touches nothing of what all patients, and most therapists, fear—closeness and intimacy.

2. Reich mentions that the expectation of "free association" during the initial stages of any relationship is unrealistic. If it is unlikely under ordinary conditions, it would be impossible in a context of total reserve. I would go further to say that a significant source of what has been called *negative transference* is a response to this impossible presumption. Trust is the end-product of long hours of meaningful in-depth contact.

3. I would go even further and say that most *enduring* nega-tive transference is realistic, and apart from its being (a) a reaction to the unnatural setting of, and conditions for analysis, it is (b) usually a reaction to the therapist's insensitivity. Granted that the patient's way of handling his negative feelings is a problem to him, his negativity is usually legitimate. A good example is to be found in an experience I had some years ago with a patient who had been given LSD for therapeutic purposes. The first part of her trip had been a quiet, joyful experience, a significant departure from her usual feelings of depression and paralysis. The "trip" was taken on a day during which I became progressively more ill from incipient influenza so that by the end of the day I was barely able to go on, but I was unaware of my deteriorating physical and mental condition. In the post-"trip" dinner we discussed what happened and because of my fatigue I regressed—lost sight of the important event—the warmth, peace, and joy and concentrated on analyzing the negative aspects of the experience. During the next few weeks the patient was negative until she was finally able to vent her feelings of resentment about my destructive response to her experience for which I apologized. Even as I had undermined her good feeling, I had been vaguely aware of it.

Enduring negative transference is often an appropriate re-sponse to the analyst's approach to "resistance."[5] In theory resistance is defined as an attempt to block awareness of the inner self. In practice, the therapist experiences the patient's resistance to the therapist's concept of a therapeutic process. This can range all the way from the "basic rule" of free-association to the existentialist's insistence on personal responsibility and personal decision and the rationalist's insistence on logical thinking and to my concept of contact. The aspect of a patient's personality which interferes with the therapist's design for treatment was conceived during the history of psychoanalysis as something to overcome (Freud)[3] or something to analyze (Wolstein).[13] Both approaches basically destroy the possibility of new experience and new living for the patient.

Apart from the principal issue of isolation and the fear of personal contact, the analyst interferes with people's growth in a variety of ways. He is terrified of dependency, his own or anyone else's. He generally evades responsibility, caring, initiative, and has a horror of insanity; in fact, he avoids in his work every human attribute which I consider necessary to human growth. The effects of such alien and unnatural behavior on people and on the world is devastating.

My major interest in this paper is to spell out a more meaningful philosophy that will foster change. Action and activity are basic to my fundamental guide—natural human development.

Action and activity are essential human behavior. Activity is the expression, verbal and nonverbal of ourselves—our feelings and our thoughts. Within this context of the survival of the human race and of any individual, constructive expression is an essential goal. Constructive expression may be angry or tender, but it must lead to growth to be considered significant.

Although growth, development and movement are our measure they do not always make the patient or others in the patient's environment happy. As one woman said to her husband recently in my presence, "As I see it now I have a choice between killing myself or getting a divorce and I think I have decided that I would prefer to get the divorce." In this instance her growth and this expression of it made her husband unhappy. The measure of constructivity is movement in the individual towards responsible human growth. When it comes out of a destructive way of life, someone, perhaps everyone, is bound to be hurt. The resolution of a bad situation cannot be totally good.

A therapy without activity is nontherapeutic. However, a legitimate concern for everyone is a clear notion of how that activity fits into our morality and our ethics, whether it stays within or exceeds the limits.

I have said at another point in this paper that I consider structure as a fundamental expression of nature. Structure is constructive, provided it is not confused with rigidity. Growth, new experience, in my opinion can come only as nature meant it to come, and whereas anarchy is its enemy on one end of the spectrum (schizophrenia), rigidity is its enemy on the other end of the scale. If a therapist begins by saying what is possible and what is impossible in a contract for growth, then in my opinion he has already destroyed the possibility for productive change.

Structure sets up guidelines—not "iron curtains." I often wonder how much "living" most psychiatrists and psychologists have actually done when they lay down rigid rules for behavior in therapy. I wonder what animal they are really treating— hardly the one I meet in my home, on the streets, in the army, at school, in marriage. In my professional life the realities of everyday behavior and the mores of our society coincide only in the most superficial encounters.

I have honestly come to feel over the years that most therapists either know little or nothing about real people or that they are just dishonest in their dealings with patients. When in our practice do we really take into account Fromm's description of each man as being the entire spectrum of human behavior and feeling? "Murderers, rapists, lovers, philanthropists, pimps, whores, sadists, and saints." These are the people I meet in and out of practice, capable at any time of anything. Our expectations and our rule for behavior in and out of therapy have little to do with the real animal we are. What do most of our sterile concepts of psychopathology have to do with Bettleheim's "descent into hell"? I sincerely question the depth to which most analysts are aware of their "own hell."

There is the issue for example, of physical contact along its entire continuum. A developmental model of therapy which concerns itself with the deepest level of dissociated material does of necessity concern itself with the earliest and certainly the pre-logical stages of development. If we postulate that needs which were significantly unmet or misused in childhood must be relieved with the therapist as a prerequisite for growth, physical contact, physical care and nonverbal communication must occupy central roles.

It is argued that people develop a style of therapy based on their own personality. The therapist who touches needs to touch and communicates best in this manner. There is, of course, truth to this point of view. However, the therapy I propose is a rational therapy based on species inherent characteristics of growth. Whatever the stage of development or the appropriate learning mechanism at that age (interjection, association, imitation) it must take place in a context of other people and in interaction with these people. The therapist who will succeed in reaching the patient where he really hurts has to comfortably touch, hold, cuddle, caress, fondle, and talk with his hands, his body. When with conviction we speak through the "laying on of hands," we practice the most ancient and fundamental of all the arts, the art of healing.

My practice of therapy is heavily in this middle group of the spectrum of contact. I find it most difficult to isolate one example from the thousands which characterize the need and the value of physical warmth in growth and change. (The subject will occupy the better part of a book.) Though this need is most obvious for those who *cannot* communicate verbally, it is *basic to life*. Touch is the experiential area where the most profound failures of development occur.

Touch is basic to and is the basic form of communication. The following examples illustrate this.

1. One brilliant young lady was referred by her college instructor. Like so many, she was totally cut off from feeling. Her talk about herself was so abstract when it came at all that it was meaningless and, for the most part, it did not come. She was lost.

I moved next to her. I held her. She sank into my arms and

stayed. Gradually some verbal communication took place but for the most it was just holding. She cried. She had had no father and her mother was a detached, possessive alcoholic school principal. She had been the housemaid for herself, her two older brothers, her mother and her mother's lovers who came for the night. What was there to say. Later she formed a close homosexual relationship with the wife of a college instructor which was enormously important in the same way. Her course was not simple, but there was a course, one which led to basic human satisfaction and security with this one woman and now with men on all levels of communication.

2. Another young lady (age 29) is typical of many whose "holes" in their personality are related to feeling defective as warm, giving women. She saw herself and played to the hilt the role of the hard woman, constantly angry, nagging and complaining about all of my inadequacies. As she left one day I took her hand and cautiously offered to hold her. She came and took hold of me. For the first time in her life she broke down. She sobbed my name for a long time with a primitive pleading wail like a young animal hurt and lost in the forest. She could not believe that I could stand to touch her. Over a period of time she began to feel what I felt—a round, soft, warm, satisfying woman.

Caring is the vital spark of life and the central issue in therapy. For most of our patients caring means death and not caring is a living death. Tillich wrote that "neurosis" is the way of avoiding non-being by avoiding being." Caring is central to being. Non-being is non-caring. I endeavor to do nothing in my work with a patient which will discourage the growth of caring, most especially if that caring is for me. I carry this consideration as a *sacred trust*, for my contact with many people may be for them that one rare opportunity to care and come to life. When it happens I breathe easier. I celebrate.

Many people believe that physical pain inflicted by one person upon another is invariably a humiliating and destructive experience, an excellent example of rigid thinking as destructive as the rigidity of a Grand Inquisition. There are times, and it is in my opinion dishonest and ridiculous to deny it, when hitting another person is an inescapably productive act. For many children the gravity or seriousness of the effect of their behavior on another person cannot be conveyed in any other fashion. At times, any lesser response would convey a lesser feeling on the part of the parent. This is true for patients in therapy. It is often so much easier to walk away and say "to hell with you" than to stay, to strike back and become engaged. The feeling that no one really cared as expressed by the fear of their parents (far too many reasons than we have time to discuss here) to punish them, to react violently, is one of the most common themes in my practice, especially with young people. The parent's fear becomes the child's feeling of weakness with a pervasive sense of alienation. "Who will show me that they do not fear me? Who will show me that I will not break if I am really hurt? Who will take the trouble to break through my detachment and depersonalization? Who cares?" Can psychiatry accept a beating out of love—out of a person's need to be reached or learn—as a productive act? Probably not. Love, as Bettleheim says, "is not enough" in its most tender forms. A smack in the face is a lot less derogating than a pious "thou know not what thou dost." In what amounts to about 25,000 hours of psychotherapy time, I have struck patients a total of six times—each time productive. I refuse to say that it should never happen again. I do not need patients to beat. Someone may need to be beaten in order to grow, and the analyst who denies this possibility is talking about a theoretical race of animals which does not now exist.

On the other end of the scale is sex. Psychiatrists are phobic about the spectrum of physical contact in between violence and sex—tenderness, affection, cuddling and warmth—the heartland of all human flowering. They are frantic about the subject of sex in the therapeutic situation, so frantic as to lose sight of the real issues involved for both the patient and the doctor.

I do not see any inherent need on the part of two people undergoing together a process of growth to engage in sexual intercourse. I would consider it as an issue to be an extreme rarity. On the other hand I consider it to be a fundamental technical error to set an a priori code of behavior. The setting of rules in therapy should be a flexible ongoing process arrived at through hard work over real issues between therapist and patient as these issues arise. Rigidity will engender the following problems:

For one kind of person, it closes the door to feelings which have been almost totally locked away and to whom such hard and fast rules are a further proof of the inadvisability of even discussion. Frequently this kind of person is unable to distinguish between words and action. An admonition to not act is an admonition to not speak.

For some the rule is a safety factor which takes the risk out of talk, makes the words and, therefore, the experience meaningless.

A third person is one who has difficulty initiating any behavior in life that might risk rejection. The most fundamental rejection is one which says "your body disgusts me."

These are the people who depend on the therapist's initiative to make the first move—who touches them first—who they can see enjoys the experience of touching and being near them. It would be tragic to say categorically where and how contact with these patients must begin and end. Let me quote Freud[2]: "We cannot avoid taking some patients for treatment who are so helpless and incapable of ordinary life that for them one has to combine analytic with educative influence; and *even with the majority,* occasions now and then arise in which the physician is bound to take up the position of teacher and mentor."

We have patients, as Freud indicates, who cannot act for themselves—who simply cannot be "analyzed." A woman depends upon a man's positive response to her to be a woman. This is true for men, as well. There is that touch which tells us that we are all right. The argument which says that people can develop the sense of a "good me" by themselves is spurious.

There seems to be some kind of notion about growth that people develop by magic. They develop by experience. A man cannot know what kind of man he is except through the experience of him by others. Identity is a human experience, not a fantasy. This is as true for sexual identity as for any other. They would not come for help in the first place if they could handle it on their own. Many patients cannot risk invalidation or rejection on the outside even after endless hours of analysis.

There is another kind of person who sees any hard and fast

role as a challenge. This is especially true in the area of sex. It may be argued that this is grist for the mill—the major first subject of therapy. Its existence must indeed be noted as a major issue in the person's life. To become immediately engaged in a battle over rules is, however, only to repeat the person's life experience to date. It adds nothing new in going beyond a way of relating which is obviously safer, if not more satisfying, than any other they have known.

Though Freud acknowledged that sex is fundamental in all human behavior, "To begin with we knew none but sex objects," psychoanalysis along with almost every other institution in society has literally denied the basic feelings of man and woman as a natural force of energy for good (man to man and woman to woman as well). That feeling, that attraction, that energy is a natural resource which if allowed to flow, carries us to awareness and knowledge beyond the models of reasonable inquiry upon which we rely. To announce that there will be no sex before a relationship begins, even if there is to be none, destroys this vital driving force. Psychoanalysis has reinforced, by its practice, those forces of repression which it has always attacked in theory.

This energy is always basic to real growth. Like a flame it varies in intensity of heat and light and may at times burn more brightly than at other times. To unilaterally extinguish that flame, to kill this feeling in myself or in anyone who wishes to grow and flourish, obviates therapy.

For some people, hard and fast rules are a new experience. I have seen many such people. Their most immediate needs may be different from the needs of those mentioned above. Structure may be a priority issue in therapy. The point is that therapy has to be an extremely flexible operation. "Hard and fast rules," made unilaterally as a general principle, destroy the essence of the very concept "change" or "growth" or "new experience."

That the physician may enjoy experience does not make it inherently bad, immoral or unethical. In fact, his genuine enjoyment of the patient in some situations may be the experience which the patient needs. The patient may try to deny subsequently that either they or the doctor enjoyed each other.

But because it was a mutually experienced event the facts are more difficult to deny.

Much of our trouble in life and in the world comes from our learned association of good as being evil and immoral. A popular "hippie" saying that "if it feels good—do it," is a reaction to our calvanistic civilization.

We must have a general guide in life. The hippie saying is only a clue. For the most part we have been taught that "if it feels bad it must be good for you," and it was literally true that medicine that tasted good was considered ineffective. The application of that general principle that "if it feels good it is bad" has been a recurrent theme among my patients for fifteen years. If it feels good to the therapist or the patient, it is not necessarily bad any more than sulfur and molasses was necessarily efficacious.

We are appropriately very concerned about hurting our patients. If we act in therapy then we increase the possibility that we will act badly. The principle of caution is a good one. No therapist should ever place himself in the position of deciding that who he is is necessarily good for someone else. We must be genuinely prepared to be wrong. If, for example, I was certain in the heat of an interaction that holding or hitting a patient was the best thing I could do, I must be ready to admit that I may be wrong and to apologize if I am.

Let me explain why I believe that caution is carried to damaging extremes in therapy. The normal process of free behavior in life depends upon the ability to make, accept, admit and repair mistakes. If we are not prepared to make mistakes we are not prepared to live.

I consider that no matter how much we would like to deny ourselves as "models of reality" we are that probably more than anything else we may fancy ourselves to be. The therapist who is able to act and is not paralyzed by his fear of error or failure is a living example for his patient that one survives one's mistakes. No words could tell him better or make him more ready to take risks than the repeated risks taken by the therapist.

The therapist whose lack of self-knowledge is great or whose controls over his impulses are poor should not be a therapist except perhaps under the most controlled therapeutic conditions. If, in order to have the privilege and freedom of being a therapist you automatically reduce the chance for growth in your patient by reducing appropriate activity, you are certainly in the wrong profession.

Countertransference is the therapist's contribution to that which interferes with productive contact leading to new experience. The type of therapy which envisions growth coming out of the repeated identification of distortion or out of repeated association of past experience with present behavior is to my mind interesting but an almost total waste of time and energy. Such identification or insight is a welcome enrichment of one's total self but it comes after the fact of seeing oneself *now* rather than the other way around. To use an extreme example, I am not concerned that the patient I smacked reminds me of my great aunt Mary whom I had always wanted to hit. They might be very much alike and perhaps both should be bounced on the head. However, if it is appropriate to "now," the past matters very little. Allport says much the same thing when he points out that people's natural thrust is forward and psychoanalysis' natural thrust is backward. The inhibitions placed upon our activity by the traditional concept of countertransference have no place in a responsible therapy of "now." The test of that responsibility is immediate, today.

Once more I must emphasize that risk-taking and mistake-making by the therapist are vital to the patient's growth. Also basic to this growth is new experience in a structured but realistic, nonrigid atmosphere that takes a broader and less academic view of man than psychiatry has taken to date. Even more central is the extreme consideration the therapist must give to nurturing, sustaining, and encouraging the smallest sign of the patient's caring for anything or anyone, especially the doctor. The patient's life may depend upon this consideration.

If we aim for a psychotherapy of the total person we must follow nature as our guide. *By nature I mean the principles of human development*—the issues of absolutes in the stages of evolution of emotional and cognitive maturity. Nature has laws, systems and controls. The term seems to erroneously connote anarchy and the absence of structure. When I use the word "nature" I *do not* mean an absence of disciplined thought and behavior. Structure is basic in my frame of reference. It is basic in nature.

It is in the nature of man to achieve his basic satisfactions in a free flow between himself and other animals, especially those of his own species. My goal is to free people for this satisfaction and my emphasis must be the natural order of things, the contact between my patient and myself. The people I see frequently cannot make this contact by themselves. If they could they would not come to me. I must take the initiative and maintain it in a context of respect. I must not repeat the mistakes of the patient's earlier life or reinforce his withdrawal by isolating him. I must pay attention to his primary needs and emphasize the positive rather than the negative. When the latter interferes with contact I call this interference transference. I value it only as a response to a broad range of stimulation and not only as a response to reserve, aloofness, and isolation.

The most profoundly concealed feelings which the patient eludes in his daily life, and which would not enter the real world without the therapist's activity and initiative, emerge in response to the kind of intense contact I have described. Special techniques of uncovering may be used *provided they are within the context of interaction as defined here.*

As they enter the mutual awareness of patient and doctor, the doctor constantly responds. The patient expresses feeling or acts; the therapist reacts. The patient expects a catastrophe of either nothingness or destruction; the therapist provides a new experience for the patient. He is there totally with the patient in the heat and center of the drama. He validates in motion—his words are emotional, his actions are a new and different reality from the old reality. Longings which have caused pain and fear for many years are pleasurable and exciting and, in some situations, behavior which was never set into realistic limits is structured and disciplined. One girl who sneered at any gesture of help after a long period of special attention had her face smacked every time she told me that I didn't care and for the first time in her life she felt cared for. She began at this point to care for me and gradually for others and for living. One young man whose parents had never been able to punish him felt he needed some kind of limitation *by someone who cared.* One day, when he was finally convinced that I did care, he hit me and we fought. Though he was half my age, I put everything I could into it and held my own. His grandiosity was reduced and manic-depressive states disappeared and later he experienced an intense desire to simply be an infant in a womb, a role he had previously acted out, unbeknowst to himself, for a long time.

A profoundly depersonalized and extremely talented young lady could not exist because in her own eyes she was a despicable person because she had never murdered her mother who had severely debilitated her. She could not bear herself in any form. She played no part in her own life because she was too contemptible to exist. She had also failed to make her parents care for her. This was further proof of her incompetence and absolute worthlessness. Since she could not exist until she satisfied these two conditions of her worthiness, I hurt her so that she could, for a moment, stop punishing herself (Gestalt therapy technique) and she came to life, existed, and at first tried to kill me. Instead her existence was accompanied by passion and she was aroused and aroused me for the moment. The feelings were good, her power was realized; she felt good and made me feel good without killing. Subsequently she tried to return to her nonexistent state and could not completely do so. She was still unable to risk a more complete existence. The process of appropriate intense interaction will have to be repeated many times before she can realize her strength. She may eventually come to know it as a positive rather than as a dangerous force. She can then risk getting involved in life in a sustaining and satisfying fashion.

Another young lady had lost the use of her senses to experience and her mind to integrate. As a child there was no place for experience or expression of strong feeling. From the start there was incredible preparation for "high-society" and severe discipline. Authority was obsessive (father), intimidating (governess), and exploitive (mother). Strong feelings became the "unknown" and a source of terror. She coped with any approach by another person, or to another person, with instant inner deadness—nothingness. A long period of respectful gestures towards meeting some basic needs for physical contact and physical care and by taking the initiative for clarifying and establishing communication gave her the feeling that I cared. Then I began to exist for her by *my* response to objects around us with increasingly powerful expressions of sensation and thought until she would scream in sympathetic vibration rather than go dead. She experienced intense feeling. But, of course, she deadened herself and accused me of attacking her. When I accepted her need to retreat to this level of contact we could start again with the goal of having her one day express feeling and risk being intimidated, or exploited, or analyzed. She was able to have a new experience with me in which she positively realized her hidden self, her passion and her energy.

I have illustrated my point with extreme examples for emphasis. This level of interaction is as necessary, or even more so, for so-called neurotic patients. As I have previously mentioned they are in the greatest danger of having their core insanity totally missed in the heat of the analyst's struggle to analyze the "neurotic's" well-developed pseudo-mutual contacts resistance.

The mere awareness of a hidden self is not a new self. Growth is rooted in nature, we cannot supersede our own nature. We can grow only as God meant us to. Growth in nature is "experience-between" rooted in a contact which leads to basic trust and which finally galvanizes awareness into realization in the overwhelming heat of a new powerful and emotional interaction between therapist and the patient's hidden self.

A word of charity for the therapist. The work I propose is exhausting. It requires inordinate amounts of time and energy and an almost inhuman amount of intimate contact. It is, in my opinion, the only way in which people can grow. We are not prepared for this involvement. To quote the architect Ian McHarg,[10] we live by "economic determinism" rather than "ecological determinism." We are worth our weight only in gold.

It is unfair to expect a man to transcend his own species and society and live alone by values which may severely penalize him and his family. A fundamental change in values in the direction of cherishing pleasure over power is a prerequisite for a therapy based on the natural history of development. We are so totally disinterested in (or afraid of) who we are that only a minute fraction of our major security system—the economy —finds its way to the study of man.

It has, for example, been clear to me that the first man-made machine to become the master of man is the clock (Mumford).[11] The possibility of working in such a way as to end this enslavement and give people time according to their needs rather than on a scheduled arrangement would enhance growth in therapy as I conceive it. The fifty-minute hour is made for therapy as it is conventionally conceived; its very limit is its philosophy. The time arrangement proves itself—leads people to become what psychoanalysis says they must be. Our way of working is a self-fulfilling rationalization for why we do it. We create a frustrated "monster" whose monstrous feelings are proof of his "illness" and proof of our obligation and right to avoid and isolate him. *Time* is the analyst's first line of alienation. *Space* is the second line—decorator-designed space in which no one may urinate, defecate, or fornicate. What can a man produce artificially in fifty minutes in a department store window except artificial fantasy? What is a man supposed to do with his real feelings on Tuesday when his appointment is on Friday?

The concept of working flexibly is a society in which we are sorted out and measured dime for dime, dollar for dollar, by our "money's worth" is impossible. Psychoanalysis was designed for this society. Both are dying. The natural process of growth requires a world which values its own nature. It has not yet come to be. However, the time has come for each man to choose his place and make his stand. I have chosen and in this paper I begin to make my stand.

REFERENCES

1. Bettleheim, B.: *The Empty Fortress*. New York, The Free Press, 1967, pp. 10-11, 83.
2. Freud, S.: Advances in psychoanalytic therapy. In *Standard Edition*. London, Hogarth Press, 1958, Vol. XVI, p. 165.
3. Freud, S.: Introductory lectures on psychoanalysis. In *Standard Edition*. London, Hogarth Press, 1958, Vol. XVI, pp. 436-437.

4. Fromm, E.: Personal communication.

5. Glover, E.: *The Technique of Psychoanalysis.* New York, International Universities Press, 1958.

6. Greenson, R.: *The Technique and Practice of Psychoanalysis.* New York, International Universities Press, 1967, Vol. 1, pp. 32-33.

7. Heider, J.: Personal communication.

8. Laing, R.: *The Divided Self.* Baltimore, Penguin Books, 1965, pp. 91-92.

9. Maslow, A. H.: *Toward a Psychology of Being.* Princeton, D. Van Nostrand, 1962, p. 144.

10. McHarg, I.: *Design with Nature.* New York, National History Press, 1969, p. 29.

11. Mumford, L.: *Technics and Civilization.* New York, Harcourt, Brace and World, 1934.

12. Rado, S.: Emergency behavior. In P. H. Hoch and J. Zubin (Eds.): *Anxiety.* New York, Grune & Stratton, 1950.

13. Wolstein, B.: *Transference,* 2nd ed. New York, Grune & Stratton, 1964, pp. 151-152.

Dr. Gerald Berenson, a graduate of the Adelphi University Postdoctoral Program in Psychotherapy and a family therapist trained in the Ackerman tradition, brings both of these backgrounds to bear in this interesting paper on the potential for both constructive and nonconstructive acting out in family therapy.

Dr. Berenson introduces his paper with an excellent discussion of the evolvement and relevance of family therapy. He proceeds to enumerate the dangers inherent in a therapist's "misuse of self" in family therapy, a situation uniquely conducive to acting out by the therapist of his own unconscious problems.

An awareness of the positive potential of the constructive use of countertransference is crucial for this particular type of therapy, as Berenson illustrates in several brief case histories taken from his personal experience as a family therapist. Berenson concludes with some suggestions for therapists who practice family therapy, among which is the use of videotape to facilitate the therapist's continual examination of his own unconscious feelings and attitudes.

Dr. Berenson directly and strongly stresses the importance of knowing oneself even more as a family therapist than in any other type of treatment situation in order to avoid the frequent situations conducive to acting out. The potentially destructive pitfalls in this type of treatment are pointed out in this thoughtful paper—all of us having been forewarned are forearmed.

D.S.M.
G.D.G.

Chapter 18

Acting Out Potentials and the Use of Self in Family Therapy

GERALD BERENSON

As WE PROGRESS IN THE latter half of the twentieth century we are becoming increasingly aware of the varied sources of pollutants in our environment and have begun to think more in ecological terms. Similarly, there have been movements in the area of psychotherapy which are taking us far from the traditional one-to-one relationship in an equivalent attempt at understanding the varied forces at work on our psyches. Family therapy belongs to this developing area of ecological psychology. As in any beginning area of knowledge the dangers are at first overlooked in favor of the excitement of discovery.

I fear we have come to a point in our work with family therapy where the dangers of misuse of self are clearly present and in fact frequently practiced. Thus, a promising area of research and practice can fall into disrepute. Very few types of therapy provide the therapist with more opportunity to "act out" his own problems than does family therapy. The immediacy of the revelation of pathology in family therapy is striking—unlike what most of us expect as a result of our more traditional training. In the confusion of being inundated by highly relevant content we can easily lose sight of the change agent in therapy, namely the working through and sharing of a relationship on conscious and unconscious levels. Family therapy offers the therapist almost unlimited opportunity to use himself, but coupled with this there is the danger of acting out his unconscious problems.

Carl Whitaker[7] notes that the stress of family therapy creates a tendency to act out as a means of releasing affect in the manner of a safety valve. Bellak[3] feels that the intolerance of frustration leads to acting out, and family therapy can be one of the most frustrating of modalities. In fact, one may say that family therapy was born out of frustration. Work in child guidance clinics where the family was traditionally split by the agency by sending different members to different therapists frequently was disappointing and incomplete. The idea of seeing whole families together did not come only out of a clearly thought out philosophical position. We must be prepared to see where some irrationality may be. The activity of family work can get frantic, and the therapist who gets right into things and "mixes it up" may be doing so out of his frustration with the lack of human change, especially his own. This is not to say that we should be passive. We should, though, be aware that activity may be a substitute for thought and that without thought we can do nothing in therapy of a serious nature. The essence of the acting out stance is the substitution of action for thought so that in this sense the newly developing therapies, which involve more activity on the part of the therapist, may in themselves be a part of the "neurosis of our time."

There have been many warnings of the breakdown of the family as we have known it. The ease of mobility of life in modern America has speeded up the pace of breakup, or breakdown as the case may be. Anxiety has become so frequent a symptom in our lives that we take it for granted and relegate it to the modern pace of living, Boeing 747's and the like. The Freudian revolution went a long way toward removing superego restraints which had become chains with which we were enslaving ourselves. The removal of those chains, however, did not generally lead to personal freedom as we had hoped. Patients who are lonely and alienated from themselves come to seek help from therapists who are likewise struggling to free themselves from their own isolation and alienation. These are our major symptoms in a therapeutic practice which has seen character problems come to the fore as our primary focus of work. Thus, the more active therapies must be dealt with not only as rational, humanistic attempts to deal with human difficulties, but also as countertransference responses to our own alienation. It is my contention that family therapy is a powerful therapeutic agent which can enable us to bind up some of our narcissistic wounds, but it is a double-edged sword. Focusing on the countertransference problems of the therapist is strangely absent in the voluminous literature of family therapy. The doing receives more than its due. The whole area of counter-transference is noted as if in passing with a nod to the analysts. Why is this so? To distinguish between the use of self and acting out is a subtle task, yet absolutely necessary in such an involving therapy. I will try to outline some countertransference possibilities and integrate the clinical aspects of use of self.

Ackerman[2] acknowledges that countertransference study is as fully important as transference work in relation to the necessity for the therapist to be more open, more human than heretofore. He feels that treating the whole family arouses greater ambivalence and anxiety than any other form of treatment. Whitaker, Felder and Warkentin[8] feel that primary process dynamics are involved in family therapy as contrasted with group therapy in which secondary processes are dealt with to a large degree. I feel this is too neat a means of separating family therapy from other therapies. We are dealing with a primary group in family therapy, not necessarily primary process. It is the therapist for whom the difficulties with primary process thinking can be insurmountable. The likelihood of arousal of anxiety to the point where this happens is greater when one deals with a primary group. To put it the other way around is to avoid the issue of countertransference. Burgess[4] talks of the family's loss of extrinsic functions such as education, religious training and physical protection as leading to the trend toward specializing in the giving and receiving of affection. This more internalized function of the family would lead to greater primary process feeling and possible expression, particularly if needs are frustrated.

There is a widening split in the field of family therapy which at the base revolves around countertransference issues. The so-called communication people emphasize the interpersonal to a very great extent and tend to demean exploration of the intra-psychic as unnecessary because it does not get people to do anything. It is true that we can get lost in the morass of unconscious associations in intrapsychic exploration, but we must not lose sight of the fact that there is no real change which starts with other than an awareness of oneself in relation to the world around us. We cannot settle for apparent change, for this means we are unwilling to face our own devils. The idea that family therapy is "faster" than other therapies plays into the need we all have to avoid pain and deny difficulty. This issue at hand is one in which we enter the family system, a most powerfully unbudgeable one, to the point where anxiety is minimized and rage subdued. How long this lasts after we leave the system is a moot point.

I recently saw a family which had been in continuous family therapy for three years with apparently good resolution of conflict. The father's rage at his wife had diminished and her masochistic defenses apparently broken into. The son was no longer as blatantly phobic as he had been. The therapist's approach was based almost solely on an attempt to get the parents to "communicate." As long as the therapist was there, things went relatively well. The enormous hatred and hurt in the family broke into the open once the son experienced the freedom to go off a bit on his own. The threat to the homeodynamic balance of the parents was more than they could take. The previous therapist's inability to challenge his rage at his own parents did not permit the patients' rage to be worked through. It was covered over by the veneer of "relating and communicating." Thus, intrapsychic phenomenon could not be explored, or as Ackerman says,[1] be "reprojected into the field of family interaction." The use of self with such a family would entail exposure to the murderous rage, immersing oneself in it and sharing one's own hurts and disappointments so that a new direction could be seen in which living with hurt and working through are possible. A real shift in the dynamic balance could be maintained on the basis of intrapsychic shifts. This is not to say that the current emphasis on communication is wrong or bad, but only that it should not be used to blind ourselves; it is an external manifestation of an internal state. Behavioral change does not necessarily indicate internal change, but it does help the therapist avoid feeling impotent. In the above cited case, the family respected the therapist's fear of his own rage by toning down theirs, thus depriving him of working through his own blocked feelings. To repeat, the countertransference problem involves conflict over our own use of power and exposure of our hurt. Family therapy is an extraordinarily seductive form of treatment on that basis. We feel we are getting helped ourselves and frequently are. The family becomes our new family, a place to heal our wounds. One aspect of the fear of family treatment on the one hand and the wish to do it on the other is that we can try to heal ourselves, but that it involves exposure. The attempt at healing without exposure is reflected in that only recently have formal training programs in family therapy evolved. The resistance to this stems in part from the anxiety induced in the therapist who has all kinds of unconscious plans for "his" family. Szurek[6] and Johnson and Szurek[5] point out that vicarious gratification of the parent is related to the child acting out the parents' forbidden impulses. In a similar manner, if we see ourselves in an omnipotent role as the leader of the family, we can get them to act out our needs, as in the case cited above, with little concern for their own. This leads to a significant area of counter-transferential feeling, namely being one's own parent. The family members become identified not only as members of one's own original family but as pieces of oneself.

I once saw a very deprived family which was referred to as "hopeless" by the referring person. This set up a series of feelings and events in me which led to what turned out to be, almost inevitably, a very early therapeutic failure. I was going to do well with this family and, in a sense, repair my own deprivation. As a side issue there was the competition with the referring source which said, in essence, that I can do anything, despite the world being against me. These thoughts, needless to say, occurred to me afterward when I became sadder, though perhaps not wiser. My identification with the father-son break was immediate. The mother and daughters hardly received much attention in the beginning. After a very short time I took over the father's role by physically comforting the crying boy who was weeping for his lost love, his father. In a few minutes the realization that I had not really attempted to heal this family but instead heal my own wounds hit me squarely and I immediately asked the father to switch chairs with me so that he could comfort his son. This, too, was doomed to failure for the father was not ready to accept this role. Thus, the exposure of need was clearly there as was the difficulty in communicating it. What was not there, though, was enough awareness of my countertransference which would have led to a more respectful use of self, respectful of the integrity of the family and the individuals in it. Allowing the hurt, sadness and anxiety to develop and commenting on my own feeling would have been a much more appropriate use of self. The need to tell the father, my father, how to deal with the son, myself, slanted the issue of what the family was about. The fact that the women were secondary was also revealing of how I viewed my family in its priorities. Seeing the boy as the needy part of me propelled me toward him with the wish to undo the hurt as soon as possible. The father's inability to emotionally touch his son not only aroused my feelings about my own father but also my natural reticence concerning my own emotional life. Thus, the need to take over and do better than one's parents can lead away from the reality of the family we are dealing with toward an attempted internal resolution which has little relationship to the current reality. The force with which this motivation sometimes occurs must be dealt with on a level of awareness which is at the base, psychoanalytic.

Not only are we faced with a new family and the opportunity of being one's own parent and doing it better, but we can alternately be father, mother and child. It is inevitable that this be so, for it is imbedded in the nature of the therapeutic system. To feel that we can transcend these roles is to blind ourselves to the power of a family system. No matter how well analyzed we are, we can never get away from the familial. The task is to know where we are and how we are affected by it. The roles assigned to individuals in families are powerfully overdetermined. In individual analysis there is a much greater possibility of presenting oneself to the therapist in an other-than-family-determined role. To be with the family physically is to confront the system while trying to restructure it, a formidable task. This is why I feel that therapists who engage in family therapy must have rigorous training in individual therapy first, with a primary emphasis on countertransference phenomena. To allow oneself the luxury of being the child again, feeling it not only in relation to the therapeutic family but also with respect to one's own family, and coming up for air is no mean task. We need to separate the respective roles in order to let the family know that we feel what they are up to, even if they don't. This use of one's own life experiences as related to a specific family member or family dynamic is most useful to the one who has been scapegoated. If, on the other hand, we overidentify with the hurt child, we cannot do the family, or the child, any good for this will have aroused a feeling of hate in us which renders us impotent. It is particularly true in psychotic families where hate is a frequently experienced feeling. Winnicott[9] talks about hate in the countertransference as being especially important in dealing with psychotics.

Problems with authority are seen everywhere in the symptomatology of the acting-out neuroses. The therapist must with great care tap his unconscious need to take over the authority role, which will generally be given over quite willingly in the regressive stance of the "patient." Actually the role is not so easily given up; it is a game we have learned at an early age. Do what mommy and daddy say and you will be properly taken care of. A despot is a despot, no matter how benevolent. In the effort to be better than our parents, we can ignore the basic human dignity of our patients. I observed a family interview in which a black family was being treated. The therapist was taken by the cuddly infant one of the daughters had brought and commented on the baby several times. After a short span of time, he held the baby, taking it from the hands of its mother who at the time was fumbling for a cigarette. It seemed a natural thing to do. However, he held the baby for the entire session, thus arrogating to himself the role of paternal protector. It did not occur to him that he was putting down the father, only that he felt good holding the baby. Now the reaching out to the family through the baby was an attempt not only to break through the initial distance but through the black-white barrier as well. In the process, though, he was trying to be a better father than his own had been. This subtle line between acting out and human use of self in order to be more real, less defended and distant is an elusive goal to achieve. There are many more blatant countertransference problems in relation to authority figures which often end in the therapist killing off the parent (his own parent) during the course of a session. Sometimes this is done in order to show the family how it is to have a "real man" in the picture. What we often do not see is that our response can be a counterphobic reaction to our own impotence. Rape never improved a real, loving relationship. It involves a total lack of respect not only for the family and for the therapist, but for the dignity and mutuality of the treatment process itself. At times a shock effect is necessary in order to get the family out of a destructive bind in which all members are helplessly mired and are continuing to suffer greatly. This technique must be used with great caution in order to avoid our own infantile gratification. One's own integrity as a human being may be attacked by an overwhelming family. Defending oneself from destruction is a valid reason for a more active approach. One must try to be sure that he is able to somehow let the family know what it has provoked, otherwise an ascending spiral of rage, hurt and distance will develop with possible termination of therapy or a power struggle in which the symptoms of the loser will be repressed.

Just as I had finished writing the above lines the phone rang. It was a teen-age girl whose family is in treatment with me. She had run out of her house after a battle between her parents in which her father caused her mother's neck to bleed in the process of choking her. He stopped when he saw the blood and gave the mother back to Betty so that she could take care of the mother. Betty was now at a girlfriend's house, having been driven there by another friend. Now I was in the process of writing this on a lazy and wet Sunday evening in my dirty work clothes. As I look back on it now, four hours later, there was no careful countertransference exploration on my part. My first thought was that I would intervene somehow, just how was not clear. I was pleased that Betty called me as there had been some recent difficulty in the treatment process in relation to the parents feeling that I was threatening their unstated covenant that important matters, notably sexual ones, would not be talked about. After Betty had filled me in on some of the details, I volunteered to pick her up at my office if she could get her friend to drive her there. From there we would go to her home. She was afraid to go home. As luck would have it the telephone at her house was out of order, a fact I verified with the telephone operator. Betty had been unable to contact her uncle; I seemed the next logical person. Her friend was not able to drive her to my office and so I told her I would pick her up and take her home. In this family crisis I had no thought that perhaps this was a sexual countertransference for me to explore, or one involving playing the omnipotent god. I simply felt responsible to the family and included myself in as a member for whom the integrity of the whole was important. In this very human response I was perhaps confusing the boundary between myself and the family but my feeling was that emotionally I was a member of the family, not an interested observer. The fact that I could come out of the morass in which the family was entangled and view what had happened with some dispassionate feeling was extremely helpful to all the members of the family. My not being afraid of the rage inherent in such a situation enabled them to stop the recycling of hurt and murderous anger. I did not leave that evening until we had been able to get into some intrapsychic and intrafamilial motivation for the blowup. Crisis intervention which stops with the symptom only reinforces the family's dependence upon external objects and consolidates its systematized impotent approach to the world of emotion.

A core concept in psychoanalytic theory, the Oedipal struggle in all its ramifications in terms of transference and counter-transference exploration, takes on a new dimension in family therapy. With all members physically present we are given the opportunity to test out reactions against a supposed reality base. This reality of the marital partner being there has been called a safeguard in terms of the therapist acting out a sexual counter-transference. Just why this is thought a safeguard, and for whom, eludes me. Are we not denying or at least minimizing the sexual implications in the therapeutic process by doing this? And if so, what kind of message are we communicating to the patient? Even if we say the same things as we would if the situation were individual therapy, the loosening of our control over sexual impulse implicit in the "safeguard" thesis would at the minimum take us away from internal process toward a pointing out of realities in a communication-oriented discussion. Not that this is bad, but it is incomplete. One major objection therapists have to family therapy is the point that we cannot talk about sex with the children there. Sex, however, can be talked about on many levels ranging from the philosophical to the practical. We should not counter or provoke patients' resistance with our own. The collusive stance taken, then, is that of the child who goes along with parental prohibition about forbidden topics. I submit we have to be even more aware of our sexual feelings in a situation where splits and alignments rapidly emerge and change. The need to risk being ourselves with all the vulnerability this implies is nowhere greater.

A family came in for an interview where the father suddenly blurted out that he wished his wife would have an affair for she was supposedly inept in bed and could benefit from some learning experiences. This was in association to his feelings of the lack of joy in his life. There are many alternatives open to the therapist in such a situation. According to the "safeguard" thesis I could have made a joke about offering myself to the wife. This could challenge the husband, shake up the wife, cause envy in the children and terminate the therapy. I say *could* because the follow-up of such a statement in terms of how the therapist uses his own feelings is all important. Actually, I did make such a statement but only after there was an interchange between the pair which indicated an acknowledgment of their internal stresses. If I had offered myself to either parent as a better lover, father and/or mother to stem the tide of depressive affect in the wake of the father's statement, I would have been operating out of my own seductiveness, guilt and competitiveness. We can get into countertransference problems by ignoring the sexual completely via the communication avenue, or putting ourselves into it before the family has a chance to share the hurts and disappointments of love. The urge to do something fast may be overwhelming in terms of the family's acting out. The potential for this acting out is, as Wynne[10] points out, greater between sessions than in group therapy. It is certainly greater than in individual therapy.

The area of nonverbal communication takes on new significance in family work. When viewing oneself on videotape one is struck by body posture as reflecting internal, unconscious feelings. In talking to a rigidly authoritarian, guilt-ridden couple about what it is to be a man, I saw myself slouching in the chair. I did not feel that I was a man with this pair, but was unaware of it. A clue I could have used was that I was talking too much. Again, I was struck by my body posture in viewing a session with a particularly needy family. I moved forward toward each of them and spoke. This was an indication of how needy the family really was and of how they get nurturance. A discussion with them of my reactions on viewing the film elicited very important and workable material about the "being-given-to" part of their system. It would serve us well as therapists and people if we were to stop short and view our external and internal stance. Of course, using the patients' body movements to cue us in on what is happening is of great significance. The beauty of being videotaped is that we can see this in ourselves.

Family therapy could easily become an establishment form of treatment by an emphasis on family life to the detriment of the individuals living in it. We are in an era of changing concepts. Communal living is one alternative to the established mode of family life; others will surely come. If we, in our own need to establish order out of chaos, direct treatment toward the family unit as we know it, it may be a step backward. Keeping this in mind will enable us to concentrate on the interrelatedness of our families without the shackles of feeling there are no alternatives. The family is the most powerful creative force mankind has ever experienced. The change that it is undergoing and which seems so chaotic and generally attributed to the nebulous "generation gap" is an exposure of hypocrisy. The great strength of family therapy is that it can capture this hypocrisy, this emotional deception, right on the spot. To do this, one must be continually aware of one's own hypocrisy or at least open to it when our patients expose it, and expose it they do.

If it seems that I feel family therapy demands an extraordinary dedication to learning about oneself, I absolutely do. It is deceptively simple to fall into family systems and be rendered impotent. The courage to explore onself is transmitted to our families and is of enormous value to them. We cannot ignore the truths of psychoanalytic practice in an attempt to plunge headlong into the "cure" of families and societies. If we do this we are abdicating fundamental responsibility to ourselves and can help no one. The promise of family therapy is bright; let us not denigrate the practice of it by shoddy thinking in the rush to "do something."

REFERENCES

1. Ackerman, N. W.: A dynamic frame for the clinical approach to family conflict. In N. W. Ackerman; F. L. Beatman, and S. N. Sherman (Eds.): *Expanding Theory and Practice in Family Therapy*. New York, Family Service Association of America, 1967.
2. Ackerman, N. W.: *Treating the Troubled Family*. New York, Basic Books, 1966.
3. Bellak, L.: The concept of acting out: theoretical considerations. In L. E. Abt and S. L. Weissman (Eds.): *Acting Out*. New York, Grune & Stratton, 1965.
4. Burgess, E. W.: The family in a changing society. In A. Etzioni and E. Etzioni (Eds.): *Social Change*. New York, Basic Books, 1964.
5. Johnson, A. M., and Szurek, S. A.: The genesis of antisocial acting out in children and adults. In S. A. Szurek and I. N. Berlin (Eds.): *The Antisocial Child*. Palo Alto, Science and Behavior Books, 1969.
6. Szurek, S. A.: Childhood origins of psychopathic personality trends. In S. A. Szurek and I. N. Berlin (Eds.): *The Antisocial Child*. Palo Alto, Science and Behavior Books, 1969.
7. Whitaker, C. A.: Acting out in family psychotherapy. In L. E. Abt and S. L. Weissman (Eds.): *Acting Out*. New York, Grune & Stratton, 1965.
8. Whitaker, C. A.; Felder, R. E., and Warkentin, J.: Countertransference in the family treatment of schizophrenia. In I. Boszormenyi-Nagy and J. L. Framo (Eds.): *Intensive Family Therapy*. New York, Harper & Row, 1965.

9. Winnicott, D. W.: *Collected Papers.* New York, Basic Books, 1958.
10. Wynne, L.: The study of intrafamilial alignments and splits in exploratory family therapy. In N. W. Ackerman; F. L. Beatman, and S. N. Sherman (Eds.): *Exploring the Base for Family Therapy.* New York, Family Service Association of America, 1961.

DR. TED SARETSKY, one of the first graduates from the Adelphi University Postdoctoral Program in Psychotherapy, offers a thoughtful and provocative paper which discusses the therapist's countertransferential acting out so others of us could be more aware of both the dangers and the constructive alternatives.

Dr. Saretsky introduces his paper with a review of the literature concerning selection of patients for group therapy and observes that there exists a gross neglect of countertransferential processes in connection with this selection procedure. To clarify the importance of this issue, Dr. Saretsky indicates a variety of ways that countertransference could affect that placement of a patient in a particular group. It could be, for example, an unconscious wish for vindication on the part of the analyst, an exclusion of minority group patients rationalized as protecting the rights of the individual, or an acting out of positive countertransferences.

Dr. Saretsky recounts his own experience with this problem in terms of his unconscious practice of channeling his "bad" patients into one group and "good" patients into another. His conclusion, based on his own experience, is that once a therapist is cognizant of the role his unconscious attitudes play in the group selection process, he may take concrete steps to insure a more balanced placement of patients and a more constructive awareness toward his own "acting out."

Dr. Saretsky, by focusing on a specific area of acting-out behavior that he has observed in himself and other therapists, has helped us be more aware of the entire countertransference issue.

D.S.M.
G.D.G.

Chapter 19

Countertransferential Acting Out in the Selection of Patients for Group Therapy

THEODORE SARETSKY

A SURVEY OF THE extensive literature covering the procedure for the proper selection of patients for group therapy is bound to make the reader very confused. The only assumptions that hold true for almost every worker in the field are that patients cannot be haphazardly thrown together without consideration of mutual suitability and that not every patient is necessarily going to benefit from group treatment.[6] Even this moderate consensus is confounded by the fact that there are continuing differences between therapists regarding the specific criteria for inclusion. Moreover, all the kinds of patients that certain workers are most pessimistic about (addicts, severe character disorders, alcoholics, border-line psychotics), have been successfully treated in a group setting by other therapists.[3] Nevertheless, there does seem to be a recent trend in the field toward greater individualization with less of a concern about screening out a patient on the basis of his formal diagnostic classification.[5] Instead, compatibility, willingness to expose weakness before a peer group, tolerance for tensions aroused by hostile expressions of others toward himself, and desire for mutuality of experience are all seen as of more paramount importance than diagnostic labels. Along these lines, many workers have written about getting a good interaction going in terms of such variables as age and educational spread, homogeneous versus heterogeneous personality combinations, the mixing of sexes, the placement of new patients into ongoing groups, and putting people together from different socioeconomic, racial or religious backgrounds.[8]

In view of the amount of attention devoted to selection procedures at symposia, in introductory texts and in the various journals of group psychotherapy, it is quite remarkable that the countertransference aspects of this process are rarely recognized— just a few paragraphs in two articles in the past twenty years.[1, 7] In my opinion, this gross neglect is only partially related to the lack of reliable criteria for the most effective grouping. Under the present ambiguous circumstances almost any selection procedure can be easily rationalized in terms of current theory and practice. More important, whatever neurotic expectations and distorted values the therapist's philosophy of life may contain are obscured and camouflaged by these rationalizations. Thus, my main interest in presenting this paper is to help clarify the following issue: to what extent are the criteria for selection subject to the therapist's countertransferential problems versus how much is placement in a particular group meeting the real needs of the individual patient and the rest of the group.

1. To start with, is it possible that referral to group therapy itself can sometimes represent countertransferential acting out? A therapist struggling with a difficult case, feeling himself particularly exasperated, frustrated and at an impasse, wondering what dynamics he might be overlooking, could understandably see group as the solution. The Kleinians, for example, have described in considerable detail the power dynamics of the transference-countertransference situation in individual therapy, whereby depressive, masochistic patients render the analyst impotent and gain the upper hand by repeatedly rejecting his interpretations.[2] Under these circumstances, sending the patient to group could represent a wish for vindication on the part of the analyst. The analyst's own set of internalized accusing objects which were put into motion by the patient's resistance to change could not be appeased by exorcising the bad, unyielding traits of the patient. Thus the therapists are sometimes prone to unconsciously orchestrate their groups like Greek choruses, pressuring the patient to shape up and surrender their stubborn defenses to restitute the therapist's bruised ego.

2. Then there is the policy of systematically excluding patients who are markedly different from the rest of the group. Under this heading we could begin by taking note that there are many clinics in this city that for the first time are beginning to get a substantial number of black referrals and are systematically forming segregated all-black groups, most often serviced by black leaders. Along these lines, many therapists in private practice have reservations about putting a blue-collar factory hand in work clothes, ghetto blacks, and even gentiles in with their middle-class Jewish patients. While there may be some validity to arguments that emphasize protecting the rights of the individual ("He'd feel uncomfortable"; "He'd be ostracized"; "His problems would be different—he wouldn't get the kind of understanding he needs"; "They'd feel more at home with a black leader"), Kadis[4] has pointed out that this attitude can be rationalized and used to defend against decisions that might be beneficial to the patients but threatening to the therapist. While we are on this topic, I could also list a number of other culturally tabooed patient types who are often arbitrarily refused admission into ongoing groups (drug addicts, psychopaths, homosexuals, borderline psychotics). There is considerable research evidence to suggest that these patients can be helped in non-homogeneous groups; moreover, heterogeneous grouping significantly improves the breadth of discussion, makes for less programmed interaction, and provides a way of circumventing denial mechanisms by generating less predictable reactions that are more difficult for patients to ward off.

I think that the countertransferential reaction implicit in keeping people with differences out, has to do with our general fear and suspiciousness of strangers. At bottom, this infantile paranoia is related to the primitive tendency to dissociate ourselves from and declare as not part of me, any feeling or experience that is not consonant with my self-image. Hence the presence of patients who are different is seen as a return of the repressed, as a disturbance and a threat that must be externalized and dispensed with rather than properly integrated.

3. I have also noticed the inhibition that many therapists have about mixing young adults (19-23-year-olds) together with

older adults (40-50-year-olds). Many texts rationalize this separation in terms of a lack of overlapping interests and an inability to easily identify with each others age-specific problems. Early in my practice, I began to question my own resistances to the obvious advantages that cross-fertilization might offer. It then occurred to me that the insecurity that I felt in the adult professional role accompanied by the nagging feeling that I was still a relative beginner and incompletely trained made me feel vulnerable to anticipated criticism by the older patients. By keeping the younger patients apart from the older patients, I was denying their existence and guarding against the possibility that I might be associated with the "kids" and thereby lose the adults' respect. The other side of the coin was that I shielded the younger patients from the older patients in order to keep their youthful allegiance. In fantasy, I imagined that the younger patients would feel awkward and tongue-tied in the presence of people their parents' age. By forcing them into such an unpromising situation I worried that they would turn against me for no longer being their pal, the good older brother.

In more classical terms, the anxious need to keep the two groups apart reflected a lack of integration between my own impulses and controls. With the adult group, my whole manner encouraged a sense of freedom and expansiveness, youthful enthusiasm, act, don't think, unbridled sexuality, and a "what the hell" attitude, much of which was really a disguised way of tweaking my own uptight superego. On the other hand, with the youthful group, I fulfilled their transference expectations by acting like a restraining force, simultaneously identifying with their youthful carousing, cynical antiestablishment attitudes and general irresponsibility while at the same time preaching a more realistic, practical accommodation to the power structure. The phony joining of their adolescent acting-out tendencies while really "spying" on them and undercutting by trying to tame the impetus of these impulses was a roundabout way of punishing my own wayward needs and drives.

4. The acting out of a positive countertransference can also be a problem here. A therapist may have a very favorable impression of a patient. The patient may make good progress, be very

receptive to the therapist's interpretations, and characterize that constellation of personality features which the therapist would prize as a catalytic force in the group. In exchange for introducing this special patient into the group, the therapist may expect the patient to live out the role of the therapist's ego ideal and perform well. This complimentary fit may actually make for considerable patient progress so long as the patient operates according to the therapist's wishes. If the patient disappoints either through active rebellion, growth and development, or simply by behaving differently than the therapist would have predicted, the therapist may repudiate and deny this piece of behavior and the honeymoon will be over. This often leads to escalating regressive behavior on the part of the patient and perplexity for the leader. The analyst finds himself in the strange position of being irrationally irritated and impatient, wishes the patient would behave in such a way so that he would stop feeling like this, wonders whether he is doing anything to elicit such disappointing behavior and generally winds up quite confused.

5. Finally, I would like to describe a group phenomenon that has received very little notice in the literature. About five years ago I was in a supervisory session describing a problem that I was having with one of my groups. The people in it seemed in a chronic state of resistance. They were passive, inhibited, not interactive enough, and rarely expressed feelings openly. I was presenting the impasse in terms of what group dynamics might be operating and what techniques might help to break through the heaviness. What I came to realize was that I had unconsciously gathered an extremely difficult assortment of people to work with. While I was trying to bring them out, mentally, I was blaming them for not being freer. Very self-righteously I said to myself, "Here I am doing everything I can to get them to relate and they're still sitting there withdrawn and unresponsive. Boy, if I were a patient in that group, I'd know how to provoke them and get things rolling." I contrasted this group with another one of my groups that was so much more verbal, vibrant and alive. After considerable exploration, it became clear to me that I was referring my "better patients," those who were more outspoken, confronting and spontaneous to the "good

group." Unwittingly, I had polarized the two groups into good and bad by collecting all my most difficult cases and channelling them to the bad group. This consisted of people who were referred to me by other therapists who could not make progress or people whom I placed in group with the hope that the group could reach them in ways that I could not. This insight was interesting but I was still intrigued by my resolute resistance to the supervisor's suggestion that I mix the "good group" and the "bad group."

Further investigation revealed that the "good group" was my showpiece group. They represented living proof that I could be respected and accepted. They were like children one could be proud of, or parents one need not be ashamed of. With regard to the "bad group," it would appear that I unconsciously constructed this inhibited, unassertive group out of impatience with my own shortcomings. While sitting sympathetically with these patients, I could gain a sense of mastery and vicariously escape more honest self-examination by exorting them to be more open and direct, take responsibility for their actions, trust people, risk taking a chance, and all the little platitudes that therapists enjoy telling their patients. So long as my masochistic identification with their passivity and sense of failure continued, this group was bound to resist my "sincere" overtures by stubborn withholding, quiet hostility, and general self-defeating negativisms. When I finally worked through my problems around switching patients more freely from one group to another and changing the original composition of this group, many significant changes took place. The group became much more resourceful, constructive and goal directed, the climate became more flexible, and many individuals began to show strengths that they had not previously demonstrated.

In conclusion, let me say that there are an infinite number of countertransferential acting-out possibilities in the selection and combination of patients for a therapy group. Many of the inexplicable dead spots and impasses experienced throughout the different stages of group treatment are probably related to the unconscious and preconscious attitudes and expectations of the therapist, each participant, and the group as a whole. I think that it would be particularly helpful for group therapists to stop masking their ambivalences behind the cliched guidelines provided by the traditional literature and look for illumination in the special personal meaning to them of the selection procedures that they seem to follow so matter-of-factly.

REFERENCES

1. Foulkes, S.: Meeting of the group analytic society. *Group Analysis,* *1*:15-23, June, 1969.
2. Guntrip, H.: *Schizoid Phenomena, Object Relations and the Self.* New York, International Universities Press, 1968.
3. Joel, W., and Shapiro, D.: Some principles and procedures for group psychotherapy. *J. Psychol.,* 29:77-88, 1950.
4. Kadis, A.: Failures in group therapy. Presented at EGPS, 1962.
5. Leopold, H.: Selection of patients for group psychotherapy. *Amer. J. Psychotherapy,* *11*:634-637, July, 1957.
6. Mullan, H., and Rosenbaum, M.:*Group Psychotherapy.* Free Press of Glencoe, 1962.
7. Olivera, W.: The analyst in the group analytic situation. *Group Psychoanalysis and Process,* *1*:85-99, Winter, 1968.
8. Ziferstein, L., and Grotjahn, M.: Psychoanalysis and group psychotherapy. In F. Fromm-Reichmann and J. L. Moreno (Eds.): *Progress in Psychotherapy.* New York, Grune & Stratton, 1956.

DRS. ROSLYN AND LEONARD SCHWARTZ, a husband and wife team who do couples therapy as co-therapists, give us a firsthand review and critique of this form of analyzing and treating character problems. Both are long-term members of the Adelphi psychology fraternity and bring to this volume not only expertise but a freshness and clarity that is coupled with a warm humanness.

Their paper has an excellent introduction that provides perspective on the effectiveness of the marathon and encounter movement in treating acting-out character problems. Sections on couples therapy, encounter techniques and marathon therapy follow in order; two case histories and a summary round out this chapter. The Schwartz' vividly present their treatment technique and the rationale for their methods.

The current encounter scene opens up new avenues of approach in the treatment of character problems. The Drs. Schwartz offer us insights into couples therapy with their excellent clinical review of this treatment modality.

D.S.M.
G.D.G.

Chapter 20

Therapeutic Acting Out – the Use of Encounter and Marathon Groups in Couples Therapy[1]

ROSLYN SCHWARTZ AND LEONARD J. SCHWARTZ

PSYCHOTHERAPY HAS UNDERGONE drastic changes in the last decade. Three notable innovations are the redefinition of "the patient," the use of encounter techniques and the introduction of marathon therapy. There has been a growing awareness among clinicians that the internal struggle between ego, id and superego is frequently manifested in the ego-syntonic character traits of patients rather than as an ego alien symptom. The traditional psychoanalytic concept of the therapist forming an alliance with the patient's ego in order to cope more adequately with the id and superego forces cannot be readily applied to character problems.

Since character problems are a form of acting out, successful therapeutic intervention begins with enabling the patient to view his behavior as an unsuccessful attempt to solve an internal struggle. Once the patient is aware of the self-defeating nature of his behavior he is both motivated and prepared to take steps to undergo changes. This initial therapeutic intervention frequently involves getting the patient to act out his "acting-out" behavior in an exaggerated form, thereby forcing him to defend against the unacceptability of his typical behavior. For example, an extremely hostile patient who constantly ingratiates himself with others through his cooperative, friendly, helpful manner is given the task in a group of putting each member down by

---

[1] Adapted from article in *Voices*, Vol. 5, No. 3, entitled "Growth Encounters."

being overly sweet and complimentary. This exercise enables him to experience the hidden meaning behind his characteristic behavior. When he defends himself against his typical sweetness and friendliness he can allow himself to accept and express his hostility more directly.

The above example is one instance of the use of an encounter technique designed to cope with the egosyntonic, and therefore out of awareness, hostility which this patient finds unacceptable. The initial therapeutic intervention must be so designed as to activate the ego to defend against the powerful superego by being more directly and openly expressive of the id as a lesser "sin" than hiding the unacceptable impulse in the life style.

The therapist's need to find novel ways of confronting patients with their acting-out behavior has led to the creation of new therapeutic structures. The couples' encounter group has been a potent vehicle to help isolate, define and examine the patients' acting-out behavior. The use of encounter techniques helps patients confront their acting-out behavior, thereby becoming aware of the hidden messages imbedded in their life styles. Marathon therapy is employed to intensify the encounter group experience and to support those changes initiated in other therapeutic structures.

Couples therapy grew out of the recognition that people form relationships to support defensive character traits and neurotic behavior as well as for self-fulfillment. Frequently the individual seeking help reflects symptoms of a disturbed marital relationship rather than solely that of his internal psychic makeup. In order to deal with such a problem, psychotherapy must be structured to include the couple as "the patient." The notion of the "marriage" as the third patient in a coupling arrangement has been discussed by Warkentin and Whitaker.[7]

To focus on a couple in psychotherapy requires a constant awareness of those forces within and between both participants. The interplay between individual frustrations and the working contract between husband and wife becomes the raw material of the treatment. The process and achievement of personal satisfactions are related to the structure of the marriage itself. Recognizing this format becomes the aim of such therapy.

Marriage partners form hidden ties that are often unknown to one another. Occasionally, one partner assumes that an understanding exists which the other member is quite unaware of. Not uncommonly there exists an implicit acceptance of a mutually unrewarding relationship between husband and wife. One function of the therapist is to help make explicit and clarify the nature of such relationships. Symptoms of anxiety, phobias, depression, etc., are related to the marital pact. In couples therapy, the focus is on the process and structure of the *interaction between* the couple.

ENCOUNTER TECHNIQUES

Encounter techniques in group therapy were devised to clarify and make explicit the nature of interpersonal ties. Patients are encouraged to deal directly with areas of their relationship that remain unresolved. The methods employed by Schutz[6] and Malamud and Machover,[3] are designed to create an interaction that concretely depicts a problem in interpersonal living. Thus, a "one downmanship" outcome is realized by having the individuals place their hands on each others' shoulders and literally try to put one another down on the floor. Or a couple that argues repetitiously (going around in circles) are placed in the middle of the room and asked to circle one another without verbalizing. Competitive behavior designed to avoid closeness is manifestly depicted by arm or leg wrestling. The physical experience offers the participants a new perspective in which to view their conflict. The novelty of the exchange induces authentic responses rather than stereotyped behavior. The game-like nature of the exercises creates an atmosphere of levity and friendship vital to the supportive function of the group. Encouragement and social rewards usually are spontaneously offered by other members of the group.

One gratifying aspect of the use of encounter techniques is the opportunity for the therapist to design, and participate in, exercises that accurately express the "here and now" of a relationship. Moreover, group members observe the therapist's flexibility and involvement and become motivated to create their own "happenings" to make explicit some of their hidden contracts with each other. With such exercises they learn to listen more concretely to themselves and others. Thus, for example, the remark, "It's impossible to pin you down," may lead to an offer to actually pin the person down. The immediacy, physicalness and spontaneity shown by the person, otherwise seen as elusive, abstract and uninvolved, breaks a mental set and helps to establish a new basis for a relationship. Since neither partner has likely experienced this method of resolving a conflict, they both approach the situation with alert openness heretofore unavailable to them.

That the authors are themselves a married couple naturally influences the group. Their participation includes efforts at making explicit that which is hidden in their own relationship. Occasionally, they may feud over a problem during the group session. At such times the attentiveness of everyone is heightened; there is instant group cohesiveness and a collective attempt to resolve the therapists' problem. An encounter may be suggested by a patient to deal with this conflict. Thus, for instance, when one therapist felt her freedom restricted by the power, perception and self-directedness of the other therapist, they were asked to be seated on the floor, to remove their eyeglasses and to face one another. The effect of being in the middle of the group, facing one another with impaired vision while being directed by a patient, quickly led to a "levelling" relationship between the therapists and evoked fresh creativity on the part of the therapist who previously felt restricted.

MARATHON THERAPY

The authors employ a variety of therapeutic techniques and structures in their work. They have had experience in orthodox Freudian analysis, Sullivanian, client-centered, experiential, Gestalt, assaultive and accommodation therapies. In addition, they utilize the structures of individual, group, family, couples and marathon therapies. From this background of professional experience, the authors employ those orientations and structures that seem most appropriate in helping patients adapt to themselves, to others, and to their environments.

Marathon therapy is a time-extended group therapeutic session running between twenty-four and thirty-six hours. Usually, there are thirteen to sixteen participants. Some marathons are uninterrupted, others are held with a recess for sleep. Some groups are led by one therapist; others by multiple therapists. While participants are mostly screened and balanced for such factors as age, sex, profession, and personality types, some marathons are open to the first fifteen people who wish to attend. A few groups are highly structured; others are self-actuating and follow the spontaneous directions and rules of the group itself. They are held in therapists' offices, in motel rooms, or in retreat-type settings. Food and soft drinks are brought into the room; rarely are liquor and drugs used. Bach[1, 2] and Mintz[4, 5] discuss some of the various formats used in their marathons.

The marathon is an intimate happening where people learn to experience the impact they make on one another. This time-extended encounter and confrontation group stresses the development of self-awareness and spontaneity while offering an opportunity to enhance authentic and productive communication and interaction with others. Self-pursuit is encouraged in an atmosphere that welcomes and rewards exposure and vulnerability. Creative situations are fashioned in the marathon to enable individuals to experience their potential in an intimate experiential setting.

The authors conduct approximately one marathon a month, usually having twelve to sixteen participants. Some are held in the living room of our home; some in the conference room of a nearby hotel. We begin on Saturday at 1:30 P.M. and run through Sunday at 4:30 P.M. Usually there is a "time out" between 4:00 A.M. and 9:00 A.M. for sleep. At such times individual sleeping arrangements are made for the participants. All meals are brought into the room and the session continues during eating. Usually an effort is made to balance the composition of each group through a screening for age, sex, profession, personality types, singles and couples. In the early hours of the marathon we are often directive in structuring encounters to help individuals identify and deal with their defenses and resistances to spontaneous behavior. While these initial experiences are sometimes seen as "contrived," their value rapidly becomes apparent to the participants. Our leadership blends into that of participants as we encounter various group members and each other. Gradually, individuals join with the therapists in fashioning exercises that help depict specific conflicts.

The unique therapeutic dimension offered by a marathon evolves from the extended period of group interaction. Four factors are operative which seldom obtain in any other therapeutic structure. First, the intensity of participation mounts as one individual after another begins to unfold his story, breaks through a previously cherished defense and has a fresh insight into his condition. Each succeeding experience tends to carry over and add to the collective emotionality. Tolerance for anxiety increases as the group is exposed, without let up, to these life dramas. This additional capacity to cope with anxiety permits the release of deep feelings such as profound grief, utter despair and overwhelming love. Secondly, the continuity of the group does not allow for the typical reestablishment of defenses observed in shorter forms of therapy. Participants are deprived of their usual environments wherein they maintain life styles and roles. Those character traits and patterns of behavior dependent on such external support and reinforcement thus become more accessible to change. Thirdly, the fatigue factor is important in helping to break down defenses and resistances, leading to a more authentic spontaneous expression of interpersonal relations. After these many hours of heightened experiences it is rare to find an individual who is unaffected. Fourthly, as the hour for termination approaches, the pressure to expose conflicts and problems increases. Knowing that the group will cease to exist shortly, each participant is struck with his personal responsibility to get from the marathon what he came for. This urgency may become desperate; in fact, during the final hours of a marathon there is a release of emotion seldom seen in any other setting.

The authors have conducted over thirty marathons and have learned to use them in a variety of ways. While most everyone gets something useful and memorable out of a marathon, those patients who are, or have been, in psychotherapy appear to benefit the most. They seem able immediately to grasp and integrate new insights. Ongoing individual and group therapy tends to enhance such insights, enabling the patient to make meaningful changes in living. The authors therefore use marathon therapy alone and in combination with individual, couples, family and group therapies.

The marathon is sometimes employed for patients with particularly rigid character defenses in order to help "soften" them up. It is also used to consolidate previous therapeutic gains. That is, validation and feedback from a new social group, of a self-image that is novel and unsettled for a patient, can save much time in building confidence with such an image. Unresolved crises are often dealt with quite effectively through the group's sharing and support of those feelings that were suppressed during the crisis. There is also a cluster of interpersonal "hang-ups" for which the marathon can be useful.

A husband or wife who complains that if only their mate would act differently they could be happier frequently "selects" the one person in the group who behaves most like his marital partner. Sometimes during the marathon, an encounter is arranged whereby these two interact with each other, or with receptive new partners in order to clarify and pinpoint those self-defeating patterns previously blamed on others. In this fashion marital, parent-child, sibling, friendship, business relations and a host of other interpersonal patterns can be exposed, clarified, diagnosed and altered in the marathon structure.

In addition to monthly marathons, the authors conduct three weekly encounter groups; two for couples and one for singles. Marathon therapy is used as a supplement to the work of these ongoing groups and frequently is the means through which change is implemented in individual group members. Specific patients as well as couples are referred to the marathon when they have reached an impasse. Patients usually attend the marathon motivated to resolve this conflict and to explore alternate ways of relating.

CASE HISTORIES

The following case histories illustrate how encounter techniques and the marathon structure are employed in couples therapy.

Gloria and Bill

Gloria was seen initially in individual therapy. She ascribed her depression and chronic unhappiness to her son who had been diagnozed schizophrenic and who seemed to be going downhill. In that first interview her focus shifted from her son to her relationship with Bill, her husband, her difficulty in getting close to him and her corresponding feelings of isolation and loneliness. She was discouraged and frightened about the future. She blamed Bill, complaining that when she tried to get him involved in a meaningful conversation, he put her off. At the end of that initial session Gloria was urged to come to a couple's group with her husband. She said she would like to come but was positive Bill would not agree as he didn't believe in psychotherapy. She was asked to have her husband call. When Bill phoned, he readily agreed to "try" a couple's group.

In the couple's group Gloria seemed the more highly defensive of the pair and the more difficult to get to, even though she had initiated treatment and was, ostensibly, better motivated. She behaved toward Bill critically and self-righteously. Of the two, she appeared the more averse to intimate contact. When this was pointed out she became defensive. The initial therapeutic plan centered on how they related to other people in the group rather than how they related to each other.

Within two sessions, several incidents occurred which generated a turning point in their relationship. The first incident concerned Gloria's rejection of the other group members and her air of superiority. This attitude was challenged by the group. She expressed surprise that she was seen as feeling superior when she felt quite inadequate. She was encouraged to encounter each group member with her feelings relative to them. Each person in the group stood as she approached, verbalizing her inadequacy to:

Sally—"You're younger and prettier."
Lynn—"You have a college education."
Joe—"You're musical."
Len—"You're powerful."
Roz—"You're sure of yourself."

Although the completion of this task brought her some relief, Bill was displeased, claiming she really didn't feel inferior in all those areas. Both Gloria and the group pointed out how difficult it was for him to accept her feelings of inadequacy. Gloria indicated that this was also true for their children.

The area of Bill's fathering was then opened up and he was given the task of fathering each member of the group. While most of the group felt that Bill was sensitive to their fathering needs, Gloria criticized him for being phony, saying things just to please the group rather than expressing how he really felt. Bill's fathering was strongly supported by the group, however, and he was grateful for this. He had, he said, lost confidence in himself as a father because of his son's illness and because Gloria held him responsible for it.

The therapists noticed that one of the Gloria-Bill problems was that they fought by being critical of each other, apparently too "chicken" to fight openly. We, therefore, suggested they have a chicken fight in the group. Each was to hold one foot while they hopped about on the other trying to throw each other off balance. Although Gloria protested the unfairness of such a fight because of her smaller size, she agreed to try. They hopped about, circling each other warily, with Bill waiting until Gloria came at him. Gloria fought hard to get Bill off balance, thereby continually losing her own equilibrium. Bill never attempted to get at Gloria but held firm in his position. Encouraged and prodded by the group, Bill finally did engage Gloria, knocking her down. To their surprise, she was relieved rather than hurt, and Bill did not feel like a bully as he had anticipated. Subsequent to this encounter Bill decided to take over the management of their son and Gloria agreed to stay out of it. They also agreed that when Gloria interfered, Bill would push her out.

They both were pleased with this arrangement, particularly as they began to see results in terms of their son's behavior.

After the above, Bill's involvement with the group deepened. Gloria still had difficulty accepting the support of the group, however, because she felt it would increase her feelings of helplessness. She kept herself in reserve, and it appeared that her experience with the group had not lessened her depression, her bitterness towards life, or her sense of hopelessness. We felt something else was needed and considered three possibilities for her:

1. An environment heavily laden with emotion for a prolonged period.

2. An intense encounter experience.

3. A group experience without Bill so that she would not have to be concerned that, if she "broke down," she would look weak in his eyes.

Hoping to break through Gloria's resistance we had her attend a weekend marathon without Bill. At the beginning of the meeting she was tense and anxious; she verbalized the fear that she would be devastated at the marathon. She was literally shaking as she spoke. Her way of coping with the fear was to become numb and paralyzed. She stayed that way throughout the first day. At dinner time, when the large group broke into small conversation groups, Gloria had a private talk with one of the therapists. She volunteered a long story about her favorite sibling, a brother, who died when she was fifteen. The death, which she had never mourned, had had a marked effect upon her. Afterward, all the color went out of her life and the world had been grey ever since. This story was related with her typical control and emotional deadness. After the group broke for the night, we (the therapists) talked about this story and decided it would be important for Gloria to tell it to the group, thus to reexperience the loss of her brother.

Her apparent numbness continued into the second day of the marathon but the tension was mounting. At one point one of the men in the group (Jim) approached her and wanted to involve her in role playing his mother. The break in her control became apparent in her refusal to become involved with Jim.

She cried out, "Don't come near me or I'll kill you." At that particular time the two leaders were sitting next to each other and made room in between them, asking Gloria to come sit there. She came without coaxing but, as she sat down, turned to Len and said, "Please don't touch me because I'm afraid I'll start to cry and, if I do, I'll never stop." Len put an arm around her shoulder, held her firmly and she began to sob. She was told repeatedly, "It's all right to cry," and little by little her sobs became less stifled until she finally gave in. When her crying abated, she was asked to talk about her brother. She retold the story of his death, displaying more and more of her grief. The whole episode with Gloria took about an hour. When she came back to the present she was able to be an excellent mother for Jim. In an uncanny sequel to her story she helped Jim "bury" his dead brother and verbalized for both of them, "Now that we've buried our dead we can both start to live."

With Gloria, the marathon structure helped her get beyond an impasse that existed both in her marriage and in the weekly encounter group. Because her experience in the encounter group replicated the struggle in her marriage she had to attend the marathon, separated from her husband. Both Gloria and Bill experienced her return from the marathon as that of a bride. Subsequently she was able to use a newfound ability to express feelings with her children and in the encounter group, as well as with Bill.

Tom and Sylvia

The first prolonged contact with this couple was through Tom who came for individual treatment. He suffered from phobias which had become especially debilitating in his job. Also, he had severe, frequent stomach disorders. After long-term treatment, most of the presenting symptoms dropped off. At this point Tom began to deal with his feelings of manliness, particularly with respect to Sylvia, his wife. Even though he was successful in his job, he felt his masculinity was diminished every time he came home. His wife consistently and continuously put him down and "made him less of a man." He was put off by her lack of sexual responsiveness and by her obesity which he felt limited his sexual desire. Two years prior to their coming to the couple's group Sylvia had gone into individual therapy and continued this for a year and a half. In the six months after she discontinued treatment both she and Tom felt stalemated and increasingly hopeless about their marriage.

When they joined the group Sylvia openly stated that her frigidity and obesity were the cause of their marital difficulties and she sincerely wanted to do something about it. At the same time, however, she saw the group as Tom's group because of his previous relationship with the male therapist. Generally she was critical and sarcastic with the group members, as well as with the two therapists. Sylvia's first direct encounter with the group centered around her criticalness. She was asked to verbalize in what way she personally resented each person in the group. When it was Tom's turn, her anger toward him was direct and intense; she resented him for confining his lovemaking to the bed and for not recognizing her value as a person. She complained, as he did, that she felt continually put down in the marriage.

It became clear that both felt inadequate, particularly as sexual individuals, and each turned to the other for some response which would enhance their positive self-image. On this score both were invariably disappointed. Each felt justified in blaming the other for their feelings of inadequacy as man and woman. As long as they focussed on their deprivation they could avoid any effort to change the status quo.

In a later session, when Sylvia was complaining about her deprivation for the umpteenth time, the therapists gave the whole group the task of giving something to her. Members of the group alternately hugged her, admired her pretty face, praised her for her courage and appreciated her motherliness. Everyone except Tom was able to gratify Sylvia. When it was the turn of the male therapist he gave Sylvia a prolonged, sensual kiss. Tom expressed contempt for the kiss as a therapeutic ploy, and the female therapist verbalized her jealousy about the kiss, saying it didn't have to last that long nor be that sensual. Sylvia's obvious satisfaction with the kiss was enhanced by the female therapist's jealousy, and literally she blossomed during that session. She believed in the kiss as a spontaneous interaction and experienced herself as desirable and womanly.

Several things occurred as a result of this episode. Firstly, it was brought out to Sylvia that her frigidity was not real and that she was capable of responding to passion in herself and others. This evoked several stories from her about her youth when she behaved with a passion of which she was both ashamed and proud. Secondly, the female therapist spoke openly to her own husband about her feelings of jealousy when he became involved with someone other than her. This prompted Tom to conjecture that perhaps he had to see the kiss as a therapeutic ploy to allay his jealousy. Thirdly, Sylvia and the female therapist became more involved with each other and had several direct encounters around the theme of the therapist as a mother figure who could accept Sylvia's sensuality.

Shortly after this the therapists brought a quarrel into a group session. The male therapist was angry because he felt his wife had been insensitive to him, particularly because she accused him of trying to inhibit her assertiveness and independence. Although the argument reflected some of the Tom-Sylvia configuration, Sylvia supported the male therapist (or Tom) position and pointed out how he could not "make" the female therapist dependent or independent. Tom was angry with Sylvia for supporting the male therapist when she would typically put him down (Tom) for taking the same position. At this point the group chastised Tom for not being able to stay with Sylvia's positiveness and for using it instead to start another quarrel between them.

Sylvia began to see that Tom could not be held responsible for making her feel feminine. She had to find something womanly in herself and use it with Tom before he could treat her as a female. At the same time a similar realization was emerging within Tom. His feelings of manliness became almost immediately apparent, and he started to behave in the group with a great deal of power. When he tried to use his authority with Sylvia, however, she would invariably and with dreadful accuracy, cut him down.

In order to clarify for the entire group the nature of the bind between Tom and Sylvia, we tied them together with two fifty-foot ropes. One rope was looped around Sylvia's neck and Tom's waist, and the other was looped around Sylvia's waist and Tom's neck. Thus tied, they were directed to move about the room. Tom gathered up all of the excess rope between them so that they were separated by only six feet. Sylvia had to follow him or be chocked because he held the rope and so was protecting his neck. In an attempt to get more maneuverability, Sylvia removed the loop from her neck and then resisted Tom with the rope around her waist. Actually she was stronger than she appeared and, once she removed the yoke that choked her, she was able to pull extra rope from Tom, thus allowing both of them a little more freedom.

Clearly both of them needed more room and, taking a cue from the ropes, we began to focus on helping Sylvia become more independent. More autonomy on her part, as well as the possibility of gratification from some source other than Tom, would decrease her hostility and her need to cut him down. At this point we thought of inviting Sylvia to a marathon.

When this idea was presented to her in the group Tom became tyrannical in his opposition. When we dealt with his anxiety, it centered around his fantasy that in a marathon "she might have a sexual affair." Until this time Tom's position relative to Sylvia had been that of injured party, and he would be only too happy to see her become more independent and lean on him less. Evidently, however, this was not true. Sylvia had left her own therapy because Tom could not tolerate her increasing independence and now she was deciding not to go to the marathon because of the threat to him. Tom revealed that what threatened him really was that he could no longer use her as a scapegoat for his not being a man. When Tom revealed this, Sylvia was enraged at his keeping her down so that he might have an excuse for not being manly. At this point she decided to attend the marathon.

Though Sylvia came to the marathon quite frightened, she opened up early with a man who acted fatherly and seductive. She responded with obvious femininity and passion; also, she expressed sadness about the kind of fathering she had missed. After that incident she became an active, involved member of the group and played a strongly positive role with others. She was both loving and loved, participating in the group with an abandon that was delightful to observe. By the end of the marathon Sylvia saw herself as a passionate woman and, for the first time, accepted herself as a female person. She was pleased with herself and, while she found it difficult to leave that "beautiful group," she was eager to go home and share her new-found passion with Tom.

At the next couple's meeting Tom came fuming with rage. He was certain that if Sylvia didn't have an affair at the marathon, she would have one in the immediate future. Sylvia was still beautiful and feminine and did not seem intimidated by his anger. The group dealt with Tom's anger by helping him recognize the absurdity of his position in that he was furious about something that had not happened. Finally, he was able to laugh at himself, a welcome change from his taking himself and his masculinity with such deadly seriousness.

Sylvia, now convinced that her obesity and frigidity were her way of maintaining the status quo in the marriage, was determined to change. She had already lost weight and vowed that she would continue to diet. As the weeks passed, she was able to maintain her positiveness and self-acceptance and no longer needed to test Tom's manliness by trying to castrate him. While they still quarreled, it was with a sense of fun; they appeared to have broken their long-term "put down" contract. Shortly before the group recessed for the summer, Tom bought a boat (despite Sylvia's objections) and both of them share the pleasure and enjoyment of his new toy.

SUMMARY

The authors have been struck by the constant need to discover and collate new methods of interventions in couples therapy. Marital relationships, whether of a family or professional nature, require ongoing evaluation and encounters in order to remain authentic and fresh. Sharing our respective and mutual problems with our patients helps to create a structure as well as a vehicle to "keep us honest." Searching for new ways of clarifying and resolving a marital or therapeutic impasse generates spontaneity, enabling us to live and work closer to our growing edge.

REFERENCES

1. Bach, G. R.: The marathon group: Intensive practice intimate interaction. *Psychol. Rep., 18*:995, 1956.
2. Bach, G. R.: Group and leader—Phobeas in marathon groups. *Voices,* 3:41, 1967.
3. Malamud, D. I., and Machover, S.: *Toward Self-understanding: Group Techniques in Self-confrontation.* Springfield, Thomas, 1965.
4. Mintz, E. E.: Time-extended marathon groups. *Psychotherapy, 4*:65, 1967.
5. Mintz, E. E.: Isabel in the marathon. *Voices,* 2:104, 1967.
6. Schutz, W. C.: *Joy: Expanding Human Awareness.* New York, Grove Press, 1967.
7. Warkentin, J., and Whitaker, C.: Serial impasse in marriage. *Psychiat. Research Report.* American Psychological Association, 1966, pp. 73-77.

NAME INDEX

Achilles, 90
Ackerman, N. W., 313, 317, 318
Adler, A., 24
Aichhorn, A., 42, 200, 201, 206, 208
Alexander, F., 42
Allport, G., 307
Angell, J. R., 24
Angyal, A., 116
Anthony, M., 90
Arnheim, R., 117

Bach, G. R., 345
Barraclough, C. A., 188
Beach, F. A., 150
Beckett, S., 80
Bellak, L., 316
Benjamin, H., 185
Berenson, G., 313-327
Bergmann, M., xviii, 263-278
Berne, E., 205
Bernheim, H., 26
Besdine, M., xvii, 77-91
Bettelheim, B., 51, 283, 294, 299, 302
Bibring, E., 276
Bieber, I., 155, 191
Bion, W., 48
Blanck, G., 119
Bolles, R., 33
Bonaparte, M., 16
Boss, M., 66
Bowlby, J., 82
Breuer, J., 26
Bromberg, W., 43
Bronner, A., 42
Brown, R., 74
Bry, T., 41
Buber, M., 65
Burgess, E. W., 317
Bychowski, G., 97

Caesar, J., 90
Camus, A., 80, 81, 88
Capote, T., 81
Casriel, D., 197-214
Cezanne, P., 80
Chafetz, M., 217
Challman, R., 154
Charcot, J., 26
Cohen, A., 251, 255, 256
Conrad, F., 153
Cory, D. W., 149

Darwin, C., 34, 35, 36, 82
Dederich, C., 202
deFreitas, L., 183-196
Delany, L. T., 228
Denes-Radomisli, M., 55-75
Dewey, J., 24
Diamond, M., 194
Dollard, J., xv
Doorbar, R. R., 192

Edwards, G., 251
Ekstein, R., 113
Ellis, A., 119, 149
Emch, M., 41
Erikson, E., 81, 82
Eysenck, H., 185

Fairbairn, W. R. D., 79
Felder, R. E., 317
Fenichel, O., 14, 41, 98
Ferenczi, S., 24
Fine, R., xvii, 3-20
Fliess, R., 46
Ford, C. S., 150
Fox, R., 215-247
Franks, C. M., 240
Freud, A., 5, 6, 28, 29, 57, 58, 81, 82, 268

357

SUBJECT INDEX